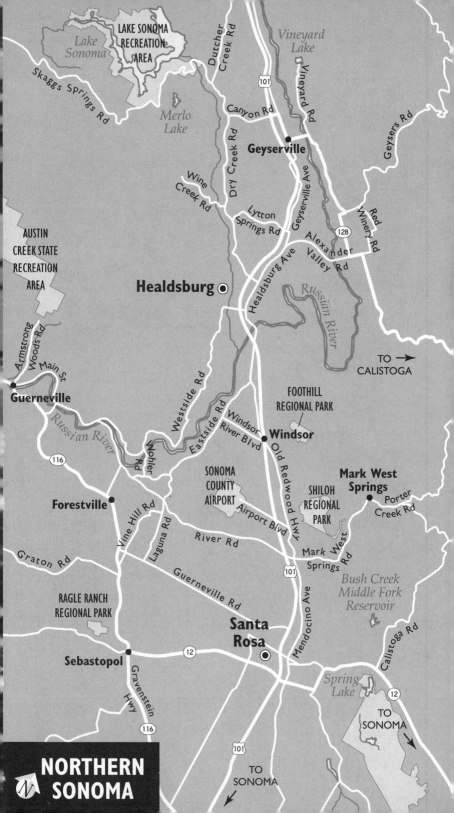

LAKE SONOMA RECREATION AREA

Lake Sonoma

Skaggs Springs Rd

Merlo Lake

Dutcher Creek Rd

Vineyard Lake

101

Vineyard Rd

Canyon Rd

Geyserville

Dry Creek Rd

Wine Creek Rd

Lytton Springs Rd

Geysers Rd

128

Red Winery Rd

Alexander Valley Rd

Geyserville Ave

AUSTIN CREEK STATE RECREATION AREA

Healdsburg

Healdsburg Ave

Russian River

TO CALISTOGA

Armstrong Woods Rd

Main St

Guerneville

Russian River

Westside Rd

Eastside Rd

Wohler Rd

Windsor River Blvd

Windsor

FOOTHILL REGIONAL PARK

Old Redwood Hwy

116

SONOMA COUNTY AIRPORT

SHILOH REGIONAL PARK

Mark West Springs

Porter Creek Rd

Forestville

Vine Hill Rd

Laguna Rd

Airport Blvd

River Rd

Mark West Springs Rd

Mark West Springs Rd

Graton Rd

Guerneville Rd

101

Bush Creek Middle Fork Reservoir

RAGLE RANCH REGIONAL PARK

Mendocino Ave

Calistoga Rd

Santa Rosa

Sebastopol

12

Gravenstein Hwy

Spring Lake

12

TO SONOMA

116

101

TO SONOMA

NORTHERN SONOMA

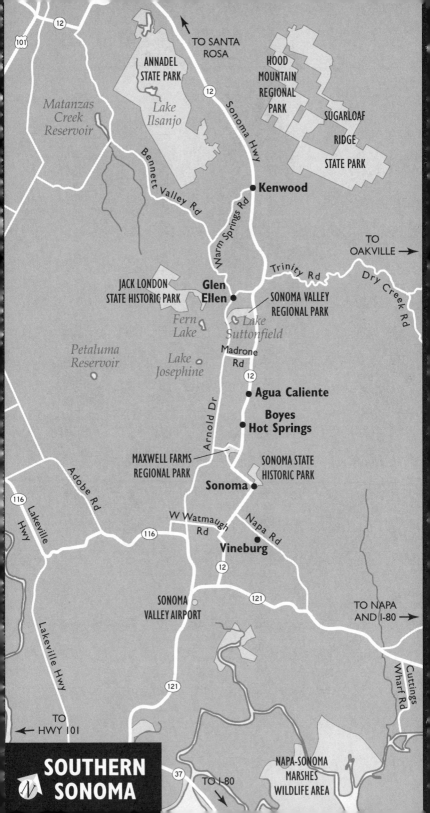

SOUTHERN SONOMA

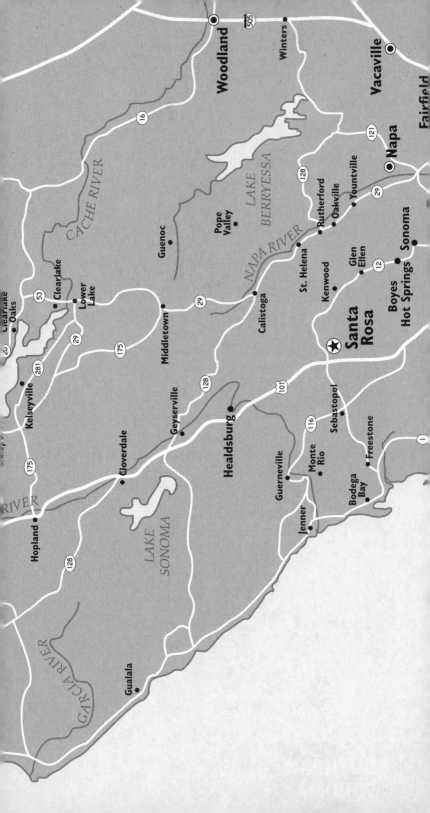

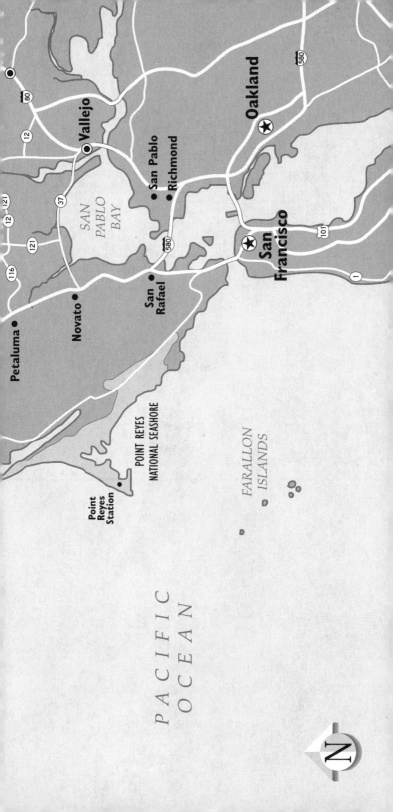

NAPA VALLEY

TO CLEAR LAKE

Petrified Forest Rd
PETRIFIED FOREST

TO HEALDSBURG AND HWY 101

Calistoga

Silverado Trail

Bell Canyon Reservoir

BOTHE-NAPA VALLEY STATE PARK

Deer Park Rd

Howell Mountain Rd

LAS POSADAS STATE FOREST

HOOD MOUNTAIN REGIONAL PARK

SUGARLOAF RIDGE STATE PARK

Pratt Ave

Pope St

St. Helena

Napa River

Lake Hennessey

Rutherford

Silverado Trial

Oakville

Oakville Cross Rd

Trinity Rd

Dry Creek Rd

Oakville Grade

NAPA RIVER ECOLOGICAL RESERVE

Glen Ellen

Rector Reservoir And Dam

Yountville Cross Rd

Redwood Rd

Yountville

St. Helena Hwy

Napa River

Sonoma

ALSTON PARK

Redwood Rd

Trancas St

Browns Valley Rd

1st St

WESTWOOD HILLS WILDERNESS PARK

Old Sonoma Rd

3rd St

Napa

Praise for Best Places® Guidebooks

"Best Places covers must-see portions of the West Coast . . . with style and authority. In-the-know locals offer thorough info on restaurants, lodgings, and the sights."
—NATIONAL GEOGRAPHIC TRAVELER

"Best Places are the best regional restaurant and guide books in America."
—THE SEATTLE TIMES

". . . travelers swear by the recommendations in the Best Places guidebooks . . . "
—SUNSET MAGAZINE

"Known for their frank yet chatty tone . . . "
—PUBLISHERS WEEKLY

"Best Places San Francisco has frank assessments of restaurants and accommodations . . . "
—THE SEATTLE TIMES

"Best Places Northern California is great fun to read even if you're not going anywhere."
—SAN FRANCISCO CHRONICLE

"Best Places Southern California is just about all the inspiration you need to start planning your next road trip or summer vacation with the kids."
—THE FRESNO BEE

"Best Places Southern California and Best Places San Diego are quite good, and any traveler to the area would do well to pick one up."
—LIBRARY JOURNAL

"Eat, surf, and shop like a local with this insider's guide, Best Places San Diego."
—AMERICAN WAY

"For travel collections covering the Northwest, the Best Places series takes precedence over all similar guides."
—BOOKLIST

"The best guide to Seattle is the locally published Best Places Seattle . . . "
—MONEY MAGAZINE

TRUST THE LOCALS

COMPLETELY INDEPENDENT
— No advertisers
— No sponsors
— No favors

EVERY PLACE STAR-RATED & RECOMMENDED

★★★★	The very best in the region
★★★	Distinguished; many outstanding features
★★	Excellent; some wonderful qualities
★	A good place
NO STARS	Worth knowing about, if nearby

CALIFORNIA WINE COUNTRY

BEST PLACES®
DESTINATIONS

CALIFORNIA
WINE COUNTRY

1ST EDITION

EDITED BY ERIKA LENKERT

SASQUATCH BOOKS
SEATTLE

Printed in the United States of America.
Distributed in Canada by Raincoast Books, Ltd.
First edition
07 06 05 04 03 02 01   5 4 3 2 1

Series editor: Kate Rogers
Assistant editor: Laura Gronewold
Cover design: Nancy Gellos
Cover photo: ©Bob Rowan, Progressive Image/CORBIS
Foldout map: GreenEye Design
Interior design adaptation: Fay Bartels, Kate Basart, Millie Beard
Interior composition: Jenny Semet

ISBN: 1-57061-300-1
ISSN: 1536-2787

SASQUATCH BOOKS
615 Second Avenue
Seattle, WA 98104
(206)467-4300
books@SasquatchBooks.com
www.SasquatchBooks.com

Special Sales

BEST PLACES® guidebooks are available at special discounts on bulk purchases for corporate, club, or organization sales promotions, premiums, and gifts. Special editions, including personalized covers, excerpts of existing guides, and corporate imprints, can be created in large quantities for specific needs. For more information, contact your local bookseller or Special Sales, Best Places Guidebooks, 615 Second Avenue, Suite 260, Seattle, Washington 98104, 800/775-0817.

CONTENTS

MENDOCINO COUNTY

LAKE COUNTY

ACKNOWLEDGMENTS

The beauty of Wine Country is that it's not something that falls into your lap; you have to get out there and experience it—one tasting room, restaurant, and backcountry road at a time. I have to thank now-defunct WineShopper.com for my ability to carve out the days in which I ventured through Northern California Wine Country. If it weren't for the absurd deadlines, breakneck pace, and woefully scarce opportunities to wine taste, I wouldn't have decided to seek a better, slower life in Napa Valley—and thus find the time to write this book. Also greatly appreciated is the traveling companionship, discriminating perspective, and wine passion of Lee Stipp, who, along with exploring Sonoma with me, jumped on his motorcycle, hit Lake County in search of adventure, and reported his findings. Huge kudos to Sasquatch editors Laura Gronewold and Kate Rogers, who are not only supportive and fun to work with but also always seem to say the right thing just when I need to hear it. Finally, thanks to my mom, Faith Winthrop, for instilling in me a love for things that taste good.

—*Erika Lenkert*

ABOUT THE EDITOR

Erika Lenkert is a San Francisco native who currently calls Napa home. She is a contributing writer and food critic for *San Francisco Magazine*, as well as editor-in-chief for the upcoming *Connoisseur's Guide San Francisco*. She was most recently the editor-in-chief of Wineshopper.com, and she has authored, co-authored, edited, or contributed to dozens of guidebooks to California—in addition to editing the premier edition of *Best Places Southern California*.

ABOUT BEST PLACES GUIDEBOOKS

California Wine Country is part of the BEST PLACES® guidebook series, which means it's written by and for locals, who enjoy getting out and exploring the region. When making our recommendations, we seek out establishments of good quality and good value, places that are independently owned, run by lively individuals, touched with local history, or sparked by fun and interesting decor. Every place listed is recommended.

BEST PLACES® guidebooks, which have been published continuously since 1975, represent one of the most respected regional travel series in the country. Each guide is written completely independently: no advertisers, no sponsors, no favors. Our reviewers know their territory, work incognito, and seek out the very best a city or region has to offer. We provide tough, candid reports and describe the true strengths, foibles, and unique characteristics of each establishment listed.

Note: Readers are advised that the reviews in this edition are based on information available at press time and are subject to change. The editors welcome information conveyed by users of this book, as long as they have no financial connection with the establishment concerned. A report form is provided at the end of the book, and feedback is also welcome via email: books@SasquatchBooks.com.

HOW TO USE THIS BOOK

ACTIVITIES

Each town throughout this area has a variety of activities and attractions from which to choose. For quick and easy reference, we've created basic symbols to represent them, with full details immediately following. Watch for these symbols:

Architecture and historical sites

Arts and crafts, galleries

Bicycling

Bird-watching, other wildlife viewing

Entertainment: movies, theater, concerts, performing arts, events

Fishing

Food and drinks

Golf

Gourmet food, cooking

Hikes and walks

Horseback riding

Kayaking and canoeing

Kid-friendly, family activities

Local produce, farmers markets, street fairs

Museums and memorials

Parks, wilderness areas, outdoor recreation

Shops: clothing, books, antiques, souvenirs

Spas

Views, scenic driving tours, attractions

Wineries, wine touring, wine tasting

RECOMMENDED RESTAURANTS AND LODGINGS

At the end of each town section you'll find restaurants and lodgings recommended by our BEST PLACES® editors.

Rating System Establishments with stars have been rated on a scale of zero to four. Ratings are based on uniqueness, value, loyalty of local clientele, excellence of cooking, performance measured against goals, and professionalism of service.

(*no stars*)	Worth knowing about, if nearby
★	A good place
★★	Some wonderful qualities
★★★	Distinguished, many outstanding features
★★★★	The very best in the region

 Watch for this symbol throughout the book, indicating those restaurants and lodgings that feature valley views.

Price Range Prices for lodgings are based on peak season rates for one night's lodging for two people (i.e., double occupancy). Off-season rates vary but can sometimes be significantly less. Prices for restaurants are based primarily on dinner for two, including dessert, tax, and tip. Call ahead to verify, as all prices are subject to change.

$$$$	Very expensive (more than $200 for one night's lodging for two)
$$$	Expensive (more than $100 for dinner for two; between $150 and $200 for one night's lodging for two)
$$	Moderate (between $40 and $100 for dinner for two; between $100 and $150 for one night's lodging for two)
$	Inexpensive (less than $40 for dinner for two; less than $100 for one night's lodging for two)

Email and Web Site Addresses We've included email and web site addresses of establishments, where available. Please note that the web is a fluid and evolving medium, and that web pages are often "under construction" or, as with all time-sensitive information in a guidebook such as this, may be no longer valid.

Checks and Credit Cards Most establishments that accept checks also require a major credit card for identification. Credit cards are abbreviated in this book as follows: American Express (AE); Diners Club (DC); Discover (DIS); MasterCard (MC); Visa (V).

Directions Throughout the book, basic directions are provided with each restaurant and lodging. Call ahead, however, to confirm hours and location.

Bed-and-Breakfasts Many B&Bs have a two-night minimum-stay requirement during the peak season, and several do not welcome children. Ask about a B&B's policies before you make your reservation.

Smoking Most establishments in Wine Country do not permit smoking inside, although some lodgings have rooms reserved for smokers. Call ahead to verify an establishment's smoking policy.

Pets Most establishments do not allow pets; call ahead to verify, however, as some budget places do.

Index All restaurants, lodgings, town names, and major tourist attractions are listed alphabetically at the back of the book.

Reader Reports At the end of the book is a report form. We receive hundreds of reports from readers suggesting new places or agreeing or disagreeing with our assessments. They greatly help in our evaluations. We encourage you to respond.

NAPA
VALLEY

NAPA VALLEY

Given that Napa Valley is the country's most extensive adult play-ground for food, wine, and luxury lovers, it's almost fitting that the 35-mile-long stretch of grape-strewn real estate surrounding rural Highway 29 is right up there with kid-oriented Disneyland as one of the most-visited destinations in California. Over 4.9 million visitors annually make the grape escape to the valley's towns and world-renowned wineries, resorts, and restaurants, which means, regardless of the time of year, roads and attractions are more tightly packed than a cluster of heavy-hanging Chardonnay fruit. In high season (March through November) the traffic on the one main road that gets you to your next winery can be as loath-some as big-city gridlock. But no matter. When spring is blessed with vibrant green hills and bright yellow mustard blossoms, summer brings everyday sun and hillsides fat with fruit, fall explodes with brilliant autumnal colors and the excitement of harvest, and winter makes for even more excuses to indulge in some of the world's best food, you're quick to realize road con-gestion is a small price to pay for paradise.

Contact Napa Valley Conference and Visi-tors Bureau; 1310 Napa Town Center, off 1st St, Napa; 707/226-7459; www.napavalley.com; for maps and exten-sive Wine Country information.

GETTING THERE

Forging the fastest route from San Francisco to Napa Valley can be a tricky business. When there's no traffic, going through the East Bay (Interstate 80 north to Highway 37/Marine World exit going west to Highway 29) shaves a good 15 minutes off the otherwise 1¼-hour jaunt. But when 80 is slow (usually between 4 and 7pm on weekdays), the ride, which is far less picturesque than the route through Marin County following Highway 101, requires Sid-dhartha-like patience. Conversely, Highway 101 (Highway 101 N onto Highway 37 E to Highway 121 N to Highway 29) has its share of rush-hour traffic, too. Whichever route you take, do it before afternoon when the suits start leaving their offices.

THE CITY OF NAPA

At the southernmost end of Napa Valley is the sprawling part-pretty, part-industrial city of Napa, where about half of the county's 72,585 residents live. Although its name is synonymous with wine, most of the valley's wineries are actually several miles north of town. Though most tourists previously zoomed past the city for the more pastoral Wine Country towns to the north, Napa, founded in 1848 and boasting stunning Victorian structures, is coming into its own. Thanks to ridiculous housing prices to the south and the much-anticipated upcoming $70 million COPIA: The American Center for Wine, Food & the Arts, the town is undergoing massive renovation and restorations. As a result, downtown commercial space is hot, hot, hot, and homes saw a 56 percent rise in prices from 1999 to 2000.

ACTIVITIES

Getting Acquainted. Napa Valley Conference and Visitors Bureau (1310 Napa Town Center; 707/226-7459; www.napavalley.com) doles out a $10 comprehensive information kit, which includes The Napa Valley Guide, a map, brochures, and coupons. To order the guide via phone, call the bureau.

Art Preserve. Nature and art are rarely celebrated as well as they are at the di Rosa Preserve, which brightens up even the highway with its two-dimensional cows standing in a field beyond its entrance. After over 40 years of privately collecting the works of America's great contemporary artists, such as Robert Arneson, Nathan Oliveira, and William T. Wiley, Rene and Veronica di Rosa decided to share their treasures with the public. Now you can make an appointment and tour the grounds and the couple's 1,800-plus pieces, which are exhibited throughout the 53-acre property, including on the banks of the huge lake and charming century-old winery that is now the di Rosas' residence. Visits are by appointment only, and the 2- to 2¹⁄₂-hour tours are guided. (5200 Sonoma Hwy (Hwy 121/12); 707/226-5991; $10 per person)

Antiquing. Plan to spend at least an hour and bring a good jacket if it's a very cold day, because both the Red Hen and Riverfront Antiques are co-op collections housed in chilly and enormous warehouses. You could spend days sorting through the hundreds of stalls, most of which are teeming with individual collectors' wares, ranging from dime-store toys to antique bedroom sets. (Red Hen: 5091 St. Helena Hwy, on Hwy 29 at Oak Knoll Ave W; 707/257-0822; open every day 10am–5:30pm. Riverfront Antiques: 705 Soscol Ave, near 3rd St; 707/253-1966)

To avoid the heaviest traffic, take the verdant Silverado Trail, which parallels Highway 29, up and down the valley.

 Outlet Mall. Bargain hunters can't help but take the First Street exit off Highway 29 and head to the Napa Premium Outlets, a huge strip mall boasting designer destinations like Esprit, Jones New York, Max Studio, BCBG, and Barney's New York. It's classic outlet shopping, for sure, which means you'll have to sort through lots of schlock for the truly great deals. But on the bright side, there are great well-priced kitchen accoutrements, and the sprawl of shops allows you to walk off some of the calories you've been collecting since your arrival or are bound to accumulate as you head north. (707/226-9876; open Mon–Sat 10am–8pm, Sun 10am–6pm)

Walking Tour. Introduce yourself to the town by taking a self-guided walking tour of downtown Napa's architectural highlights. A detailed map outlining everything from a Victorian Gothic church to an art deco brewery to a Beaux Arts bank is available for free at the Napa Valley Conference and Visitors Bureau (see the contact information above), or you may purchase a $3 booklet with descriptions of relevant buildings and a corresponding numbered map at Napa County Landmarks. (1026 1st St, at Main St, in the Community Preservation Center; 707/255-1836; open Mon–Tues 1–5pm, Wed–Fri 9am–1pm)

Golf. Appropriately, Wine Country's luxury life includes various locations where you can play luxury sports. The farthest south such spot, Chardonnay Golf Club (2555 Jamison Canyon Rd, off Hwy 29; 707/257-1900), is home to two 18-hole championship golf courses. Its Vineyards course, which is open to the public, is set amid 500 acres complete with 140 acres of working vineyards and lakes, and traverses Fagan Creek five times. The Club Shakespeare course is private and available through reciprocal play—i.e., if you're a member of any private golf club (Vineyards rates, which include greens and cart fees, Mar 14–Nov 30: Mon–Fri $65, Sat–Sun $95; Dec 1–Mar 13: Mon–Fri $60, Sat–Sun $75; rates include green fee and cart fee; Club Shakespeare rates $110). Napa Municipal Golf Course at Kennedy Park (2295 Streblow Dr, off the Silverado Trail; 707/255-4333; www.playnapa.com) is an 18-hole public course,

City of Napa • 5

PICNIC SUPPLIES

You need only spend two days of wine tasting divided by lunches and dinners before the revelation hits: it's far too exhausting and rich for your tummy to dine out twice a day. The good news is Napa Valley is prime for picnicking. During high season, when traffic can take a bite out of your time and patience, it's best to buy in your vicinity. But true gourmands will want to drive the extra few miles to the destination markets where everything you could possibly want—and more—is available and beautifully packaged. Either way, in summer don't forget a cooler, or by the time you get to it your sandwich will be a soggy heated mess, and to make the most of your surroundings consider charting your lunchtime path toward a winery with picnic facilities or a park. In the city of Napa, your best bet is Genova Delicatessen (1550 Trancas St, W of Jefferson St, Napa; 707/253-8686), which makes fine sandwiches, roasted chickens, pasta, and a variety of salads and sweets. You can even sit at the espresso bar and order an Italian soda, a gelato, or a great cup of joe. Convenient, yes, but it's not

Want a facial like those that cost $125 in the spa at Auberge du Soliel for less than half the price? Call Peg de Graaf, who helped develop the Auberge skin-care program. When she's not slathering on soothing products at the exclusive resort, she is giving Napa locals facials, dermabrasion, and glycolic acid treatments at her clinic Face to Face (1095 Trancas St, in Jason Square; 707/253-7546).

which is less picturesque, but substantially cheaper at $28 for nonresidents on weekdays, and $38 on weekends. Farther north, a quick turn off an industrial stretch of Highway 29 leads to the refined Napa Valley Country Club (3385 Hagen Rd; 707/252-1114). The club is private, but reciprocal for private-club members, and offers a breathtaking view of the valley from the back nine. Silverado Country Club (1600 Atlas Peak Rd; 707/257-5444) is the most chichi of private resorts, harboring two beautiful 18-hole courses designed by Robert Trent Jones Jr. The traditional-style course is challenging, but forgiving. (Tee times for resort nonguests 2 days in advance only; greens and cart fees for nonguests $150, half-price after 4pm; winter rates Dec–Feb for nonguests: Mon–Thurs $70, weekends $80; summer rates for guests $130; winter rates for guests $75 Mon–Thurs, $85 Fri–Sun)

Spa. Although all the big boys in luxury are "up valley," Napa locals rely on spa veteran Sonja Akey, a German-trained and licensed aesthetician who's been helping people look *nearly as exciting as culinary mecca* **Dean & DeLuca** *(607 S Main St/Hwy 29, N of Zinfandel Ln, St. Helena; 707/967-9980), the best (and most expensive) fine foods and wines warehouse. Their cheese selection is astounding (free tastes!), the prepared food selection on the back wall offers feasts fit for kings, shelves everywhere teem with chocolate and treats, foie gras, gourmet mustards, marinades, cookies, and—ooh-la-la!—it's hard to get out of here without buying the whole store. Farther north on Highway 29 is* **Oakville Grocery Co.** *(7856 St. Helena Hwy at Oakville Cross Rd, Oakville; 707/944-8802), a local icon disguised as an old-fashioned country market that is not a scene for the claustrophobic; any given noontime will find this homey establishment clogged with tourists lined up to buy gourmet deli treats. But those who brave the scene will find a fine variety of local wines (including a good selection of splits), a small espresso bar tucked in the corner, and pricey but delicious picnic supplies ranging from pâté and caviar to turkey sandwiches and several freshly made sweets.*

luminous for more than a decade. Her Greenhaus European Day Spa is modestly situated in a tiny freestanding building in the historic Hatt Building parking lot. But in Napa you won't find a better spa offering manicures and pedicures, skin care and body treatments, massage, waxing, and baths and scrubs. Call well in advance; they book up a few weeks ahead, especially on weekends. (1091 5th St, at Main St; 707/257-8837; www.greenhauspa.com)

 Hiking/Biking Trails. Just 2 miles east of downtown Napa is a pristine mountain escape. Follow Imola Avenue east to Skyline Park, pay $4 to park, and 26 miles of hiking trails await you. Trails are wide and even, which makes it appealing to all levels of athletes as well as horseback riders (BYO horse) and mountain bikers, the latter of which are required to wear helmets. Along the way you'll stumble upon a beautiful mountain lake, valley views, and plenty of spots to feel alone with nature. Be sure to bring sunblock and water—it gets hot and dry in these parts. (2201 Imola Ave; 707/252-0481; open 8am–5pm, extended hours in summer)

Want to grab a new novel or catch up on Napa Valley history? Stop by downtown Napa's bookstore Copperfield's (1303 1st St; 707/252-8002) to browse its large selection.

American Center for Wine, Food & the Arts.

Though it's yet to open as this book goes to press, Napa residents are wondering how 12-acre COPIA: The American Center for Wine, Food & the Arts will change the face of their predominantly blue-collar city. The $70 million project, which was completed in fall 2001, boasts Robert Mondavi as its chairman of the board, and its stated mission is to "explore our culture, highlighting American innovations and investigating our distinctive approach to food and drink." Planned offerings include classes, exhibitions, and demonstrations on viticulture, enology, agriculture, cuisine, artistic and literary expression, and the history, science, and politics of food, nutrition, and health. Part of the aim is to bring chefs, winemakers, and artists together with wine, food, and art lovers, all in the name of "sharing their connections with food and wine as expressions of American culture." (500 1st St; 707/259-1600; www.Americancenter.com)

Barrel Tour.

Ever wondered how your Chardonnay gets that toasted oak flavor? Find out firsthand at the only U.S. outpost of French barrel makers Seguin Moureau Napa Cooperage. Here oak staves are roasted, toasted, bent, shaved, and specifically designed to enhance the wine that will age within them. Learn about specific types of oak and watch a step-by-step demonstration. (151 Camino Dorado; 707/252-3408; open Mon–Fri 8am–5pm; reservations recommended)

Brandy.

The art of making table wine isn't the only libation education in Napa. In fact, RMS Brandy Distillery, a classic brandy distillery in the Carneros region of Napa, bordering Sonoma, has been following France's 400-year-old Cognac production tradition since 1982, and boasts the status of oldest alembic brandy distillery in California. Tours walk you through the production process from start to finish. Unfortunately, the distillery is not allowed to hold tastings because its products have higher alcohol content than table wine, but you do get the opportunity to sniff and purchase its three brandies and pear liqueur. (1250 Cuttings Wharf Rd; 707/253-9055; open every day 10am–4:30pm; reservations recommended)

Wine Train Ride.

Think of the Napa Valley Wine Train as a land cruise. The cushy 2½-hour ride chugs through Napa, Yountville, Oakville, Rutherford, and St. Helena as passengers sip fine wines and sup on a meal, all the while gazing at the lush countryside from a historically preserved vintage railcar. More a spectator sport than a journey, the Wine Train allows you to skip the traffic and tasting rooms, which is great for those who want a snapshot of the basic layout, but not so great for anyone anxious to get out and scout the valley. Most tours feature food and views without any stops along the way; some specialized trips include live jazz, winemaker dinners, or food and wine pairing extravaganzas. One option allows for leg stretching in Yountville and a wine-tasting stop at Grgich Winery in Rutherford. (Off Soscol Ave and 1st St; 707/253-2111 or 800/427-4124; $29.50–$110, depending on type of ride)

WINERIES

 Acacia Winery. Almost as enjoyable as a visit to Acacia is the drive there. While the convoy of tourists follows Highway 12/121, you can't help but feel like a rebel as you pass Domaine Carneros and disappear onto rural Duhig Road and its surrounding vineyards that stretch from the hills to San Pablo Bay. Right about the time you think you're lost, you arrive at humble and friendly Acacia. Eschewing all the fancy facades, Acacia struts its stuff primarily through award-winning Carneros Chardonnays and Pinot Noirs, but sparkling wine is usually being poured as well. Now part of the Chalone Group's winery portfolio, the company, founded in 1979, continues its emphasis on regionally specific wines and requires an appointment due to permit restrictions. *2750 Las Amigas Rd; 707/226-9991; www.acaciawinery.com; open Mon–Sat 10am–4:30pm, Sun noon–4:30pm; tasting free, reserve tasting $5 with keepsake logo glass; tastings and tours by appointment.*

Artesa Vineyards & Winery. Artesa is off the beaten track, but of the hundreds of wineries in the valley, few boast as many reasons to make the drive. The grounds, complete with vast valley views, modern sculptures, and fabulous fountains, are absolutely magical. The winery, built into the mountainside and covered in fescue grass, is glorious from the outside, sleek and inviting on the inside. Although Artesa, owned by Codorníu of Spain, was dedicated solely to *méthode champenoise*

NAPA VALLEY'S WINE TRAILS

Napa's wineries are mainly clustered along Highway 29 and the Silverado Trail, two parallel roads running the length of the valley. The place is a zoo on weekends—especially in the summer and early fall, when the traffic on narrow Highway 29 rivals rush hour in the Bay Area. With the increased number of visitors, most vintners now charge a small fee to taste their wines and some require reservations for tours (don't let the latter deter you—the smaller establishments just need to control the number of visitors at any one time and make sure someone will be available to show you around). A tip from veteran wine tasters: pick out the four or five wineries you're most interested in visiting over the weekend, and stick to your itinerary. Touring more than a couple of wineries a day will surely overwhelm and exhaust even the most intrepid wine connoisseur, although if you really want to see several wineries in a short period, skip the grand tours and just visit the tasting rooms. If you're new to the wine-touring scene, you'll be relieved to know you won't ever be pressured to buy any of the wines you've sampled—the tasting room hosts are just delighted to expose you to their line of products. Winery maps, as well as details about parks, hot-air balloon rides, and other recreational pastimes, are readily available at many locations, including most hotels and the Napa Valley Conference and Visitors Bureau (1310 Napa Town Center, off 1st St, Napa; 707/226-7459).

sparkling wine production at its 1991 inception, six years later it made a name change and a $10 million turn to focus on award-winning premium still wines. Today you can taste around a dozen wines, including various region-specific Chardonnays and Pinot Noirs, a Sauvignon Blanc, Cabernet Sauvignon, Zinfandel, and two sparklers. There's also a fantastic gift store that's worlds better than most in the valley and a small museum featuring the history of the Carneros region. Unfortunately, Artesa's permit does not allow food to be sold or enjoyed on the perfect-picnic property. *1345 Henry Rd; turn N onto Old Sonoma Rd off Hwy 12/121, left on Dealy Ln, right on Henry Rd; 707/224-1668; www.artesawinery.com; open every day 10am–5pm; free production tours every day at 11am* *and 2pm; tasting $2 per 2-ounce pour or $6 for any six wines, $3 per 2-oz. pour of reserve wines or $6 to taste all three reserves.*

🍷 **Darioush Winery.** Persian-American Darioush Khaledi dreamed of being a winemaker. So after immigrating during the Islamic revolution and spending decades building up equity through a successful Southern California grocery store chain, he bought some vineyard land, hired the winemaker from neighboring winery Signorello Vineyards, and opened this winery in 2000. Although the winery is selling its 80 percent reds (Cabernet, Shiraz, Merlot) and 20 percent whites (Chardonnay, Viognier, Vin Gris) out of what is fondly called the "Darioush double-wide" trailer, ground has been broken on an ambitious winery project, which is sure to merit a stop for a look at its traditional Persian gardens, state-of-the-art facilities, and impressive buildings with tile imported from Iran. But now a visit allows guests the opportunity to learn about the winery's commitment to classic Bordeaux varietals and techniques (they even handpick their grapes), taste some delicious wines, and familiarize themselves with a winery that, though in its infancy, is poised to be a contender. Plus every wine taster gets a bottle of Evian or juice. *4240 Silverado Trail; 5 miles N of Trancas St; 707/257-2345; www.darioushwinery.com; open every day 10:30am–5pm; tasting $5, fee credited toward purchase.*

🍷 **Domaine Carneros by Tattinger.** Perched on a hill that overlooks Highway 12/121, this grandiose château is the first unmistakable sign that you've entered big-business Wine Country. The majestic building, constructed in 1988 and modeled after Louis XV–style Chateau de la Marquetterie in Champagne, France, is surrounded by meticulously kept grounds. Inside, the old-world illusion falls short in the rather corporate tasting room and gift shop. Nonetheless, if it's sparkling wine you're interested in, they've got delicious examples here along with their sole still wine, Pinot Noir. Tastes come by the glass for $5 to $10 along with free herbed goat cheese and toast. Caviar service is also offered. If it's not too hot, it's best to enjoy your bubbly on the terrace. Those who want to know more about *méthode champenoise*, France's traditional sparkling winemaking process, can drop in on the free 40-minute tour, which includes an educational film and a glimpse of the aging cellar and production line. *1240 Duhig Rd; 707/257-0101; www.domainecarneros.com; open every day 10:30am–6 pm; tours*

ROBERT LOUIS STEVENSON'S TIME IN NAPA

The Scottish author Robert Louis Stevenson came to California in search of Fanny, a married woman, 10 years his senior, whom he'd met and fallen in love with in France. After arriving by ship in San Francisco, and half dead from bronchitis, he waited for Fanny to divorce, and the couple married in May of 1880. In an attempt to restore the groom's health, the poverty-stricken couple spent their last $10 on a honeymoon cabin at a hot-springs resort in Calistoga—a region that even then was famed for its restorative powers. With their money gone, they spent the summer in the old bunkhouse of an abandoned silver mine on Mount St. Helena.

every day on the hour 11am–4pm, except mid-Nov–Mar, when weekday tours are at 11am, 1pm, and 3pm.

The Hess Collection Winery. There may be no more majestic place to view the works by contemporary artists Francis Bacon, Frank Stella, and Robert Rauschenberg, see barrel and bottling rooms, and sample Chardonnay and Cabernet Sauvignon than the Hess Collection. While most wineries welcome you from the valley floor, this secluded, dramatic stone structure showcases its winemaking facilities, wines, and wonderful contemporary American and European art collection high in the hills of scenic Mount Veeder. A self-guided tour winds through two 1903 buildings, which were renovated in 1989 to beautifully merge modern design with their historic walls. *4411 Redwood Rd; from Hwy 29 exit W on Redwood Rd/Trancas St, follow Redwood Rd 6 miles; 707/255-1144; www.hesscollection.com; open every day 10am–4pm, excluding major holidays; tasting $3.*

Silverado Vineyards. After its 1981 inception, Silverado wasn't even open to the public for six years, and when it did open its doors, they didn't really tell anyone. But in 2001 they debuted their new 30,000-square-foot Italian hillside town-inspired facilities. Perched atop a knoll overlooking the northern half of the Stags Leap District, the winery is understated, charming, and refreshingly clean of gift-shop items. From an architec-

The writer admits more than healthy environs was a draw to Napa: "I was interested in California wine. Indeed, I am interested in all wines, and have been all my life. . . ." To this end, he spent time with Jacob Schram, who founded Schramsberg Vineyards.

While Stevenson idled on the mountain with Fanny, his family accepted the news of his marriage. The couple returned to Scotland, where Stevenson wrote Treasure Island. *Mount St. Helena is said to be the inspiration for Spyglass Hill.*

Today, at Robert Louis Stevenson State Park, you can hike up rugged, solitary Mount St. Helena to the site where the newlyweds squatted.

tural perspective, it's interesting to note that the cobblestones on the plaza and terrace come from old New York City streets and the tasting room's antique overhead beams were imported from British Columbia. From an aesthetic perspective, it's absolute bliss to look over the winery's 95 acres of Cabernet, sprinkled with a few Merlot vines, from the landscaped patio. Within the airy new 4,000-square-foot tasting room (complete with huge fireplace) guests can sample four of the winery's six or seven current releases, which include Cabernet, Sangiovese, Chardonnay, Sauvignon Blanc, and Merlot. Step into the hallway to peek through French doors at the enormous new barrel room, where 1,000 barrels of Cabernet and Merlot age in oak. Newly designed tours escort guests through the winery's history and winemaking process and into the gorgeous new tasting room and blissful terrace. *6121 Silverado Trail; 707/257-1770; tasting $3.*

Stag's Leap Wine Cellars. Picture perfect from the front walkway's wildflower gardens to the $5 million caves, Stag's Leap helped put Napa Valley on the wine map when in 1976 its Cabernet bested French competition in the now-famous Parisian blind tasting. The winery intends to develop a new tasting room, but for now sampling is done in a rather cramped nook beside stainless steel tanks. It's not surprising they haven't gotten around to it yet: their brand-new caves, which premiered in 2001 and are open by appointment, went over budget by four years

Don't be intimidated by wineries that offer tours and tastings by appointment only. In most cases exclusivity is not intentional, but rather a result of operating-permit laws.

and $4 million. They were worth the wait, however; take the tour and you'll wander barrel-flanked corridors and into the Round Room, where a pendulum keeps time. Tastings are $5 and include five current releases (perhaps Cabernet Sauvignon, Merlot, Petite Sirah, Chardonnay, Sauvignon Blanc, and white Riesling) and a keepsake glass, or you can fork over up to $35 for estate tastings. The 1-hour tour runs through everything from the vineyard to production facilities and caves. *5766 Silverado Trail; 707/944-2020; www.cask23.com; open every day 10am–4:30pm.*

Trefethen Vineyards. Along a quiet crossroad between the Silverado Trail and Highway 29 is historic Trefethen's main building, which was built in 1886 and today boasts the status of Napa's only wooden gravity-flow winery. Although the antiquated method is no longer used, daily free tours review the old facilities as well as the grounds, 100-year-old vines, and herb gardens, which contribute to the winery's annual summer demonstration cooking class series. Tastings are complimentary and include samples of Chardonnay, Cabernet Sauvignon, Merlot, Cabernet Franc, and Dry Riesling; the reserve tasting is $5. *1160 Oak Knoll Ave, E of Hwy 29; 707/255-7700; www.trefethen.com; open every day 10am–4:30pm; tours by appointment only.*

RESTAURANTS

ALEXIS BAKING COMPANY AND CAFE ★★

"ABC," as the locals call it, is the best all-around casual standby cafe in downtown Napa. Fresh, cute, and cheap is the winning combination that inspires locals to grab the newspaper, stand in line, and order from the counter. Breakfast promises the town's most popular pancakes, which are made from scratch, come in flamboyant varieties such as cornmeal or lemon ricotta, and are served with real maple syrup. At lunch, which stretches into the dinner hour of 6pm, it's a tough choice between the signature focaccia smoked turkey sandwich, burger, or grilled chicken, the latter two of which are snuggled in homemade potato buns. Once you've battled the what-to-order dilemma and cleared the oft-impatient counter staff, all is utterly relaxed—from the funky-fun local art adorning the high walls and the light pouring in through huge windows to the few coveted sidewalk seats. It's a far cry from the fancy stuff of restaurants to the north. But for anyone seeking a refreshingly unfussy retreat, that's exactly the point. And take heed: it's nearly impossible to leave without one or two sweet treats—ranging from chocolate macaroons to luxurious chocolate caramel cake. *1517 3rd St, Napa; 707/258-1827; $; MC, V; local checks only; breakfast, lunch every day; beer and wine; no reservations; between School St and Wilson.*

BISTRO DON GIOVANNI   ★★★

An absolute favorite for locals, Bistro Don Giovanni manages to be all things to all people. The bar, which extends the length of the restaurant, is a preferred perch for gathering and chatting over a glass of wine and, quite often, a complete dinner. The bright main dining room is comfortable and bustling. Patio dining is perfect year-round thanks to heat lamps, Tuscan-style decor, and vine views. Donna and Giovanni Scala also own Scala's Bistro in San Francisco's Sir Francis Drake Hotel, but as far as food goes, this is their flagship. Perfectly al dente penne with rich duck ragout is so good it's difficult to stray. But flat, crisp pizzas are worth exploration, the beet and haricot vert salad has garnered a large fan club, and seared salmon is sure to send you. The wine list, although skewed toward expensive California vintages, is extensive and imaginative, and dessert beckons with such offerings as watermelon granita and textbook tiramisu. *4110 St. Helena Hwy/Hwy 29, Napa; 707/224-3300; $$; AE, DC, DIS, MC, V; local checks only; lunch, dinner every day; full bar; reservations recommended; on Hwy 29, just N of Salvador Ave.*

CELADON   ★★✦

By the time you find this restaurant, hidden behind a downtown office building and overlooking the creek, you will have worked up an appetite. And that's good news, because you'll be in the right place to satisfy it. Chef Greg Cole fuses an eclectic blend of spicy international flavors into a small, rotating menu. Some of the constants are grilled tuna salad with macadamia nuts and spicy sesame greens; an udon noodle bowl with shiitake mushroom broth; and a "Jamaican-inspired" pork chop with black beans and grilled pineapple salsa. The impressive wine list is not surprising once you know that Cole once worked at Napa Valley's Robert Sinskey Vineyards, where he made it a point to learn all he could about wine. His by-the-glass prices are some of the more reasonable in the area. The decor of the small indoor restaurant is unpretentious and serene; outdoor creekside dining is an option in warm weather. To find the restaurant, take the outdoor walkway to the rear of the Main Street Exchange Building. *1040 Main St #104, Napa; 707/254-9690; $$$; AE, DC, MC, V; local checks only; lunch Mon–Fri, dinner Mon–Sat; beer and wine; reservations recommended; at Pearl St.*

COLE'S CHOP HOUSE   ★★◗

Some may have considered opening an expensive American steak house in predominantly blue-collar Napa a raw idea, but from the beginning owner Greg Cole has welcomed brisk business to this bright, airy restored historic building, built in 1886. The loyal clientele, which was developed at his other restaurant, Celadon (see review), didn't hesitate to up the ante to pay close to $30 for aged steak without any accompaniments served in downtown's most upscale environment. Whether you mosey up to the bar, dine alfresco on the charming courtyard patio, or soak in the old-meets-new ambience of stone walls, hardwood floors, cush booths, and beamed ceilings, you need not stick with steak: additional menu classics include a tangy Caesar salad, rich oysters Rockefeller, veal, lamb, and a few vegetarian dishes thrown in for modern measure. Old-school side dishes such as creamed spinach, which are ordered à la carte, can quickly jack up the bill, as can the wine list, which emphasizes expensive reds. A city-smart cocktail menu rounds out the retro drinking and dining options. *1122 Main St, Napa; 707/224-6328; $$$; AE, DC, MC, V; local checks only; dinner Tues–Sun; full bar; reservations recommended; www.coleschophouse.citysearch.com; behind the big pink movie theater on Soscol Ave, just N of 1st St.* ⎃

A GOOD DAY IN . . . NAPA VALLEY

Rise at the crack of dawn, drag your weary bones out of bed, and exhilarate your morning with a hot-air balloon ride over Napa Valley. After the included Champagne breakfast hit the wine trail. Stop by **Artesa,** *take a tour at* **di Rosa Preserve** *(reserve in advance), and sip a glass of bubbly at* **Domaine Chandon** *before lunching on the patio at* **Tra Vigne.** *Take an afternoon nap, then hit one or two more wineries before settling in to a dinner seat at* **Terra.** *If you've got any energy left, expend it at* **1351 Lounge** *over cocktails and revelry or catch a flick at the* **Cameo Cinema** *across the street.*

FIRST SQUEEZE CAFE AND JUICE BAR   ★

When your body is craving respite from luxury food and your wallet is begging for mercy, First Squeeze is your simple savior. Birkenstocks-casual, the funky green and yellow painted eatery offers a bountiful breakfast, which includes zesty huevos rancheros, breakfast burritos, eggs Benedict, and honey wheat pancakes. Lunch features a slew of fresh sandwiches, fresh juices (carrot, apple, etc.), and smoothies, all of which are ordered at the counter and devoured at cafe-style tables and banquettes. *1126 Main St, Napa; 707/224-6762; $; AE, DC, DIS, MC, V; no checks; breakfast, lunch every day; beer and wine; no reservations; at Coombs St, in the Clock Tower Plaza.* &

FOOTHILL CAFE   ★★★

Foothill Cafe, a hidden gem favored by locals who know to turn off the main streets and into the eastern Napa neighborhood for great food at amazingly low prices, has been outed. In 2001 the friendly kitsch-casual restaurant was named one of the top 100 Bay Area restaurants by the *San Francisco Chronicle*. Now the 42 seats are even harder to come by. Despite the growing attention to chef/owner Jerry Shaffer's (of San Francisco's Masa's and St. Helena's original Miramonte) American restaurant, the space maintains its sense of whimsy; even decorative items, such as wrought-iron artwork

House-brewed ales, a central location, happy hour, basic grub, and live music make Downtown Joe's (902 Main St; 707/258-2337) a great place to savor local flavor.

by a local artist, are fanciful. Sure things are virtually anything from the big oak oven, such as oak-roasted baby back ribs, which come in snack and fill-'er-up sizes, or eight-hour-smoked prime rib with potato Stilton gratin, homemade horseradish, and a melange of seasonal vegetables. Then again, it's hard to go wrong with sautéed salmon fillet with cracked black pepper, ginger, Cabernet balsamic reduction, and garlic mashed potatoes. Dessert favorites include classic vanilla-bean and Cognac crème brûlée. Like the rest of the menu, wines are affordably priced. *2766 Old Sonoma Rd, Napa; 707/252-6178; $$; AE, MC, V; local checks only; dinner Wed–Sun; beer and wine; reservations recommended; from Hwy 29 go W on Imola Ave, right at Foster Rd, left on Old Sonoma Rd; in J&P Center.* &

LA BOUCANE   ★★

Housed in a restored Victorian, Napa Valley's bastion of classic French cuisine has a small teal-and-rose dining room that glows with candles. The wine list, with its healthy mix of Bordeaux and Burgundian varietals from California's top vintners, is perfectly matched to owner/chef Jacques Mokrani's traditional French fare: crisp roasted duck in a zesty, bittersweet orange sauce; perfect poached salmon in a delicate Champagne cream sauce; and thick, flavorful tournedos forestière in a reduction of game and beef stock with fresh herbs and red wine. All entrees come with a richly flavored soup such as crawfish bisque or cream of turnip, artfully arranged vegetables, a salad, and a divine dessert such as soufflé glacé praliné, *mousse au chocolat*, or crème caramel. Despite the restaurant's old-fashioned decor, the atmosphere is delightfully unstuffy. *1778 2nd St, Napa; 707/253-1177; $$$; MC, V; local checks only; dinner Mon–Sat (closed in Jan); beer and wine; reservations recommended; 1 block E of Jefferson St.*

PAIRS NAPA VALLEY   ★★

Anyone who's had it with French- and Italian-inspired "Wine Country" cuisine will revel in Pairs' dramatic culinary departure. Though the restaurant name reflects chef/owner brothers Craig and Keith Schauffel's intent to match food and wine, at this chic, rustic-modern restaurant the mates are Asian fusion and the uncommonly worldly wine list. It's a bold move, but after establishing themselves for seven and a half years in a modest 50-seat restaurant in St. Helena, the Schauffels are ready to stir it up a bit. And they do. The design alone—a sleek, bamboo-fence-enclosed front patio, river rock and bamboo landscaping, a gorgeous, swerving, wood-topped river-rock bar, and a split dining room graced by shades of brown and a sexy overhead bamboo lattice below dangling globe lights—declares this is no tribute to stereotypical Napa Valley. Of even greater interest is what's on the plate. Starters include absolutely addictive, zingy and crunchy lemon calamari, which consists of battered and fried tender squid, potato, onion, and lemon shavings with a tangy citrus aioli; rather doughy vegetarian spring rolls; and a light and crisp Caesar. Pasta and sandwich offerings include a juicy basil burger and, on occasion, roasted mussels in tomato coconut broth with cilantro lime fettuccine, which is a very tasty, albeit curious cross between Italian and Thai. If the sea bass with daikon mushroom sauce and nori is on the menu, get it. Lack of a liquor license may have been the inspiration behind the sake martinis, but the wine list, which includes a good selection of French, German, and California wines and lots of by-the-glass selections, is hard to pass up. *4175 Solano Ave, Napa; 707/224-8464; $$; AE, DC, MC, V; no checks; lunch, dinner every day; beer and wine; reservations recommended; www.pairsrestaurant.com; at Hwy 29 and Wine Country Rd.* &

PEARL ★★

This homey establishment is a favorite with locals, mainly because it's been one of the few places in town where you can count on friendly—albeit woefully slow—service and consistently good fare. Owners Nickie and Pete Zeller divide duties; Nickie presides over the kitchen, and Pete runs the front of the house. The menu offers something for all tastes and budgets, running the gamut from an array of raw and prepared oyster appetizers to goat cheese pizzas to an Asian-inspired ahi tuna sandwich with red cabbage coleslaw to a hearty triple pork chop with mashed potatoes.

Pearl is located in a terra-cotta-colored stucco building, with a cute patio on the street. Inside, hex signs scare away evil spirits, and hopefully will someday soon scare away the restaurant's chipboard tables and continued tendency toward understaffing, because this food deserves a better presentation. *1339 Pearl St, Ste 104, Napa; 707/224-9161; $$; MC, V; local checks only; lunch, dinner Tues–Sat; beer and wine; reservations recommended; at Franklin.*

VILLA CORONA ★★↓

This low-key Mexican restaurant in a mall serves such clean, delicious, authentic cuisine that local chefs come here on days off. Stand in line, order from the counter, grab a number, and settle down at one of the tables amid brightly colored walls or at one of the few patio tables outside. Shortly afterward huge plates will come your way. Classic burritos—especially carnitas (pork)—are outstanding, but the homemade corn tortillas and delicious red sauce make the chicken enchiladas another favorite. Prawns are flavor-packed with garlic butter or spicy hot sauce, and all the usual suspects—chimichangas, chiles rellenos, tamales, tostadas—are just as good. Breakfast includes a concise list of favorites: chilaquiles (scrambled eggs with tortilla strips and salsa), huevos rancheros, and machaca (eggs and roasted pork scramble). Good news for those who absolutely must share the fresh-tortilla experience with friends: they ship anywhere in the United States. And if you simply want to take an order to go, call in advance or order at the takeout counter. *3614 Bel Aire Plaza (Trancas St), Napa; 707/257-8685; $; MC, V; no checks; breakfast, lunch, dinner Tues–Sun; beer and wine; no reservations; off Trancas St hidden in the SE corner of the mall.*

LODGINGS

CEDAR GABLES ★★↓

Forget any preconceived notions of B&Bs with weathered rooms, thin walls, sagging mattresses, shared baths, and funky cramped quarters. Beautiful Cedar Gables' attention to decor and service puts many of the valley's upscale hotels to shame. Innkeepers Margaret and Craig Snasdell have worked wonders with their 1892 Victorian and its nine rooms. The historic theme extends from the large and cozy family room, where guests meet each night to enjoy wine and cheese or watch TV in front of a blazing fire, to the breakfast room, where a full hot morning meal might include homemade breads, in-season fruit, French toast soufflé with strawberries and walnuts, or a Southwest casserole. Rooms are lavishly and appropriately adorned with tapestries, gilded antiques, and, in five rooms, fireplaces and/or whirlpool tubs. Bonuses uncommon to B&Bs include a decanter of port in each room, robes, irons and ironing boards, CD players, and hair dryers. *486 Coombs St, Napa; 707/224-7969 or 800/309-7969; $$$; AE, DIS, MC, V; checks OK; info@cedargablesinn.com; www.cedargablesinn.com; from Hwy 29 exit onto 1st St, follow signs to downtown, turn right on Coombs St and proceed to corner of Oak St.*

THE CHABLIS INN   ★

The 34-room Chablis looks a little old, but its rooms are decent-size, comfortable, and very cheap. Each unit has a king- or queen-size bed, phone, TV, wet bar, coffeemaker, and small refrigerator; some have kitchenettes. The small heated swimming pool and spa—a godsend during the sweltering summer months—are surrounded by cement, but the potted flowers and baby-blue-and-white umbrellas add a little zip. Continental breakfast is included. Small dogs are welcome. Ask for a room facing away from Highway 29. *3360 Solano Ave, Napa; 707/257-1944 or 800/443-3490; $; AE, DC, DIS, MC, V; no checks; www.chablisinn.com; off Hwy 29.*

CHURCHILL MANOR   ★★

Churchill Manor is an elegant, meticulously maintained mansion, incongruously set in a modest neighborhood. Built in 1889 by a local banker, it is listed on the National Register of Historic Places. The Colonial Revival house, which rises three stories above an expanse of beautiful gardens, is graced by stately pillars and a large, inviting veranda. Each of the 10 immaculate guest rooms features antique furnishings, ultraplush carpeting, and an elegant private bath; among the favorites are Victoria's Room (imposing and spacious, with a king-size bed and a claw-footed tub perched by the fireplace), Rose's Room (with a scattering of French antiques, including a carved-wood, king-size bed), and Edward's Room (the largest room, Mr. Churchill's former sanctuary also boasts magnificent French antiques and a lavish bath with hand-painted tiles). Rates include a full breakfast served in the marble-floored sunroom, fresh-baked cookies and coffee or tea in the afternoon, and a wine-and-cheese reception in the evening. When you're not out touring the local wineries, you may tickle the ivories of the grand piano in the parlor, play croquet on the lovely side lawn, or tour Old Town Napa on the inn's tandem bicycles. Owners Brian Jensen and Joanna Guidotti are attentive and welcoming hosts. *485 Brown St, Napa; 707/253-7733; $$; AE, DIS, MC, V; checks OK; www.churchillmanor.com; at Oak St.*

LA RESIDENCE ★★

Set back in the trees along busy Highway 29, this multimillion-dollar creation of partners David Jackson and Craig Claussen has 20 guest rooms scattered throughout two houses separated by a heated swimming pool and an elaborate gazebo. The main house, a Gothic Revival mansion built in 1870 by a former New Orleans riverboat captain, contains nine comfortable guest rooms beautifully decorated with designer fabrics and American antiques. Most have sitting rooms, fireplaces, and private baths. Airier accommodations can be found in the modern French-style barn across the plaza. Filled with simple pine antiques, these spacious rooms have fireplaces, private baths, and French doors that open onto small patios or balconies. A delicious gourmet breakfast is served downstairs in the barn in a cheery, sunny dining room. Although La Residence is undeniably one of the region's loveliest small inns, its location next to the highway detracts from the away-from-it-all feel that B&Bs usually try to cultivate. *4066 St. Helena Hwy, Napa; 707/253-0337; $$$; AE, DC, DIS, MC, V; checks OK; on Hwy 29, next to Bistro Don Giovanni.*

While most of downtown Napa's accommodations are on the lower end of the hotel spectrum, this riverfront newcomer, which opened in June 2000, is bent on becoming a reason to stay south of Yountville. The three buildings that make up the 66-room hotel are part of the newly reconstructed and historic Napa Mill and Hatt Market, a soon-to-be gourmet marketplace with a few restaurants and easy access to central downtown. Superior rooms located in the main building, an 1884 historic landmark, ooze romance—from their bordello red walls accented with original brick, their lovely dark wood furnishings, and their comfortable (and new!) half-canopy beds draped with cream, gold, and red patterned textiles to their overstuffed love seats with ruby red ottomans and gas fireplaces. If the adorable gold-and-cream clawfooted tubs in the luxury bathrooms don't lure you to lounge, extra perks like in-room coffee, daily newspaper, data ports, voice mail, CD clock radios, and complimentary vouchers for a full breakfast and evening cocktails at one of the adjoining restaurants will encourage you to spend some time on the property. The newest hotel building, to the left of the main hotel, offers airy, light, and modern rooms and murky-river views. Rooms in the adjoining Annex to the right of the main hotel and directly on the river are less appealing due to their somewhat loud mustard-and-brown "nautical" decor and motel-style brick interior walls. (If you must stay there, ask for a second-floor room facing the river with a window at the bathtub and a small patio.) Still, they're worlds above a lot of the area's motels that charge similar rates. During high season there is a two-night minimum. The Greenhaus European Day Spa (see activities) is located in the hotel's parking lot. *500 Main St, Napa; 707/251-8500 or 877/251-8500; $$–$$$$; AE, DC, DIS, MC, V; checks OK; www.napariverinn.com; just S of 1st St.*

OAK KNOLL INN ★★★

 If you want to know what it feels like to live like a pampered local, this ultra-exclusive four-room B&B is the way to go. The unassuming driveway, which requires a hard turn into the driveway along a pastoral stretch between Highway 29 and the Silverado Trail, is so discreet it's hard to find the front entrance. But no matter. Every accessible French door opens to the small but oh-so-charming French-country dining room and fire-front seating area, complete with an alluring selection of books, nuts, fruit, and hints of the breathtaking panoramic views beyond the back door. The cozy common quarters lead one to believe bedrooms will be equally compact, but that's not the case. Each of the four rooms in the one-level stone-walled mansion is enormous, with floral patterns, rock walls, vaulted ceilings, a wood-burning fireplace, sitting area, and private entrance. Not that an excuse is needed, but the lack of a TV is inspiration to kick up your heels on the back deck or by the large swimming pool or whirlpool spa and look over the unobstructed 600-acre vineyard and mountain view. Adding to the aura of exclusivity is the nightly wine and cheese hour for up to a mere eight guests, which is often hosted by the valley's most prestigious winemakers, and the full gourmet breakfast, which features creative dishes such as fruit pizza or baked eggs. *2200 E Oak Knoll Ave, Napa; 707/255-2200; $$$$; MC, V; checks OK; between Hwy 29 and the Silverado Trail.*

SILVERADO COUNTRY CLUB & RESORT ★★

Golfers and tennis players flock to this 1,200-acre estate, and it's easy to see why. The Silverado boasts two perfectly maintained 18-hole golf courses designed by Robert Trent Jones Jr., and the largest tennis complex in North America, holding 20 championship courts rimmed with flowered walkways. If you're not into golf or tennis, however, there's little reason to stay here; the 280 unprepossessing rooms seem to have been designed for people who don't plan to spend much time indoors. The standard rooms, in a condolike warren, start at about $165. The one- and two-bedroom suites overlooking the golf course are prettier but equally soulless; they're gleamingly modern with black-marble fireplaces and well-appointed kitchens. A few minutes' drive from the main complex are the more secluded Oak Creek East accommodations, street after street of mind-numbingly similar houses and condominiums owned by country-club members and rented out to guests. Numerous swimming pools dot the extensive grounds—popular spots to cool off on the valley's sweltering summer days. The resort's clubhouse and restaurants are located in the magnificent colonnaded Southern Gothic mansion at the heart of the main complex. Vintners Court, a formal dining room dominated by a glittering chandelier and a white grand piano, offers decent Pacific Rim fare. For a more casual meal, order a club sandwich or a hamburger at the Silverado Bar & Grill. The Royal Oak restaurant is a luxurious throwback to the days of elegant club grills. *1600 Atlas Peak Rd, Napa; 707/257-0200; $$$; AE, DC, DIS, MC, V; checks OK; www.silveradoresort.com; from Hwy 29, turn right onto Trancas St (Trancas St will become Hwy 121), then left on Atlas Peak Rd.*

YOUNTVILLE

Given that the commercial hub is about three blocks long, sleepy little Yountville, located 9 miles north of Napa off Highway 29 and founded in the mid-19th century by pioneer George Clavert Yount (reportedly the first American to settle in Napa Valley), has developed quite a reputation as a top-notch destination. Most of the hullabaloo, of course, can be credited to the French Laundry, which has been touted as the best restaurant in the United States—and the most impossible to get into. But on the heels of its success came two glorious French bistros (Bouchon and Bistro Jeanty), a handful of new and expensive inns, and more foot traffic to the small collection of boutiques.

ACTIVITIES

Hot-Air Ballooning. The only sight more quintessentially Napa than colorful hot-air balloons hovering overhead is the view *from* one of those hot-air balloons. The ride is far tamer than it looks, and it's a fun, sleepy trip down the valley. But there is a catch: balloons ascend at sunrise (weather permitting), or as early as 6am, and the price is inching closer and closer to $200 per person. On the bright side, Adventures Aloft schedules pickups from hotels as far north as St. Helena, warms your half-awake soul with coffee and baked goods before taking flight, and finishes with a full sparkling-wine breakfast at Compadres Mexican restaurant. (Vintage 1870 shopping complex, 6525 Washington St, between California Dr and Webber St; 707/944-2451)

Museum. The setting, above a redwood grove adjacent to the Veterans Home and champagne maker Domaine Chandon, couldn't be more representative of the Napa Valley Museum's permanent collection, showcasing regional art and the cultural, historical, and environmental heritage of Napa Valley. The collection includes 4,000 artifacts ranging from Native American arrowheads and winemaking equipment to fine arts, along with rotating contemporary exhibits. (55 Presidents Cir; from Hwy 29 go W on California Dr; 707/944-0500; www.napavalleymuseum.org; open Wed–Mon 10am–5pm; $4.50 adults, $3.50 seniors and students, $2.50 ages 7–17, kids under 7 free; free Mon)

Shopping. In the heart of Yountville is the beautiful brick complex known as Vintage 1870 (6525 Washington St, Yountville; 707/944-2451), a touristy mall with a few dozen shops and a handful of restaurants. The building was erected in 1870 as a winery and is listed on the National Register of Historic Places. Cooks will appreciate its cute gourmet foods and kitchenware store called Cravings. North on Washington next to Bistro Jeanty is a French antiquer's dream, Antique Fair (6512 Washington St; 707/944-8440), where gorgeous imported and restored imported 18th-, 19th-, and 20th-century furniture is complemented by great French-milled soap, honey, and silver accessories. Headed out of town, Mosswood (6550 Washington St; 707/944-8151) is a sweet boutique with oodles of gifts and knick-knacks for the home and garden. Anyone looking to add some substantial furnishings to their backyard or patio can stock up on Indonesian imports and pretty teak outdoor furniture at Venika (6774 Washington St; 707/944-8944, located at the end of the commercial stretch)

WINERIES

Domaine Chandon. The French may not have meant to, but they encouraged Napa Valley's grand European-style Wine Country with French Champagne house Moët et Chandon's

1973 introduction of its beautiful, aesthetic, expansive, and bucolic sparkling-wine facility and gardens. Along with gorgeous landscaped grounds, ever-changing art exhibits, and very comprehensive hourly tours of the sparkling-winemaking process, visitors have access to a lovely tasting room and patio where delicious bubbly is for sale by the glass, as well as a renowned restaurant (see review). The showcased art, which recently included a collection of Wine Country works from French painter Guy Buffet, is for sale. *1 California Dr; 707/944-2280; www.dchandon.com; open every day 10am–6pm.*

RESTAURANTS

BISTRO JEANTY ★★★

Philippe Jeanty was a culinary pioneer in Napa. He came from France to head Domaine Chandon's now-legendary kitchen back when the region was known more for cattle and prunes than for four-star wines. After 17 years at Chandon, he left to open his own place in Yountville, and it's been a success ever since, with the James Beard Foundation nominating it for the title of best new restaurant in the United States. Three years later Bistro Jeanty still represents the rare perfect marriage of ambience and cuisine, perhaps because Jeanty designed the whole thing himself, modeled on the small French bistros from his childhood. The details are flawless—from the window boxes with geraniums outside to the antiques and the specials chalkboard inside. A large "community table" by the front door seats diners without partners or reservations and is a favorite of locals who drop by. Patio seating is equally pleasant, even though it's adjoining a parking lot. The food remains true to Jeanty's heritage: lamb tongue salad, haricots verts, sole meunière, steak tartare, and a dreamy coq au vin—all of which are well followed by a sinfully luxurious crème brûlée, with a thin but poignant layer of chocolate mousse beneath its perfect caramelized top. *6510 Washington St, Yountville; 707/944-0103; $$$; MC, V; no checks; lunch, dinner every day; full bar; reservations recommended; at Mulberry St.*

BOUCHON ★★¹

Thomas Keller opened this small bistro, which is worlds more casual than his other restaurant, the French Laundry, and is most popular as a late-night gathering place for the valley. Bouchon looks like a miniature Paris nightclub—one with such a sophisticated, elegant atmosphere that you immediately feel stylish simply by walking through the door. A zinc bar is put to good use serving raw seafood specialties such as oysters, mussels, and langoustines, while the few patio seats recall Parisian-style dining. The fare is traditional *bistro français:* foie gras, quiche du jour, charcuterie plates, onion soup gratine, steak frites, mussels marinières, and, for dessert, tarte Tatin and profiteroles with ice cream and chocolate sauce. A short menu of appetizers, entrees, and desserts is served till 1:30am daily. While food and service can be uneven, it's hard not to have a good time here. *6534 Washington St, Yountville; 707/944-8037; $$$; AE, MC, V; local checks only; lunch, dinner every day; full bar; reservations recommended; across from the Vintage 1870 shopping center.*

DOMAINE CHANDON ★★★

Napa Valley's culinary reputation was born at this elegant restaurant with rough-textured walls and wood archways overlooking the winery's manicured gardens and vineyards. Rooted in traditional French techniques enlivened by California innovation, executive chef Robert Curry's creative and delicate cooking style is perfectly matched to Domaine Chandon's sparkling wines. Past winners from the ever-changing menu have included an exquisite appetizer of alder-smoked trout served on a bed of curly endive, and a Japanese eggplant soup that arrives not as the customary purée but as a multicolored mélange streaked with basil and red and yellow peppers. Anything from the grill—such as beef, rabbit, or the divine pancetta-wrapped salmon—packs a salt-and-peppery punch, followed by a flavorful unfolding of meltingly tender meat. Grand desserts have included such jewels as a ground-almond shortcake with strawberries and a polenta pudding saturated with grappa and topped with fresh raspberries and mascarpone. The extensive wine list features some interesting (mainly California) vintages at sur-

prisingly reasonable prices. Service is gracious and impecca-
ble. Domaine Chandon also offers patio dining during the
warm months. While the cuisine here is quite good, it doesn't
reach the past culinary heights for which it was renowned
during chef Philippe Jeanty's reign. But then again, Jeanty,
during much of his 17 years in the kitchen, had no budget and
no requirement to make profits. *1 California Dr, Yountville;
707/944-2892; $$$; AE, DC, DIS, MC, V; no checks; May–Oct:
lunch every day, dinner Wed–Sun; Nov–Apr: lunch, dinner
Wed–Sun (closed first 2 weeks of Jan); wine only; reservations rec-
ommended; www.dchandon. com; just W of Hwy 29.*

THE FRENCH LAUNDRY ★★★★

A serious dining affair awaits those who are fortunate (or
persistent) enough to snare a reservation at the French
Laundry, the top-ranked restaurant in the country. Draped
in ivy, surrounded by herb gardens, and bearing no sign
announcing its purpose, the incognito restaurant is occu-
pied by a brilliant chef offering unbelievably intricate
meals, stellar wines, and faultless (yes, rather formal) serv-
ice. Since taking over the helm in 1994, chef Thomas Keller
has created the ultimate "precious" dining experience. Here
everything is coddled, sculpted, ornamented (and often
adorned with truffles or 100-year-old balsamic vinegar),
and coaxed to beyond perfection. This is not the kind of
place you come to to have a good time as much as it is an
opportunity to witness and taste edible artistry, which
comes in small portions, but is rich and delicious enough
to require a full day of recuperation. The prix-fixe tasting
menu—always lavish, extraordinary, and *very* precious—
offers a choice of five or seven courses that change daily and
invariably are accompanied by more than one amuse-
bouche. On one evening, dinner commenced with a chilled
English pea soup infused with white truffle oil, followed by
Maine lobster poached in sweet butter, pan-seared white
quail with braised Adriatic figs and a Mission fig coulis, and
an incredible saddle of venison. In true French style the
meal was topped off by a cheese course with French butter
pears poached in white wine, followed by a divine yellow
nectarine sorbet. The service is subtle and perfectly timed,

but such perfection doesn't come quickly *or* cheaply. The French Laundry (the place was indeed a laundry when it was constructed in the 1890s) also serves a four-course lunch, which is best enjoyed on the patio next to the flower and herb gardens. Reservations are accepted up to two months in advance. Good luck getting through to a receptionist, though. *6640 Washington St, Yountville; 707/944-2380; $$$$; AE, MC, V; local checks only; lunch Fri–Sun, dinner every day; beer and wine; reservations required; at Creek St.*

GORDON'S CAFE AND WINE BAR ★★✦

There's no pretense or slick Wine Country show here. Instead, it's a good old-fashioned country-store-style cafe where homemade granola, baby oats, scones, big cookies, omelets, strong cups of coffee, individual pizzas, sandwiches (such as house-roasted turkey breast with applewood smoked bacon, Roma tomatoes, and arugula), and soups are enjoyed by a good portion of locals and tourists. After ordering from the chalkboard menu and paying the tab, diners settle into a charming and sunny dining area, which is flanked by for-sale wine and edible accoutrements and antiquated by old-hardwood floors. Proprietor Sally Gordon recently got a permit to extend her three-course Friday-night dinner to every night, but she's pacing herself by starting with weekend nights only. It's good news for anyone looking for a reasonably priced, more low-key but delicious dinner, because joints with this much authentic, small-business atmosphere are hard to come by in these parts. If you come for dinner, expect three or four selections within each category (appetizer, main course, and dessert). Previous starters have included grilled asparagus with Meyer lemon shallot relish and crumbled Humbodlt Fog goat cheese and a luxurious salad of white winter vegetables with white truffle vinaigrette and shaved pecorino. Main courses may feature pan-seared filet mignon with decadent potato and caramelized onion gratin, al dente sautéed greens, and Zinfandel black peppercorn sauce, or the even more exotic grilled fresh white prawns with Cuban-style black beans and roasted tomato salsa. Dessert, which you can't help but indulge in, might be a tangy pineapple flan with roasted fresh pineapple or devilish chocolate molten cake with coffee crème anglaise. *6770 Washington St, Yountville; 707/944-8246; $$; MC, V; checks OK; breakfast and lunch Tues–Sun, dinner Fri–Sat; beer and wine; reservations accepted for dinner; from Hwy 29, take Yountville exit, turn left on Washington St, and follow it to the N side of town.* &

MUSTARDS GRILL ★★★

Some critics call Mustards' feisty American regional cuisine comfort food, but that's too complacent a description for the vigorous, spicy, vaguely Asian-influenced bistro fare served here. Part of the Cindy Pawlcyn dynasty (which includes such highly successful restaurants as St. Helena's Tra Vigne, Mill Valley's Buckeye Roadhouse, and her brand-new St. Helena restaurant Miramonte), this wildly popular restaurant has a big open kitchen, pale yellow walls, dark wood wainscoting, and a black-and-white checkerboard floor. Appetizers range from wild mushroom toast with goat cheese to Chinese chicken noodle salad with spicy peanut dressing. The menu changes frequently, but is anchored by long-standing favorites such as the giant Mongolian pork chop with braised sweet-and-sour cabbage and garlic mashed potatoes. Mustards specializes in entrees from the wood-burning grill; try the tea-smoked Peking duck with almond-onion sauce, or barbecued baby back ribs. The desserts often change, but they're always worth the splurge, especially if they include the fresh blueberry crisp with lemon ice cream. Mustards' voluminous international wine list includes a vintage chart, and the restaurant pours a selection of domestic microbrews, including a "sassy beer of the day." *7399 St. Helena Hwy, Yountville; 707/944-2424; $$; DC, DIS, MC, V; no checks; lunch, dinner every day; full bar; reservations recommended; on Hwy 29, just N of town.*

RISTORANTE PIATTI ★★

 Piatti is a deservedly popular chain of chic nouvelle Italian restaurants with outlets in touristy towns throughout Northern California. And it all started right here in tiny Yountville. Chef Peter Hall (of Tra Vigne and Mustards Grill fame) took over from Renzo Veronese in 1997, bringing his own touch to the kitchen with such dishes as Peter's Rabbit Sausage and homemade potato gnocchi. Kick off your meal with the melt-in-your-mouth sweetbreads sautéed with mushrooms or perfectly grilled vegetables with whole roasted garlic. For a main course, try any of the plump, delicately flavored cannelloni or the risotto of the day: favorites include a creamy risotto packed with artichoke hearts, chicken, and sun-dried tomatoes, and a delicious variation with smoked salmon and fresh asparagus. Grilled items, such as the chicken and rabbit, are also consistently top-notch. Piatti sometimes goes overboard with the seasonings, forsaking balance for blasts of flavor, so select a wine with a lot of backbone. The Italian/Napa Valley wine list is extensive. *6480 Washington St, Yountville (and branches); 707/944-2070; $$; AE, DC, MC, V; no checks; lunch, dinner every day; full bar; reservations recommended; S of the Vintage 1870 shopping center.*

LODGINGS

MAISON FLEURIE ★★

Built in 1873, this beautiful, ivy-covered brick-and-fieldstone hotel was a bordello and later a 4-H clubhouse before it opened in 1971 as the Napa Valley's first bed-and-breakfast inn. Purchased by the owners of the Four Sisters Inns company (who also run the charming Petite Auberge in San Francisco and Pacific Grove's Gosby House), the old Magnolia Hotel was reborn as Maison Fleurie in 1994 and endowed with a French country feel. Seven of the guest rooms are located in the main house, with its thick brick walls, terra-cotta tiles, and vineyard views; the remaining six are divided between the old bakery building and the carriage house. All have private baths, and some feature fireplaces, private balconies, sitting areas, and patios. After a long day of wine tasting, unwind at the pool or soak your tired dogs in the outdoor spa tub. The inn also provides bicycles for tooling around town. *6529 Yount St, Yountville; 707/944-2056; $$$; AE, DC, MC, V; no checks; www.foursisters.com; at Washington St.*

VILLAGIO INN & SPA   ★★★

One of the latest additions to the luxury hotel scene is the Vintage Inn's Tuscan-inspired sister, the Villagio, which is too centrally located in downtown Yountville to be pastoral or exclusive, but well designed enough to warrant high prices for its rooms. The 112 homey accommodations are divided among a small village of patina-washed two-story buildings ("Italian cluster-style architecture," they call it) and flanked by flowers and one long tiled pond. Each is notably spacious and gorgeously appointed with rich burgundy, mustard, and cream-colored fabrics, mahogany furnishings, fireplaces, TVs with VCRs (plus movie rentals and popcorn at the front desk for $9), down comforters, a complimentary bottle of wine and bowl of apples, and crisp, gold-accented sheets sweet enough to take with you. Bathrooms are just as generous, with oversize sunken tubs, plush robes, Aveda products, and the very unusual and thoughtful addition of mouthwash. Second-floor digs boast a private patio and vaulted ceilings. Corporations book retreats here due to the great conference facilities, but it could easily also be because of the perks, which include a full-service spa complete with massage, hydrotherapy, and body scrubs and wraps; tennis courts; outdoor pools (one in the spa area, one closer to the rooms); a very small exercise room; bocce ball; a sauna; and a sparkling-wine breakfast served in the large and gracious lobby. *6481 Washington St, Yountville; 707/944-8877 or 800/351-1133; $$$$; AE, DC, DIS, MC, V; checks OK; www.villagio.com; just E of Hwy 29.* ♿

VINTAGE INN   ★★

Spread throughout a 23-acre estate and designed by the same architect who created Big Sur's Ventana Inn, the Vintage Inn provides the Napa Valley traveler with a host of creature comforts in a modern—and rather corporate—setting. The 80 large, cheery rooms, bathed in soothing earth tones and wood accents, are all equipped with fireplaces, whirlpool tubs, refrigerators, patios or verandas, ceiling fans, and plush private baths. Guests may take a dip in the heated pool or outdoor spa, play a game of tennis, order room service, sip a spirit at the bar, or rent the inn's

You don't have to stay at a fancy hotel to get an in-room massage. Massage to Go (707/252-2466) delivers strong loving hands to your door no matter where you're staying in the valley.

bikes, hot-air balloon, or private limo for a tour of the Wine Country. You'll also be treated to a continental breakfast served with glasses of bubbly. *6541 Washington St, Yountville; 707/944-1112 or 800/351-1133; $$$; AE, DC, DIS, MC, V; checks OK; www.vintageinn.com; just E of Hwy 29.*

YOUNTVILLE INN   ★★✦

Well landscaped, pretty, centrally located in downtown Yountville, and brand-new is the combination that makes for a good night's sleep at Yountville Inn. From the outside the 51 guest rooms, many of which have vaulted ceilings and tend to look out over foliage and other accommodations, may not feel as exclusive as some of the more expensive Wine Country properties. But step through the door and you'll discover they've got all the fixings: great square footage, fieldstone fireplaces, attractive Pottery Barn/country-style furnishings, a tempting snack basket, coffeemakers, TVs with VCRs, patios, comfortable beds, and, most desirable for all hotels, newness. Bathrooms are fabulous with Italian tile, double sinks, robes, and hair dryers. An outdoor pool and Jacuzzi help you wind down after a hectic day of indulgence, and each day starts with complementary continental breakfast in the warm, welcoming lobby, where vaulted ceilings, comfy couches and chairs, and a fire remind you that Wine Country is all about relaxation. *6462 Washington St, Yountville; 707/944-5600 or 800/972-2293; $$$; AE, DC, DIS, MC, V; California checks OK; www.yountvilleinn.com; at the S end of town.* ᕦ

OAKVILLE

Other than several world-class wineries, boutique Oakville's main claim to fame is the Oakville Grocery (see picnic sidebar in this chapter), an old-timey gourmet goods purveyor complete with a fading "Drink Coca-Cola" sign outside.

WINERIES

Opus One. This world-famous winery collaboration between the late Baron Philippe de Rothschild and Robert Mondavi is dedicated to producing the single and outstanding

Cabernet blend known as Opus One. Stunning architecture is only half the reason to make an appointment to tour the dramatic neoclassical building. Along the way you'll learn high-tech wine-making practices and see the way it's done when money is no object. Tastings are expensive ($25 per 4-ounce glass of wine; tours are free) and the atmosphere is quite serious, as is the extraordinary wine. You can taste without touring, but if you want the whole experience, schedule your tour well in advance; weekend spots book up a month ahead of time. *7900 St. Helena Hwy, at Oakville Cross Rd; 707/944-9442; www.opusone.com; one public tour every day; tasting 10:30am–3:30pm.*

Robert Mondavi Winery. This huge, world-famous winery, housed in a Mission-style building, offers the most comprehensive selection of tours in the entire valley. The basic one-and-a-half-hour tour of the vineyard and winery is $10 and includes wine tasting and one appetizer and wine pairing. But it's worth investing time and money in the more intimate tours, such as the 3-hour, $35 "essence tasting," where you smell various herbs, spices, and other scents attributed to wine, then taste wines that contain the same elements, or the appellation tour ($85), which examines the winery and terroir and includes a three-course wine-paired lunch. *7801 St. Helena Hwy; 707/963-9611; open every day 9am–5pm; closed Easter, Thanksgiving, Christmas, and New Year's Day.*

Silver Oak Wine Cellars. This small winery tucked on a side road in between the Silverado Trail and Highway 29 is so well known for its Cabernet Sauvignon that brand-conscious power diners are almost guaranteed to order it if it's on a restaurant's wine list. But that's not to say its two designer wines, which are either from the Napa Valley or Alexander Valley appellation, aren't justifiably power players themselves. You can decide for yourself by stopping in to taste Monday through Friday. Tours, which wander into the vineyards and include a discussion of the vines and the winery history, are available only on weekdays at 1:30pm and require an appointment. On Saturday, no tours are offered, but you can arrive unannounced to taste in the morning. In the afternoon you must make an appointment. *915 Oakville Cross Rd, at Money Rd; 707/944-8808.*

Consider visiting
during weekdays,
the misty months of
winter, or early
spring, when many
room rates are
lower and every-
thing's less
crowded, but the
valley is no less
spectacular.

RUTHERFORD

Neighboring the towns of Oakville and St. Helena, Rutherford
has no commercial center, but it does boast a number of highly
regarded wineries.

ACTIVITIES

Outdoor Play. Napa Valley may not be known for its
nightlife—or its performing arts—but every Friday, Saturday, and Sunday night in July you can catch a fantastic Shakespeare performance. Where better to watch actors and directors
from all over perform the likes of *Richard III* and *Twelfth Night*
than under the stars at Rutherford Grove Winery? (Shakespeare
Festival; 707/251-WILL or www.napashakespeare.org; tickets
$18 adults, $14 students and seniors)

WINERIES

Beaulieu Vineyards. This historic winery founded in
1900 by France's famed Georges de Latour is housed in a
historic estate and is famous for its Cabernet Sauvignon. Free
tours cover the basics of winemaking and the company's history,
but most people pop into the modest tasting area, where for a
small fee you can sample current releases. Big spenders step into
the adjoining building to savor a flight of reserve wines, which
will set you back at least $20. *1960 St. Helena Hwy, N of Rutherford
Rd; 707/967-5230; www.bvwine.com; open every day 10am–5pm.*

Franciscan Estates. While anyone who visited Franciscan in the mid-'90s will recall a friendly and large tasting
room where wine was showcased wine-shop style, the new Franciscan, which was unveiled in 2001, is a sophisticated and welcoming space in which visitors can sample the winery's complete
selection (Simi, Ouintessa, Estancia, Veramonte, and Franciscan). In the beautiful new tasting room with dark wood mer-
chandising shelves, a zinc-topped centerpiece bar, and light
pouring in from skylights, guests can taste Franciscan Oakville
Estate wines (Chardonnay, Merlot, Cabernet Sauvignon, Zinfandel) for a small fee. For a heftier chunk of change you can do an
"estate tasting," which includes samples from all the estates,

served in new, wood-paneled, library-like VIP tasting rooms. Additional comprehensive private tastings include a blending tasting called "mastering the meritage." *1178 Galleron Rd, at Hwy 29 N of Rutherford; 707/963-7111; www.franciscan.com; open every day 10am–5pm; closed major holidays.*

Niebaum-Coppola Winery. Filmmaker Francis Ford Coppola owns this incredible former Inglenook grand château, built in the 1880s. The grounds are everything you'd think a fantasy winery would be—grand, pastoral, opulent, historic—and are well worth a turn off Highway 29. Inside the visitor center is a different story altogether. Along with good displays on Coppola's film career and Inglenook's history, you'll find an enormous, modern, and expensive gift shop stocked with wine, pottery, books, T-shirts, and even Coppola's favorite cigars. Daily wine tastings are offered for a steep $7.50, and $20 tours are by appointment. *1991 St. Helena Hwy; 707/963-9099; open every day 10am–5pm.*

St. Supéry Winery. Lifetime tasting privileges for $5 and a fun, approachable self-guided tour of the winemaking setup make St. Supéry a favorite for the everyday visitor. Especially fun is "SmellaVision," which allows you to smell various scents that are commonly found in wine. Free guided tours, which start at 11am, 1pm, and 3pm, visit the vineyard's demonstration vines to discuss various grapes and how they're grown, then lead you through the self-guided tour, adding supplemental stories and information along the way. The 3pm tour also visits the historic Victorian, called the Atkinson House, which showcases 100-plus years of winery memorabilia. Tastings include current releases such as Sauvignon Blanc, Merlot, and Cabernet Sauvignon. *8440 St. Helena Hwy/Hwy 29; 707/963-4507 or 800/942-0809; www.stsupery.com; open every day 9:30am–5pm.*

RESTAURANTS

LA TOQUE ★★★

While the sometimes overly casual staff and framed chef's hat over the giant stone fireplace evoke the spirit of laid-back dining, French-inspired La Toque is exceptionally formal.

CYCLING

It doesn't take long for outdoor enthusiasts visiting Napa Valley and the surrounding wine region to realize they're going to want to spend more time sipping out of water bottles on their bicycles than out of wineglasses in the tasting rooms. The cool canyons and gently sloping country roads make Napa an ideal cycling-tour destination. Don't worry that the main highways are crowded with tourists buzzing from winery to winery in their rental cars—the best cycling routes are off the main highways anyway, and that's where you're advised to stay. The scenery is pleasant, rural, and quiet; long, low-slung canyons planted with vineyards dominate much of the landscape. Among the best areas to explore the looping country roads are in the valleys west of Highway 121 and around the St. Helena area, west toward Sonoma. The best time of year to ride is either side of summer, particularly during the fall grape harvest season, when the mornings stay cool longer and the afternoons are mild.

There are two ways to bike the valley: either contact a tour company for a complete cycle tour of the wineries and canyon roads, with tastings and even accommodations included, or rent bicycles and explore freestyle. Some reputable tour companies and outfitters in the area include Getaway Bicycle Tours (1117 Lincoln Ave, Calistoga; 800/499-2453); Bicycle Trax

Guests are advised to dress elegantly, and with only a few well-dispersed tables and a full-room view blocked only by a floral centerpiece, it's safer to overdo it than arrive in khakis and a pullover. But in truth, most people quickly turn their focus to the quiet, refined menu featuring Ken Frank's gorgeous four-course prix fixe feast. Chef Frank's culinary creativity shows both in presentation and flavor. A recent visit included an outstanding oxtail flan, clams nestled in a savory salt cod brandade, and delicate artichoke soup with a starburst of white truffle cream. The beer-battered porcini appetizer and chestnut-and-chanterelle bisque with black truffle cream didn't impress, but with the menu changing weekly, duds are quickly replaced with winners and ongoing surprises, as well as classics such as Niman Ranch beef tender-

(796 Soscol Ave, Napa; 707/258-8729); Napa Valley Bike Tours (4080 Byway E, Napa; 800/707-BIKE); St. Helena Cyclery (1156 Main St, St. Helena; 707/963-7736); and Detailed Destinations (1734 Jefferson #C, Napa; 707/256-3078).

One pleasant ride, of intermediate difficulty mostly because of its length, is the 40-mile trek through Wooden Valley along Wooden Valley Road, which begins at the Highway 121 intersection and then follows Wooden Valley Creek and Suisun Creek to the west. There are numerous possible loop connections here that will bring you back to the highway, with most of the ride in lightly traveled countryside dotted with ranch buildings and cropland. Another favorite among road cyclists is Dry Creek Road, which takes riders from Oakville north of Yountville on Highway 29 through scenic canyons and ridge lands separating the area from Glen Ellen in Sonoma County. There is also a pleasant but long 50-mile loop beginning on Dry Creek at Oakville, through to Glen Ellen via Trinity Road, then back to the Highway 29 corridor via Napa Road. All of this, of course, is through lovely ranchlands and open countryside best explored in the spring and early fall when temperatures tend to be moderate. Petrified Forest Road west of Calistoga near the Highway 29/128 junction passes through the Chalk Mountain wilderness areas, with loop connections through Alexander Valley to Santa Rosa and then Napa.

loin with roasted root vegetables and red wine. Appropriately, there's an optional wine-pairing menu. *1140 Rutherford Cross Rd, Rutherford; 707/963-9770; $$$; AE, MC, V; no checks; dinner Wed–Sun; full bar; reservations required; www.latoque.com; adjoining Rancho Caymus Inn at Hwy 29.*

RUTHERFORD GRILL   ★★✔

Midsummer, the patio and outdoor bar are prime real estate at this convivial Houston's chain–owned California-style restaurant. On rainy winter eves (and on blazing summer days) the comfortable but supper-club-style house is packed with festive diners who know the body-to-body bar is one of the most popular places to elbow up to for a martini straight up or a glass of wine and some Chicago-style spinach-artichoke dip or house-smoked salmon. Meanwhile, hordes of attractive happy visitors and families line up at the door to be seated first-come, first-served at one of the 190 seats around booths or tables. House specialties include zesty baby back ribs, tender wood-fired rotisserie chicken, and the ever-popular prime rib sandwich. Extra perks include continuous service from lunch through dinner and no corkage fee, a rarity for any restaurant. *1180 Rutherford Rd, Rutherford; 707/963-1792; $$; AE, MV, V; local checks only; lunch, dinner every day; full bar; no reservations; www.rutherfordgrill.com.* &

LODGINGS

AUBERGE DU SOLEIL ★★★★

 There are few better places on earth to escape to than Auberge. This exclusive 33-acre, 52-unit resort, inspired by the sunny architecture of southern France, is nestled in an olive grove on a wooded hillside above Napa Valley (think views for miles). Here it's all about exclusivity in the form of cottages and suites you could get lost in, complete with rough-textured adobe-style walls, white French doors and windows, and shocking pink textiles that are whimsical upon first encounter and old hat by the second or third visit. Each cottage has four guest rooms. Suites have very private entrances and patios or balconies. Upstairs rooms, which boast vaulted, exposed-beam ceilings, are particularly posh, but even the humblest accommodations here are sinfully hedonistic, with fireplaces, CD players, artwork, comfortable furnishings, candles, sitting areas, tiled floors, and to-die-for bathrooms. Two rooms in the main building lack fireplaces but have king-size beds and French doors that open onto private terraces. The other extreme are the cottages of all cottages, with 1,800 square feet of full-blown luxury, including a whirlpool spa on the terrace, two fireplaces, a living room, den, and master bedroom and bath, not to mention a $3,000-a-night price tag (off-season it's a piddly $1,500). Tack on the pool, brand-spanking-new completely fabulous spa with heated tile floors, enough treatments to keep you busy for weeks (and broke at $125 per hour per treatment), the same famous view, three additional pools, and the new gym, and there's little reason to leave. With the dining room serving Wine Country cuisine (best enjoyed on the terrace) for lunch and dinner, and a bar serving a light menu from 11am to 11pm, you really don't need to set foot off the property. And shhhh. Don't say we said so, but last we checked, the hotel was rumored to have a few reserved tables at the French Laundry, which are doled out by concierge on a first-come, first-served basis. *180 Rutherford Hill Rd, Rutherford; 707/963-1211 or 800/348-5406; $$$$; AE, DIS, MC, V; checks OK; www.aubergedusoleil.com; N of Yountville: from the Silverado Trail, turn right on Rutherford Hill Rd.*

RANCHO CAYMUS INN ★ʲ

Travelers with modern fashion sensibilities may not appreciate the old-fashioned funky-rustic Spanish colonial decor of Rancho Caymus, but people with more whimsical tastes and an appreciation for furnishings and crafts from south of the border will delight in the worldly collection amassed here. Built by architect Mary Tilden Morton in 1986, the unique structure surrounds a tiled courtyard overflowing with Chinese wisteria, star jasmine, pink jasmine, lilies, and bird of paradise. Its adobe fireplace, which blazes nightly, adds ambience to the outside seats of adjoining restaurant La Toque. Step into any one of the 26 split-level stucco rooms and you'll find antique handcrafted South American furnishings, hand-woven rugs, ceramic artworks, a queen-size bed, sofa, and wet bar. All but four have beehive fireplaces, and four suites have whirlpool tubs backed by stained glass windows. If you don't get the opportunity to dine at formal and French La Toque (adjoining next door), you can at least see the dining room during the complimentary continental breakfast (prepared by the inn). *1140 Rutherford Rd, Rutherford; 707/963-1777 or 800/845-1777; $$$–$$$$; AE, DIS, MC, V; checks OK; www.ranchocaymus.com; at Hwy 29.* &

ST. HELENA

If you continue north from Rutherford on a scenic stretch of Highway 29, you'll drive smack through the center of St. Helena, which has come a long way since its days as a rural Seventh Day Adventist village. For many years St. Helena has been entrenched in a never-ending battle to preserve its exclusive, small-town way of life—instead of becoming even more of a tourist haven for Wine Country visitors. Citizens have filed injunctions against everything from the Napa Valley Wine Train (forbidding it to stop in town) to Safeway (the grocery giant wanted to build a larger supermarket here). Needless to say, Wal-Mart was out of the question. Still, St. Helena's Victorian Main Street (a.k.a. Highway 29) and its shopping are about as chichi as Wine Country gets, with women's clothing boutiques and upscale home-furnishing stores nuzzling a few fine restaurants and gift shops.

ACTIVITIES

Cooking Demonstrations. If you have even the slightest fantasy of being a chef, a visit to the Culinary Institute of America is an absolute inspiration. The grand stone building, once a Christian Brothers winery, is on the National Register of Historic Places and is now home to aspiring professionals in the fields of food, wine, health, and hospitality. The public can no longer embark on tours of the complete cooking compound, where chefs bustle through impressive teaching kitchens to learn the nuances of roux and meringue. But cooking demonstrations are now offered every day. Gourmands need only make a reservation and pay the $10 fee to watch a chef prepare a dish, then taste it and depart with the recipe. If all that mixing, grating, and sautéing has you hankering for more, you can drop into the building's restaurant, the Wine Spectator Greystone Restaurant, and try to grab a table or a bar seat to savor its great appetizers and A-OK main courses. No matter what, make a pit stop at the gift store, an unparalleled shrine to the culinary craft. (2555 Main St; 707/967-2320; call for scheduled demonstration times and availability)

Museum. The author best known for the book *Treasure Island* is celebrated with abandon at the aptly named Robert Louis Stevenson Silverado Museum. Of the 8,000 relics that help to chronicle the valley resident's life, you can catch a glimpse of everything from letters, manuscripts, and paintings to personal belongings. (1490 Library Ln, N of Adams St; 707/963-3757; open Tues–Sun noon–4pm; free)

Olive Oil. Napa Valley Olive Oil Manufacturing Company is an authentic Italian deli and general store stuffed with goodies like dried fava beans, biscotti, salami, and fresh mozzarella. But it's most revered by locals and visitors for its incredible olive oil, which visitors buy by the half gallon. For great gifts, be sure to pick up a bottle or two. (835 Charter Oak Ave, in the white shack at the dead end; 707/963-4173; open every day)

One-Stop Wine Tasting. Cantinetta Tra Vigne (1050 Charter Oak Ave; 707/963-8888) and its charming patio seats, adjacent to the atmospheric Ristorante Tra Vigne (see review), has long been a great pit stop for enjoying espresso, focaccia pizzas, Italian sandwiches, interesting soups and salads, pastas topped with smoked salmon and other delights, and a surfeit of sweets. But in 2000 the tiny shop packed to the rafters with gourmet to-go goods introduced its wine-by-the-glass program, which features 100 selections. The Tuscan atmosphere is enough reason to walk through the door, but anyone who wants a crash course in unique wines from around the world (they recently poured Screaming Eagle) is sure to spend some time at the Cantinetta's bar.

Outlet Shopping. With headliner shops like Donna Karan, Brooks Brothers, Movado, Tumi, and Coach, you won't find so many cheap seconds in the cute square known as St. Helena Premium Outlets. There is only a handful of stores, but each promises 25 to 55 percent off retail prices. Come on the right day and you're likely to depart with at least a few bags of new fashion favorites. (3111 St. Helena Hwy; 707/963-7282; open every day 10am–6pm)

Boutique Shopping. You need only walk one of the few commercial blocks in downtown St. Helena to realize the town's charms go beyond the Victorian architecture and into the adorable shops. Though the area is condensed and walkable, you could easily window-shop your way through an afternoon. Be

Unlike in big cities, finding a good cup o' joe in the valley is harder than most residents would like. But one faithful place for caffeine fixes is Napa Valley Coffee Roasting Company, which has locations in downtown Napa (948 Main St; 707/224-2233) and downtown St. Helena (1400 Oak Ave; 707/963-4491).

sure to check out Vanderbilt and Company (1429 Main St, between Adams and Pine Sts; 707/963-1010; open every day), a haven for home and garden lovers, where paper plates and bath soap meet collectable Italian ceramic dishware and cooking ware.

 Park and Historic Mill. Peaceful paths, gorgeous wooded surroundings, and a recently renovated bale mill hark back to Napa Valley's early existence at beautiful and underutilized Bale Grist Mill State Historic Park (3369 Hwy 29 at Bale Grist Mill Rd, 2 miles N of St. Helena on the left side of the road; 707/963-2236). Wind down the wooded paths to the recently restored historic flour mill built in 1846 by a British surgeon named Bale. The 36-foot wooden waterwheel still grinds grain into meal and flour on weekends ($1 donation per person); it also appeared in the 1960 film *Pollyanna*. Next door is the 1,800-acre Bothe-Napa Valley State Park (707/942-4575), offering about 100 picnic spots with barbecues and tables, a swimming pool open from Memorial Day through Labor Day, and 50 campsites. You can hike from one park to the other by following the moderately strenuous 1.2-mile History Trail. (Hwy 29, 3 miles N of St. Helena)

Cocktails and Dancing. For years it seemed like the whole region turned off its lights and went to bed right after dinner. Enter 1351 Lounge, hands down the most festive and fancy bar in the valley. The city-smart bar is located in a wonderful former bank complete with vault, which was Napa Valley's first Bank of Italy and later a very small Bank of America. The stone-walled building was renovated under the guidance of one of the talents behind the too-chic W hotel chain. Now guests sip their flavored martinis surrounded by brown velvet, a beautiful old mahogany bar, an original pressed-tin ceiling, a disco ball, and candlelight. Despite no sign on the door, the word is out that this is the hot spot for cocktails, dancing (although there's no official dance floor) to a DJ or live blues, rock, reggae, or funk, and all-around revelry with a classy twist. (1351 Main St, in downtown St. Helena; 707/963-1969; open nightly; cover charge with live music)

Movie Theater. St. Helena's historic Cameo Cinema is sitting pretty thanks to a loving restoration by valley resident and famed filmmaker Francis Ford Coppola. Current releases and art films now show on its single screen and change frequently. (1340 Main St, between Hunt Ave and Adams St; 707/963-9779; www.cameocinema.com)

WINERIES

Beringer Vineyards. Napa Valley's oldest continuously operating winery features astounding landscaped grounds, a brand-new tasting room, and a stately old Rhineland-style mansion, which displays historical information about the winery and hosts reserve tastings. The winery, which is well known for its Chardonnay, Cabernet, and ever-popular white Zinfandel, has an extensive selection of wines to taste and purchase, great tours of the vineyards and caves, and of course plenty of knickknacks to buy in the gift shop. *2000 Main St; 707/963-7115; open every day 9:30am–6pm Apr–Oct, 9:30am–5pm Nov–March; $5 tours every half hour from 10am; reservations not necessary.*

Duckhorn Vineyards. Tucked into a quintessential meadow off the Silverado Trail, Duckhorn has long been a stop for fans of its Cabernet Sauvignon, Merlot, and Sauvignon Blanc. But as of spring 2001 there's yet another reason to pull into the parking lot: the beautiful new tasting room, which mixes Victorian farmhouse charm (think lots of sunlight, light colors, and wraparound veranda) with a sleek centerpiece bar, pendant lights, and salon-style (sit-down) wine tasting. Permits require guests to make reservations to taste or tour, but you can always stop by and grab a bottle to go. *1000 Lodi Ln; 707/963-7108; www.duckhorn.com; open every day 10am–4pm; tasting $15.*

Merryvale Vineyards. Merryvale's historic stone building makes a stunning backdrop for daily tastings and, by appointment only, informative, thorough wine-component tasting classes on Saturday and Sunday mornings. The winery is best known for its Chardonnay. *1000 Main St; 707/963-7777; $10 component tastings, $3–$12 tastings; open every day 10am–6:30pm.*

RESTAURANTS

BRAVA TERRACE ★★

Brava Terrace offers lively French-Mediterranean cuisine in an idyllic setting: the beautiful dining room has vaulted ceilings with exposed wood beams, white walls with bright modern art, glowing hardwood floors and furniture, and a big stone fireplace. Even better are the large, beautifully landscaped terraces—the perfect place for a lazy lunch, a late-afternoon snack, or dinner on a warm evening. Owner Fred Halpert breathes life into old classics like cassoulet, but he also has an inviting menu of daily pastas and risottos. The grilled portobello mushrooms with spinach and artichokes topped by a roasted garlic–walnut vinaigrette is a first-rate appetizer, and the pan-roasted chicken with "garlic-smashed" potatoes and rosemary-infused pan juices is a soul-satisfying choice for the main course. Finish with a chocolate chip crème brûlée or one of the exquisite house-made sorbets. There's a lengthy, reasonably priced wine list to boot. *3010 St. Helena Hwy, St. Helena; 707/963-9300; $$$; AE, DC, DIS, MC, V; no checks; lunch, dinner every day May–Oct; lunch, dinner Thurs–Tues, Nov–Apr; full bar; reservations recommended; fredbrava@aol.com; on Hwy 29, between St. Helena and Calistoga, next to Freemark Abbey.*

PINOT BLANC ★★

Celebrity chef Joachim Splichal (owner of LA's Patina and a trio of other Pinots in Los Angeles) migrated north to open this "country bistro." With executive chef Sean Knight in the kitchen, the food usually shines. Don't miss his salmon with a shallot- and apple-smoked-bacon crust, marinated pork chop with horseradish mashed potatoes, or any of the plats du jour (for example, braised Calistoga pig with home-made sauerkraut is served on Sunday, and Provençal-style bouillabaisse with saffron rouille is offered on Friday). The wine menu suggests trying a bottle of Pinot Blanc, but it also features more than 350 other possibilities, including a lengthy list of whites for those suffering from Chardonnay burnout. *641 Main St, St. Helena; 707/963-6191; $$$; AE,*

DC, DIS, MC, V; no checks; lunch, dinner every day; full bar; reservations recommended; off Hwy 29.

TAYLOR'S AUTOMATIC REFRESHER ★★√

Anyone who knows how tiresome fancy food can get can understand why Taylor's Refresher, a classic burger stand straight out of the 1950s, is a favorite among even the region's top chefs and the nation's best-regarded food editors. Sure, the 1949-built outdoor diner is a looker, with its yesteryear fast-food-shack design and outdoor seating. But more important, it doles out some darned good burgers and fries—juicy, thick, and served with all the toppings. Wine Country living doesn't get much better than a patty smothered with cheese and accompanied by a creamy shake or fizzy root beer float. Those who beg to differ can always belly up for a good old-fashioned corn dog; steak, fish, or chicken taco; or veggie burger. *933 Main St, St Helena; 707/963-3486; $; AE, MC, V; local checks only; lunch, dinner every day; beer and wine; no reservations; right on the highway, you can't miss it.* &

TERRA ★★★√

If you can have only one dinner out while visiting Napa Valley, have it at Terra. The incognito restaurant, housed in a historic stone building with high ceilings and arched windows, is known as a valley favorite. But with no advertising or marketing during more than a decade in business, it has managed to avoid hoopla and maintain a quiet reputation as one of the finest dining destinations in Northern California. Terra's subdued dining rooms have an ineffable sense of intimacy about them. Fervid tête-à-têtes, however, are more likely to revolve around Terra's fine eclectic southern French/northern Italian food (with Asian influences) than around *amore*. Yet this isn't the sort of food that screams to be noticed; chef Hiro Sone's cuisine never grandstands. Unusual combinations such as mild duck-liver wontons with an earthy wild mushroom sauce may sound a little forced, but they don't play that way on the palate. Broiled sake-marinated Chilean sea bass with shrimp dumplings is an addiction at first bite; spaghettini with fresh tomatoes

Unless you want to forage local supermarkets for dinner, be sure to make restaurant reservations. Wine Country tables are some of the most coveted in the state and are booked well in advance, especially between April and October.

and white bean stew is simply delicious; grilled veal chop with Pinot Noir sauce, to die for. Whatever you do, don't skip dessert. You may just discover that until Terra, you have never really understood why tiramisu means "carry me up." *1345 Railroad Ave, St. Helena; 707/963-8931; $$$; DC, MC, V; local checks only; dinner Wed–Mon; beer and wine; reservations recommended; between Adams and Hunt Sts, 1 block E of Main St.*

TRA VIGNE & CANTINETTA TRA VIGNE ★★★★

The Tuscan-inspired food at Tra Vigne is exceptionally fresh, and almost everything is made on the premises, including the anise-flecked bread, pasta, cheese, olive oils, smoked meats, and desserts. Appetizers are chef Carmen Quagliata's forte. The menu changes seasonally, but you can usually find delicately crisp polenta rounds topped with meaty wild mushrooms in a rich, gamy vinaigrette; wonderfully fresh mozzarella and tomatoes drizzled with basil oil and balsamic vinegar; and a daily seafood selection fried crisp in arborio rice flour with mustard seed vinegar. Pastas run the gamut from traditional to outrageous—such as ravioli stuffed with puréed pumpkin and sprinkled with fresh cranberries—and pizzas are delicately and expertly rendered. Entrees might include grilled Sonoma rabbit with Teleme-cheese-layered potatoes, oven-dried tomatoes, and mustard sauce; ahi tuna grilled on a rosemary skewer and served on a roasted-pepper salad with pea sprouts; and a crisp leg of duck confit on a pea-and-potato purée with spring onion sauce. Desserts are stellar: try the velvety espresso custard with a thin layer of fudgelike chocolate dusted with powdered sugar, served with a crisp hazelnut cookie. Service is knowledgeable, witty, and efficient. The wine list is excellent and includes a carefully chosen array of Italian and Napa Valley bottles. The vast, exquisitely designed dining room has soaring ceilings and taupe walls covered with big, bright Italian poster art. Even more appealing is the Tuscan-inspired courtyard, which is shaded by umbrellas, and a serious contender for the best dining atmosphere in the valley.

If you'd prefer a light lunch or want your food to go, amble over to the less expensive Cantinetta Tra Vigne. The cantinetta sells several varieties of focaccia pizza, gourmet sandwiches, interesting soups and salads, pastas topped with smoked salmon and other delights, and a variety of sweets. *1050 Charter Oak Ave, St. Helena; 707/963-4444 (restaurant) or 707/963-8888 (cantinetta); $$$; DC, DIS, MC, V; local checks only; lunch, dinner every day (restaurant), lunch every day (catinetta); full bar; reservations recommended; off Hwy 29.*

Bring bottled water with you when you hit the wine-tasting trail. The valley gets hot, and sampling wine all day is sure to make you parched.

WINE SPECTATOR GREYSTONE RESTAURANT AT THE CULINARY INSTITUTE OF AMERICA AT GREYSTONE ★★✦

When you first spot Greystone perched high atop a hill, you'll catch your breath, as it's the closest thing the United States has to a castle. The building, which formerly housed the Christian Brothers winery, was constructed in 1889 out of local tufa stone. The restaurant is on the first floor of the Culinary Institute of America (it's named for *Wine Spectator* magazine, which donated $1 million to the school's scholarship fund) and is in a large, noisy room with a fireplace and a display kitchen surrounded by a bar. The CIA's cooking students play an integral role in restaurant preparations, led by talented chef Todd Humphrey. Humphrey has steered the menu away from the Mediterranean theme of former restaurateur/chef Joyce Goldstein, into New American territory. Diners have two choices for appetizers: raw oysters or a chef's tasting menu. Choose both. Begin with oysters and the CIA's own reasonably priced house champagne, then move on to the tasting menu, which offers small morsels of indescribable variety and pleasure. Some examples from one offering: carpaccio, smoked salmon on a bed of shredded beets, potato balls, and scallops in crème fraîche. The main course brings other unique mouthwatering combinations: venison served with a confit of autumn vegetables and huckleberry sauce; seared sea scallops with saffron gnocchi, asparagus and morel sauce, and so on. A fine finish to the meal is the velvety crème brûlée accompanied by vin santo. The wine list is extensive, offering something for every taste and price range. Tours of the building are available, as are cooking demonstrations on weekends (707/967-1100). The basement houses a huge cookware emporium, complete with every gadget and cookbook imaginable. *2555 Main St, St. Helena; 707/967-1010; $$$$; AE, DC, MC, V; local checks only; lunch, dinner every day; full bar; reservations recommended; www.ciachef.edu; at Deer Park Rd.*

LODGINGS

EL BONITA MOTEL ★✈

Thanks to an extensive remodeling, El Bonita is indeed *bonita*. Hand-painted grapevines grace many of the room entrances, and inside the walls are colored a faint pink, with floor-length baby blue drapes and pink-and-baby-blue floral bedspreads. Each of the 41 rooms has a private bath, color TV, and phone; for a little more money, you can have cable TV, a microwave, a refrigerator, and even a kitchen and a whirlpool bath. Huge oak trees surround the motel, a heated kidney-shaped swimming pool sits in front, and a sauna and an outdoor whirlpool are on the premises; massages are available by appointment. The rates vary from month to month (depending on business), but in general you (and your pet) can get a reasonably priced room. El Bonita fronts Highway 29, so try to get a room as far from the street as possible. St. Helena's shopping district is a short drive or a 20-minute walk away. *195 Main St, St. Helena; 707/963-3216 or 800/541-3284; $$; AE, DC, DIS, MC, V; no checks; elbonita1@aol.com; www.elbonita.com; just S of downtown St. Helena on Hwy 29.*

HOTEL ST. HELENA ★✈

Those who'd like to stay in the heart of charming St. Helena need look no further. The amazing lobby looks like someone transported all the props from Disneyland's "It's a Small World After All" and deposited them here. Hundreds of elaborately decorated dolls and marionettes are draped over the furniture and hung from the ceiling. Fortunately, the excessive doll theme doesn't continue in the rooms, which are decorated in rich tones of burgundy, gold, and mauve, with polished antique furnishings (no smoking allowed). Most of the 18 units have private baths and TVs, although some have shared baths and run a bit cheaper. If you look hard enough beyond the lobby's dollscape, you'll see a small coffee, wine, and beer bar tucked in the back, where—with the wide-eyed plastic faces staring at you from all angles—you'll never drink alone. *1309 Main St, St. Helena; 707/963-4388; $$–$$$; AE, DC, DIS, MC, V; no checks; downtown.*

THE INK HOUSE BED AND BREAKFAST ★⁄

This gorgeous Italianate Victorian inn, built in the shape of an ink bottle by Napa settler Theron Ink in 1884, would merit three stars if it weren't for its no-star location along a busy, noisy stretch of Highway 29. The three-story yellow-and-white home has seven sumptuously decorated guest rooms, plus a lavish living room and parlor with an old-fashioned pump organ and a grand piano. The B&B's most interesting architectural feature is the glass-walled belvedere that sits atop the house like the stopper of an inkwell and offers a sweeping 360-degree view of Napa Valley hills and vineyards. The best (and quietest) room is the spacious, high-ceilinged French Room, with its richly carved mahogany bed graced by an elegant half canopy. The rooms at the front of the house are for sound sleepers only. Innkeepers David and Diane Horkheimer are incredibly friendly and helpful, and they'll nourish you with a full country breakfast, plus wine and appetizers in the afternoon. *1575 St. Helena Hwy, St. Helena; 707/963-3890; $$; MC, V; checks OK; inkhousebb@aol.com; www.inkhouse.com; at Whitehall Ln.*

INN AT SOUTHBRIDGE ★★★

This newer sister to the swanky Meadowood Resort fills the gap between Napa's ultra-luxe digs and its ubiquitous bed-and-breakfast inns. Designed by the late William Turnbull Jr., the 21-room inn is part of a terra-cotta-hued complex that dominates a long block on St. Helena's main drag. Inside, the guest rooms are almost Shaker in their elegant simplicity, with white piqué cotton comforters, candles, fireplaces, vaulted ceilings, and French doors opening onto private balconies. Guest privileges are available at the exclusive Meadowood Resort, though the on-site Health Spa

Napa Valley offers a plethora of spa treatments, plus its own swimming pool and exercise equipment. In the courtyard, a big red tomato sets the mood at Tomatina, the inn's stylish pizzeria. Sit on one of the tomato red bar stools facing the open kitchen and order the clam pie, a winning pizza combo. *1020 Main St, St. Helena; 707/967-9400 or 800/520-6800; $$$$; MC, DC, V; checks OK; www.slh.com (search for "southbridge"); between Charter Oak Ave and Pope St.*

MEADOWOOD RESORT ★★★★

Rising out of a surreal green sea of fairways and croquet lawns, Meadowood's pearl gray, New England–style mansions are resolutely East Coast. Winding landscaped paths and roads connect the central buildings with smaller lodges scattered over 256 acres; the lodges are strategically situated near an immaculately maintained nine-hole golf course, two croquet lawns (with a full-time croquet pro on hand), seven championship tennis courts, and a 25-yard lap pool. The 85 exorbitantly priced accommodations range from one-room studios to four-room suites, each with a private porch and a wet bar. The suites tucked back in the woods are the most private, while the Lawnview Terrace rooms are more central and include vaulted ceilings, massive stone fireplaces, and French doors opening onto balconies that overlook the croquet green. The vast bathrooms have hair dryers, magnified makeup mirrors, thick bathrobes, and floors inset with radiant heating to keep your toes cozy as you pad to the cavernous shower. All guests have access to the swimming pool, the outdoor whirlpool, and the well-equipped health spa that offers a weight room, aerobics classes, massages, and numerous other ways to pamper your body.

The octagonal Restaurant at Meadowood has a high ceiling and a beautiful balcony overlooking the golf course. Appetizers, like the sweet bell pepper ravioli with wild mushrooms in a browned sage butter or the Miyagi oysters on the half shell with champagne sauce and caviar, are consistently very good, though the expensive entrees vary in quality. The more informal Grill at Meadowood offers an elaborate breakfast buffet, and sandwiches and salads for lunch. *900 Meadowood Ln, St. Helena; 707/963-3646 or*

800/458-8080; $$$$; AE, DC, DIS, MC, V; checks OK; www.meadowood.com; off the Silverado Trail.

WHITE SULPHUR SPRINGS RESORT & SPA ★★

Pastoral surroundings and an uncommonly casual St. Helena atmosphere are all yours with a quick turn off Highway 29, a five-minute drive up the mountainside, and a reservation at White Sulphur Springs. No need for fancy duds here. It's just you, and 330 acres of wilderness and hiking trails, creeks, waterfalls, and natural springs that inspired the resort's original construction in 1852. Today the property continues to be upgraded, from the nine cozy creekside cabins to the 28 rooms dispersed among three structures, including the old Carriage House. All rooms are adorned with country-style furnishings; some have a fireplace or wood-burning stove and/or kitchenette. Cottages have picnic tables and barbecues and modern touches like air conditioning and heaters. Rooms at the "inn" have private entrances and showers (no tubs), and the two-story Carriage House boasts shared bathrooms for each floor (men's and women's are separate, but they recommend you bring a bathrobe for the dash to the shower and back). There's no TV, phones, or Internet access, so it's easy to forget the dramas of everyday life. Equally stress-free is the cost, which is far better than at most properties in the area. The best perk is easy access to nature and the brand-new spa, which offers everything from rock therapy and salt scrubs to massage and use of the heated outdoor pool and natural hot springs. *3100 White Sulphur Springs Rd, St. Helena; 707/963-8588 or 800/593-8873 (in CA); $$; MC, V; no checks; www.whitesulphursprings.com; turn W at Exxon gas station (Spring St) and continue 3 miles.*

Find out if a wine you want to buy is in local distribution. If so, consider buying it at a retail outlet instead of at the winery, because you'll often find much better prices at some of the good wine stores in town.

CALISTOGA

Mud baths, mineral pools, and massage are still the main attractions of this charming little spa town, founded in the mid-19th century by California's first millionaire, Sam Brannan. Savvy Brannan made a bundle of cash supplying miners in the Gold Rush and quickly recognized the value of Calistoga's mineral-rich

Leaving downtown
St. Helena and
heading north
toward Calistoga,
you'll pass under
the Tunnel of the
Elms (also called
the Tree Tunnel), a
fantastic row of
dozens of elm trees
arched across Main
Street (Highway 29)
in front of Beringer
Vineyards. They
were planted by
the Beringer broth-
ers more than 100
years ago, and
their interlaced
branches form a
gorgeous canopy
about a quarter of
a mile long.

hot springs. In 1859 he purchased 2,000 acres of the Wappo Indians' hot springs land, built a first-class hotel and spa, and named
the region Calistoga (a combination of the words California and
Saratoga). He then watched his fortunes grow as affluent San
Franciscans paraded into town for a relaxing respite from city life.

Generations later, city slickers are still making the pilgrimage.
These days, however, more than a dozen enterprises touting the
magical restorative powers of mineral baths line the town's streets.
You'll see an odd combo of stressed-out CEOs and earthier types
shelling out dough for a chance to soak away their worries and get
the kinks rubbed out of their necks. While Calistoga's spas and
resorts are far from glamorous, many offer body treatments and
mud baths you won't find anywhere else in this part of the state.

ACTIVITIES

Museum. For a trip back in time to Calistoga's pioneer
past, stop by the Sharpsteen Museum and Brannan Cot-
tage. The area's rich historic past is brought to life through a dio-
rama of Sam Brannan's resort, which was opened in 1862; one of
the original Sam Brannan cottages (moved from its original location); "Ben's Room," showcasing memorabilia of Ben Sharpsteen,
who created the museum and was a Walt Disney producer and
director; an old stagecoach that used to run from Calistoga to
Lakeport; and an interactive geothermal exhibit. (1311 Washington St; from downtown Calistoga's Lincoln Ave, turn N onto
Washington St; 707/942-5911; open every day 11am–4pm; $3
donation appreciated)

Old Faithful Geyser. They don't call it Old Faithful for
nothing. This natural wonder faithfully shoots a plume of
350°F mineral water 60 feet into the air at regular intervals. (1299
Tubbs Ln; take Hwy 29 2 miles N from Calistoga, then take a right
on Tubbs Ln; 707/942-6463; open 9am–6pm Apr–Sept, 9am–5pm
Oct–Mar; $6 adults, $5 seniors 60 and over, $2 kids 6–12)

 Petrified Forest. No, it wasn't the work of
Medusa that turned the Petrified Forest's towering
redwoods to stone. Rather, it was a natural occurrence that
resulted from an eruption of Mount St. Helena 3 million years
ago. Stop by to see the redwoods as well as petrified seashells and

other fossils that give a glimpse into the area's history. (4100 Petrified Forest Rd; off Hwy 128, 6 miles N of town; 707/942-6667; open every day 10am–5:30pm; $5 adults, $4 adults 60 and over and kids 12–17, $2 children 6–12, free under age 6)

Hike with a View. The premier challenge for hikers looking to make a day of it in the Napa Valley is the trek to the 4,343-foot summit of Mount St. Helena along Mount St. Helena Trail (difficult; 9 miles round trip), a sometimes steep and grueling climb to what has got to be the best view of the California wine region found anywhere. The trail is best tackled during the spring wildflower season—not only because it's so pretty but also because the summers at high noon are just plain intolerable here. The mountain is slated for development as a state park someday, but for now it is more of a wilderness area with few recreational improvements beyond trail cuts. (W side of Hwy 29, approximately 9 miles N of Calistoga; call the local state parks office at 707/942-4575 for information)

Shopping. Since most everything commercial is condensed into a few short blocks in downtown Calistoga, you can easily window-shop your way though town in an hour or two. Keep a lookout for Casa Design (1419 Lincoln Ave; 707/942-2293), which showcases a beautiful eclectic mix of home gifts, stunning woven sea grass armchairs, pillows, and bath and bedroom accessories. Also worth a peek is Evans Design Group (1421 Lincoln Ave; 707/942-0453), a below-wholesale factory outlet for raku pottery and glass art that you might otherwise find in shops like Saks, Macy's, and Ethan Allen.

 Mountain Biking. The ridge lands, peaks, and winding canyons surrounding Napa Valley are ideal for mountain biking, some even featuring intense climbs for those who really want to sweat it. The chief conquest is, of course, the ride to the 4,343-foot summit of Mount St. Helena northeast of Calistoga, a moderately difficult 9-mile ride on the summit fire road (clearly marked) off Hwy 29 east of the town of St. Helena. This is the main fire road leading to both the south and north peaks of the mountain, which offer spectacular views of several high Northern California peaks—including Mounts Shasta, Lassen, Diablo, and the Sierra Nevada—on clear, cool days. The best route for expert bikers is the Oat Hill Mine Road in Calistoga, an old mining road turned bike trail that climbs from 400 feet to 2,200 feet in about 5 miles. Definitely bring plenty of water on this ride. The dirt-rock road is very rutted from the days of old mining wagons, and the property on either side of it is private, so do not stray from the trail. In the spring you will see plenty of wildflowers. From Calistoga, take Highway 29 north about 1 mile and look for the trailhead to the east. Oat Hill Mine Road is to the left of the Trailhead Store. For more information, see the "Cycling" sidebar in this chapter.

Safari. In the mood for a bit of Africa? The 240-acre Safari West animal preserve, west of Calistoga, is home to nearly 400 mammals and birds. Guests spend two and a half hours on an educational tram and walking tour of the preserve. Sunscreen and a hat are recommended during the spring and summer months. Walking shoes are also essential, and don't forget the binoculars if you plan to try this unique experience. Last we checked, the basic tour ran $48 for adults and $24 for children. (From Santa Rosa, take US 101 N and exit E at the

River Road/Calistoga exit. In 7 miles, turn left on Franz Valley Rd. Proceed to the entrance gate. For additional information, contact Safari West at 707/579-2551 or www.safariwest.com)

WINERIES

🍷 **Château Montelena Winery.** This stunning French château-style winery, built of stone, has been celebrated for its Chardonnay since it brought global attention to the valley by snaring top ranking in the now-famous 1976 Paris blind tasting. Today you can taste a selection of three wines—perhaps Chardonnay, a Zinfandel blend, and estate Cabernet Sauvignon—for $10. But a visit promises more than just a feast for the palate: the beautiful setting includes a lake with two islands. *1429 Tubbs Ln; 707/942-5105; open every day 10am–4pm; tours by appointment.*

🍷 **Clos Pegase.** Architecture, art, and wine flow together in the most tasteful way at this stunning winery designed by architect Michael Graves. The impressive modern facility offers grand outdoor sculpture, a "Wine in Art" slide show every third Saturday afternoon, and good guided tours of the winery, caves, and art collection daily at 11am and 2pm. If nothing else, stop by and fork over $5 for samples of Chardonnay, Merlot, and Cabernet, which can be enjoyed in the pretty, manicured garden, or, better yet, bring a picnic, buy a bottle of Chardonnay, and set up camp at any of the prime outdoor-dining sites on the grounds. *1060 Dunaweal Ln, 2 miles S of Calistoga; 707/942-4982; www. clospegase.com; open every day 10:30am–5pm.*

🍷 **Schramsberg.** If you love sparkling wines, you'll love Schramsberg. Set amid 200 rustic acres, which were once stomping grounds for Robert Louis Stevenson, the historic estate and its 2 and a half miles of caves are magical and hark back to a time of transportation by horse and carriage. But the very comprehensive tour is led on foot through the old, damp passageways (carved in part by Chinese laborers in the 1800s and now filled with aging bubbly) and through every step of the sparkling-winemaking process. The free tour ends with an optional tasting of several delicious sparklers for a rather steep, but worthy, fee. The biggest catch: you can taste only if you've taken the tour, and you must reserve for the tour in advance.

After you've steamed or soaked away all your tensions, head over to the pretty outdoor patio at the Calistoga Inn (1250 Lincoln Ave; 707/942-4101) for a tall, cool drink. Try one of the house-brewed beers or ales, but save your appetite for one of the better restaurants in town.

Most wineries charge a tasting fee, but if you purchase wine afterward they usually subtract the charge from the wine's total price.

1400 Schramsberg Rd, just S of downtown Calistoga off Hwy 29; 707/942-2414; www.schramsberg.com; open every day 10am–4pm.

   Sterling Vineyards. Even in the thick of summer heat, from the road Sterling is reminiscent of an alpine ski resort. In truth, the only reason people make the association is because the winery, perched on a hilltop overlooking virtually all of the upper valley, is accessed by aerial sky tram. Ironically, because 2001's complete renovation of the facilities includes a large outdoor patio with umbrella, tables, chairs, and a bird's-eye view, that convivial ski-lodge vibe is sure to continue. While more than 250,000 people a year—including lots of families—pay the under-$10 fee to take a ride (which includes tasting for adults, a snack bag for kids), there's a lot more to sexy Sterling. You get an excellent self-guided tour as well as a great selection of wines to taste, and facilities have been updated to better accommodate wheelchair-bound visitors. *1111 Dunaweal Ln, 1 mile S of Calistoga, between Hwy 29 and Silverado Trail; 707/942-3300; www.sterlingvineyards.com; open every day 10:30am–4:30pm.*

RESTAURANTS

ALL SEASONS CAFE   ★★

Many restaurants in Napa Valley have elaborate wine lists, but none compare to this cafe's award-winning roster. The rear of the restaurant—a retail wine store with a tasting bar—stocks hundreds of first-rate foreign and domestic selections at remarkably reasonable prices. If nothing catches your fancy on the restaurant's regular wine list, ask to see the shop's enormous computerized catalog. The All Seasons menu is even structured around wine: the appetizers, such as crisp, herby bruschetta and creative salads, are recommended to accompany sparklers, Chardonnay, and Sauvignon Blanc; respectable California pizzas and pastas are paired with Sauvignon Blanc, Zinfandel, and Rhône wines; and entrees such as delicate roast quail with walnut-studded polenta, grilled lamb with fresh sprigs of dill, and fish with fruity sauces are matched with an excellent selection of Chardonnay, Cabernet, and Pinot Noir. So much emphasis is placed on wine, in fact, that the food sometimes suffers. However, the enthusiastic and opinionated servers can usually steer you safely to the better choices on the changing menu. *1400 Lincoln Ave, Calistoga; 707/942-9111; $$; MC, DIS, V; local checks only; lunch Thurs–Tues, dinner every day; beer and wine; reservations recommended; at Washington St.*

CATAHOULA ★★

By playfully dubbing his Wine Country restaurant Catahoula, the name of the Louisiana state dog, chef/owner Jan Birnbaum served notice that he was returning to his Southern roots—a surprise move, since Birnbaum's reputation had been built at such bastions of haute cuisine as New York's Quilted Giraffe and San Francisco's Campton Place restaurant. The discrepancy between his formal training and Catahoula's down-home fare turns out to be serendipitous, resulting in a glorious, spirited brand of nouvelle Southern cuisine. Hominy cakes served hot off the griddle are paired with fennel, potatoes, endive, and other veggies coated with a smoked-onion vinaigrette. The cornmeal-fried catfish is laced with lemon-jalapeño meunière and served with slaw, and a thin-crusted pizza is crowned with crayfish and andouille sausage. Catahoula is located in the Mount View Hotel, with its homey lobby featuring a huge hearth and overstuffed couches. The hotel saloon offers Catahoula's appetizers and light dinners on weekends, and serves other tidbits on the poolside patio in the summer. If you overindulge, you can always relax at the Mount View's well-appointed spa, or sleep it off in one of the hotel's guest rooms. *1457 Lincoln Ave, Calistoga; 707/942-2275; $$$; MC, DIS, V; checks OK; breakfast, lunch Sat–Sun, dinner every day; full bar; reservations recommended; near Washington St.*

CIN CIN ★★◗

Cin Cin's soulful Mediterranean food satisfies more than mere appetite. Dishes like melt-in-your-mouth gnocchi, served in a deep, flavorful ragout of duck, porcini mushrooms, and pancetta, offer a comfort akin to a nice warm blanket on a chilly night. The changing menu showcases delicacies of the season; one spring visit found a delicious salad of warm grilled asparagus combined with tart and juicy blood oranges. An inspired lavender and honey crème brûlée provided the perfect finish to the meal. The wine list features an international selection, with unusual vintages from France, Italy, and even New Zealand added to the usual California suspects. While the restaurant is located on Calistoga's main drag, the interior has a sophisticated big-city bistro feel, probably explained by the fact that chefs John Gillis and Gina Armanini both worked in San Francisco before opening their own place. *1440 Lincoln Ave, Calistoga; 707/942-1008; $$$; MC, V; no checks; dinner Wed–Sun, brunch Sat–Sun; beer and wine; reservations recommended; next to the Ace Hardware store.*

WAPPO BAR & BISTRO ★★

Husband-and-wife chefs Aaron Bauman and Michelle Matrux opened this zesty bistro in 1993 and immediately began collecting accolades for what Bauman describes as "regional global cuisine." Confused? Well, even Bauman admits the cuisine is hard to pinpoint, merrily skipping as it does from the Middle East to Europe to Asia to South America to the good old USA. The small menu changes often, but this culinary United Nations has embraced such diverse dishes as chicken potpie with a cornmeal-herb crust, fresh sea bass dipped in chick-pea flour served with mint chutney and lentil crepes, and Moroccan lamb stew with dried fruit and couscous. One dish that turns up often due to popular demand: chiles rellenos stuffed with basmati rice, crème fraîche, currants, and fresh herbs, dipped in a blue cornmeal batter, deep-fried, and served on a bed of walnut-pomegranate sauce. This is ambitious, imaginative cooking, and the talented chefs usually pull it off with aplomb. *1226-B Washington St, Calistoga; 707/942-4712; $$; AE, MC, V; local checks only; lunch, dinner Wed–Mon; beer and wine; reservations recommended; off Lincoln Ave.*

LODGINGS

CALISTOGA VILLAGE INN & SPA ★

Located at the northernmost end of the valley, the Calistoga Village Inn & Spa is a one-story, 41-room, sprawling white inn trimmed in slate blue, with baskets of colorful begonias hanging out in front. The rooms are spare but comfortable and spacious and include a private bath, air-conditioning, a queen-size or double bed, and a TV. The least expensive ones are in back, facing a parking lot and the rear of the Calistoga water-bottling plant. A well supplies the hot natural-mineral water to the inn's swimming pool, wading pool, and 12-person whirlpool spa, which is set under a handsome natural wood and glass-block gazebo. The pools aren't always as sparkling clean as others in the neighborhood, but they're still inviting. You can also get the full gamut of body treatments here—from mud baths to salt scrubs—although, as elsewhere in the valley, most cost as much as a night's lodging in a cheap sleep. *1880 Lincoln Ave, Calistoga; 707/942-0991; $–$$; AE, DIS, MC, V; no checks; greatspa@napanet.net; www.greatspa.com; next to the Ford dealership.*

COTTAGE GROVE INN ★★♪

It may feel a little like summer camp, with two lines of cabins tucked in a small grove and flanking a paved road, but if B&B quarters are a little too close for comfort and you want one of the best (albeit compact) rooms in Calistoga, you can't beat this place. Too bad Calistoga's busiest street is a tad close to some of the cottages (though the walls have double layers of Sheetrock to cut down on noise). Still, the 16 gray clapboard structures are storybook sweet, with white wicker rockers and firewood on the porches, two-person Jacuzzi tubs, fireplaces, hardwood floors, TVs with VCRs, CD players, and quaint quilts on the beds. An expanded continental breakfast of pastries, fresh fruit, cereal, coffee, and juice (included in the rate) is served in the small guest lounge, and wine and cheese are offered in the evening. *1711 Lincoln Ave, Calistoga; 707/942-8400 or 800/799-2284; $$$$; AE, DC, DIS, MC, V; checks OK; www.cottagegrove.com; at Wappo Ave.*

INDIAN SPRINGS RESORT   ★★

This historic inn was built in 1860 by Sam Brannan, the founder of Calistoga, on a site where Native Americans used to erect sweat lodges to harness the healing power of the region's thermal waters. A procession of 60 palm trees leads to the accommodations—17 rustic and casually furnished wooden cottages with partial kitchens, which appeal to families eager to cavort in the resort's huge hot-springs-fed swimming pool. Indian Springs also offers a playground and the full gamut of spa services (massages, facials, mud baths, and more). The spa is open to the public, but the wonderful pool is now restricted to spa and hotel guests only. *1712 Lincoln Ave, Calistoga; 707/942-4913; $$$; DIS, MC, V; checks OK; between Wappo Ave and Brannan St.*

MOUNT VIEW HOTEL   ★★

Other than Cottage Grove Inn, this National Historic Landmark hotel smack in the middle of charming downtown Calistoga is the best bet for the area. While a few years back the hotel was really showing its age, San Francisco hotel group Joie de Vivre is slowly breathing new life into the place. Today the 20 rooms and 9 suites, which tend to be on the small side, are cheerfully decorated with plenty of patterns (such as striped walls), colorful country-style textiles, overstuffed furnishings, feather beds, fresh flowers, and homey accoutrements such as coffeemakers and sparkling water. (Alas, age is still apparent in old and rather small televisions and general wear and tear.) Each morning as the rooms brighten with Wine Country sun, continental breakfast is delivered to your door. Romantics should splurge on one of the three cottages, which are located across the parking lot from the courtyard and its large outdoor pool and hot mineral whirlpool. Each cottage is fenced in for privacy and has a tiny outdoor patio (with hot tub) and wet bar. Rooms may be on the expensive side for what they are, but no other hotel in town boasts a good, festive restaurant (Catahoula) and a brand-new full-service spa offering everything from mud baths and massage to aromatherapy steams, body wraps, stone therapies, and facials. *1457 Lincoln Ave, Calistoga; 707/942-6877 or 800/816-6877; $$$$; AE, DIS, MC, V;*

checks OK; www.mountviewhotel.com; from Hwy 29 turn E onto Lincoln into downtown Calistoga.

NANCE'S HOT SPRINGS ★

Many Bay Area residents escape the hustle and bustle of city life by hiding out at Nance's, a very reasonably priced, funky, but comfortable hotel just steps from Calistoga's shops and cafes. The color scheme leaves a bit to be desired (dark green shag carpeting clashing with turquoise-and-navy bedspreads), but in a second-floor room, with a balcony overlooking the tree-covered hills, such issues fade in importance. Each well-worn room has a kitchenette, a cushioned chocolate brown Naugahyde chair, air-conditioning, cable TV (with HBO), and a phone. What more do you need? Nance's also offers massages, mud baths, and blanket wraps, and all guests have access to the 102-degree indoor mineral pool. *1614 Lincoln Ave, Calistoga; 707/942-6211; $–$$; AE, DIS, MC, V; checks OK; just E of downtown.*

QUAIL MOUNTAIN BED AND BREAKFAST ★★

Quail Mountain is a good choice for people who want to escape the bustle of the valley floor but still want to be near the action. Decorated with contemporary furnishings, artwork, and a smattering of antiques, the inn's three rooms open onto the outside balcony through sliding glass doors. During the day, you can read in the glass-enclosed solarium, swim in the small lap pool out back, warm up in the hot tub, nap in the hammock tucked in the trees on the hill above the house, or stroll through the fruit orchard and nibble on the amazing bounty. Innkeepers Don and Alma Swiers encourage guests to pick their own apricots, apples, peaches, cherries, figs, oranges, kumquats, and more. Some of the harvest always turns up at the table for breakfast, perhaps fresh with yogurt or in a brandy-wine sauce over French toast. The bad news is that this idyllic place is almost always booked; you'd be wise to make reservations several months in advance. *4455 St. Helena Hwy, Calistoga; 707/942-0316; $$$; MC, V; checks OK; from Hwy 29, turn left just after Dunaweal Ln and follow the signs.*

SONOMA VALLEY

SONOMA VALLEY

Many would argue that when it comes to comparing Sonoma Valley's 17-mile-long stretch of Wine Country with Napa's, less is definitely more: Sonoma is less congested, less developed, less commercial, and less glitzy than its rival. The valley itself boasts far fewer wineries and tourists than neighboring Napa, which welcomes 4.9 million annual visitors. But for Sonoma residents and visitors, that's exactly the point. Smitten with the bucolic charm of this region cradled by the Mayacamas Mountains to the west and the Sonoma Mountains to the east, oenophiles delight in wandering the area's back roads, leisurely hopping from winery to winery and exploring the quaint one-street towns along the way. There are moments when—sitting in the sunshine at some of the beautifully landscaped wineries, inhaling the hot camphor smell of the eucalyptus trees, listening to a gurgling brook and the serenade of songbirds as you sip a glass of chilled Sauvignon Blanc—you think that even Eden would be a disappointment after Sonoma.

GETTING THERE

Traffic permitting, it's a painless 45-minute drive from San Francisco to Sonoma. The fastest route is Highway 101 North to Highway 37 East (Vallejo/Napa exit). Follow Highway 37 to Highway 121 North, to Sonoma. Highway 121 becomes Broadway, a street that dead-ends at Sonoma's town plaza. From Oakland, take Interstate 80 north to Highway 37 W; follow Highway 37 to 121 North to Sonoma Plaza.

SONOMA

The town of Sonoma, one of the most historic towns in Northern California, is a good place to experience the region's Mexican heritage. Designed by General Mariano Vallejo in 1835, downtown Sonoma is set up like a Mexican town, with an 8-acre parklike plaza in the center—complete with a meandering flock of chickens and crowing roosters. Several authentic adobe buildings, most of which now house an assortment of boutiques, restaurants, and inns, hug the perimeter.

Learn more about the region by visiting www. sonomavalley.com.

ACTIVITIES

Getting Acquainted. Before setting out for this verdant vineyard-laced region, stop at the Sonoma Valley Visitors Bureau (453 1st St E; 707/996-1090; www.sonomavalley.com). Along with lots of free, helpful information about the area's wineries, farmers markets, historic sites, walking tours, recreational facilities, and seasonal events, they have a concierge program (707/996-1090; sonomaconcierge@sonomavalley.com), which offers referrals and reservations for hotels, restaurants, balloon rides, limos, spa treatments, and more.

 Plaza Walking Tour and Mission. Sonoma's central plaza, originally laid out by General Mariano Vallejo, is rife with history, restaurants, and shops and is virtually effortless to stroll. If you're a history buff you might want to stop by the visitors bureau (see above) to pick up one of the free maps to more than 61 historic buildings, most of which are located within the nine-block radius in and surrounding Sonoma Plaza. Of the highlighted buildings, one of the most noteworthy is San Francisco Solano Mission, on the corner of Sonoma Plaza. Founded in 1823, it was the last and most northerly of the 21 Franciscan missions of Alta California and the only one of the California missions to be established under Mexican rule, independent of Spain (open daily 10am–5pm; $1 adults, free ages 16 and under). On the plaza's periphery are dozens of interesting shops, including two excellent bookstores, Reader's Books (127 and 130 Napa St E; 707/939-1779) and Plaza Book Shop (40 W Spain; 707/996-8474) for used and rare volumes. You can find everything for a wine-country feast: cheeses and deli fare galore from the Sonoma Cheese Factory (2 W Spain St; 707/996-1931) or pâtés, hams, bratwurst, and sausages from the Sonoma Sausage Company (414 1st St E; 707/938-1215). Cucina Viansa (400 1st St E; 707/935-5656), which has the same takeout gourmet fare as Viansa Winery, also features wine tasting, an espresso bar, a lively cafe, and music on weekend nights. Listen to acoustic music at Murphy's Irish Pub (464 1st St E; 707/935-0660; www.sonomapub.com), hidden in the courtyard behind the Sebastiani Theater.

Cooking Classes. Interested in the nuances of how to prepare stocks and soups or want to learn how to best handle your designer kitchen knives? Ramekin Sonoma Valley Culinary School offers a plethora of courses to whet the appetite of any gourmand. Half-day programs are led by guest chefs, which in 2001 included at least a dozen Bay Area culinary celebrities. San Francisco's Traci Des Jardins (of the restaurant Jardinière) shared secrets to her red-wine-braised short ribs and seared sea scallops with truffled mashed potatoes, while Ron Siegel, Iron Chef culinary competition winner and chef at San Francisco's Masa's, let participants in on recipes for warm chestnut soup with sautéed mushrooms and Dungeness crab salad. Sonoma local Nancy Oakes (Boulevard) led a class on how couples can work best in the kitchen. Appropriately, some classes focus on wine, others include wine dinners, and all feature generous tastes and written recipes. The reasonably priced classes are held at the attractive Tuscan-inspired campus located four blocks west of Sonoma Plaza. (450 W Spain St; 707/933-0450, ext 3; www.ramekins.com; info@ramekins.com)

If you visit Sonoma during a summer weekend and enjoy Shakespeare, pick up the phone and call Gundlach Bundschu (2000 Denmark St, Sonoma; 707/938-5277), which offers weekend performances of the bard's works from July through September.

 Train Town. You won't find any lunch-regurgitating rides at Train Town, a 10-acre landscaped park dedicated to fun for the very little ones. Here moms chat on benches while a steam train makes the 20-minute ride around a woodsy environment toting happy kids over bridges and around the park and blowing off steam. Tickets provide access to a petting zoo and all rides, which include a carousel, Ferris wheel, and a few amusement park rides for younger revelers. (Broadway, between MacArthur St and Napa Rd; 1 mile S of Sonoma Square on Hwy 12; 707/938-3912; open Oct–May Fri–Sun 10am–5pm, Jun–Sept every day 10am–5pm; train ride $3.75 adults, $2.75 children and seniors; each additional ride $1.50 per person)

Farmers Market. Mingle with the locals and fill your picnic basket with the freshest of organic fruits and vegetables at the Sonoma Farmers Market, which takes place year-round on Friday morning from 9am to noon at Depot Park (1 block N of Sonoma Plaza between 1st St W and 2nd St W). April through October an additional market comes to life on Tuesdays from 5:30pm to dusk in Sonoma Plaza; call the visitors bureau for more information.

 Bicycling. There's no better way to revitalize from overeating and drinking than to pedal along the scenic bucolic trails of Sonoma Valley. Sonoma Valley Cyclery rents bikes for adults and doles out maps for a handful of great and easy trails, all of which are about a mile long. They can also point more hard-core athletes to more challenging terrain. Bike rentals cost $25 for 24 hours. (20093 Broadway, at Newcomb St; 707/935-3377; Mon–Sat 10am–6pm, Sun 10am–4pm)

Local Artists. If you're planning to visit Sonoma County in the fall and you love art, consider scheduling your trip around ARTrails annual weekend of open studios. More than 130 valley artists open their doors to the general public for viewing and sales of jewelry, works on canvas and paper, sculpture, and more. If you can't make the studios tour, it's worth requesting a catalog since it includes color photos of artists' works and information about where to find their galleries and see ongoing exhibitions. For information, call the Cultural Arts Council of Sonoma County (707/579-ARTS or go to www.artrails.org).

Car Racing. It's anything but classic Wine Country, but that doesn't deter nearly 175,000 racing fans from heading to Sears Point Raceway for the annual NASCAR Dodge/Save Mart 350. Car and motorcycle races at the challenging 12-turn, 2.52-mile road course with a quarter-mile drag strip are held year-round and include National Hot Road Association drag racing and AMA Superbikes. (Hwy 37 and Hwy 121; 707/938-8448, for tickets call 800/870-RACE; www.searspoint.com; trackinfo@searspoint.com; races nearly every day)

Golf. Golfers interested in casually hitting a few balls without the expense and pomp of the fancier courses can head to Los Arroyos Golf Course, where on weekdays you can play nine holes for $10 and 18 holes for $15. Weekend rates are upped by $2. (500 State Gulch Rd; 707/938-8835; open every day 7am–sundown)

WINERIES

California's world-renowned wine industry was born in the Sonoma Valley. Franciscan fathers planted the state's first vineyards at the Mission San Francisco Solano de Sonoma in 1823 and harvested the grapes to make their sacramental wines. Thirty-four years later, California's first major vineyard was planted with European grape varietals by Hungarian Count Agoston Haraszthy at Sonoma's revered Buena Vista Winery. The count is widely hailed as the father of California wine—consistently rated as some of the best wine in the world. Today more than 30 wineries dot the Sonoma Valley (there are over 100 in the county), most offering pretty picnic areas and free tours of their winemaking facilities.

Bartholomew Park Winery. Tucked at the end of a narrow road leading east of downtown Sonoma in the midst of 400-acre Bartholomew Memorial Park and surrounded by old vines and gnarled oak trees, this historic, colonial-style boutique winery harbors one of the most beautiful settings in the valley. It also happens to be an exceptional picnic spot, complete with tables, ample seclusion, and hiking trails. But there are plenty of reasons to cast attentions indoors, specifically the limited-production wines, which can be sampled for $3. A museum provides Victorian photographs documenting viticulture practices from the 19th century and information about Agoston Haraszthy. Tours, available by appointment for a fee, include a museum tour and private tasting as well as a 10 percent discount off all purchases. *1000 Vineyard Ln; 707/935-9511; open every day 10:30am–4pm; closed major holidays.*

Buena Vista Winery. California's oldest premium winery (founded in 1857) is a large estate set in a forest with picnic grounds. The historic stone building, once a working winery, is now a large and open tasting facility where everything from crisp non-oaked Sauvignon Blanc, Chardonnay, and Pinot Noir to Merlot and Cabernet Sauvignon is poured with no strings attached. Limited-production and library wines are also available to taste for a small fee in a more intimate setting. On the second floor of the property's Press House guests can view rotating exhibits of local artists' works, with the artist on hand for questions and discussion during weekends. Tours of the stone winery and the hillside tunnels are held every day from July through September at 11am and 2pm. But the self-guided tour is available anytime, describes the history of the winery and its Hungarian founder, Agoston Haraszthy, and includes photographic works chronicling "A Year in the Vineyards" in 1870. Picnic grounds in a wooded setting are appetizing, and deli items are available.

18000 Old Winery Rd; 707/938-1266 or 800/926-1266; www.
buenavista.com; open every day 10:30am–5pm.

🍷 **Cline Cellars.** Its country farm setting perfectly comple-
ments Cline Cellar's laid-back tasting room and casual
vibe. Saunter up to the bar to taste a variety of complimentary
nonreserve wines, which are likely to include Syrah and Zinfandel,
for which the winery is known; break out $1 per each reserve wine
taste; or drop a five-spot for a reserve flight. Free tours, which are
held at 11am, 1pm, and 3pm and require advance reservation,
include vineyards, winemaking, barrels, an overview of the family
history, and regional information. Picnickers are in luck: more
than 5,000 rosebushes surround the tables here. *24737 Arnold Dr;*
707/935-4310; www.clinecellars.com; open every day 10am–6pm.

🍷 **Gloria Ferrer Champagne Caves.** An elegant Spanish-
influenced building with a view of the vineyards and
Carneros region sets the stage for this sparkling-wine experience.
Fork over $3.50 to $6 for a full glass of bubbly or $2 to $4 for samples of still wines, many available only at the winery. Relax at the
welcoming tasting room with a spacious bar, grand fireplace, and
tables inside and outside on the adjoining patio (a bonus, since
many comparable rooms offer standing room only; also, unlike at
most Napa wineries, picnickers are welcome here). Or stretch the
old legs for the fun guided subterranean cave tour, which includes
information on the winery's history and winemaking. *23555 Hwy*
121; 707/996-7256; www.gloriaferrer.com; open every day 10:30am–
5:30pm; call for tour times.

🍷 **Gundlach Bundschu Winery.** Anyone fearful of a chichi,
pretentious winery experience need only head to historic
and grand Gundlach Bundschu ("Gund-lock bun-shoo"), where
rustic, fun, unassuming, self-deprecating, and friendly people
welcome you to California's oldest family-owned winery.
Founded in 1858, the winery's seen seven generations of family
members and has had plenty of time to perfect its wine-tasting
experience. Today the winery, known for its Gewürztraminer,
Riesling, and Merlot as well as its intimate setting on beautiful
grounds, offers complimentary tastings of four to five wines and
weekend tours that scan the vineyards and wine-barrel caves and
review the history of winery and its winemaking techniques. A

few picnic tables surrounded by oak trees and vineyards beg to be used, and often are. *2000 Denmark St; 707/938-5277; open every day 11am–4:30pm, except major holidays; tours Sat–Sun on the hour noon–3pm.*

Ravenswood Winery. Wind through massive oaks and eucalyptus and find the Ravenswood tasting room—a warm, rustic stone building that appears to have sprouted from the rocky hillside. It's no secret that this is home of some of the tastiest Zinfandels; thus it's likely you'll have to squeeze into the long, busy tasting bar to taste up to four wines on the house. Ravenswood's vintages run the full range of styles from jammy to peppery, so as long as you're on board with their slogan, "No Wimpy Wines," you're bound to taste something you like. But if

Zin isn't your thing you can sample the Merlot, Cabernet, Petit Sirah, or a small production of barrel-fermented Chardonnay. Tours are available by appointment for $3 per person, and picnic tables stashed among the oaks and boulders with nice vineyard views are ever ready. On weekends from Memorial Day through Labor Day there's no need to bring provisions: for a nominal fee visitors are welcome to partake in the festive barbecues. *18701 Gehricke Rd; 888/669-4679; open every day 10am–4pm.*

 Sebastiani Vineyards. In late 2001 Sebastiani moved into its old tasting facility, which underwent upgrading in 2000. Now guests can again tour the huge historic stone building that showcases the family and winemaking history and sample current releases for a $5 fee, which includes the highly regarded Cabernet Sauvignon and Merlot, various other varietals, and a keepsake logo glass. Reserve wines are available at $2 per taste. The free tour includes a view of the fermentation room and aging cellar, which holds an interesting collection of carved-oak cask heads. Gifts and snacks are available and picnic tables are scattered around the vineyard. *389 4th St E; 707/938-5532 or 800/888-5532; www.sebastiani.com; open every day 10am–5pm.*

Viansa Winery and Italian Marketplace. Modeled after a Tuscan hilltop village, Viansa's expansive facilities and grounds offer virtually everything a wine taster could want. Guests can sample three of anything from Chardonnay, Sangiovese, and Barbera to Cabernet Sauvignon and Cabernet Franc for $5. Wines, which are sold exclusively through the tasting room and mail-order wine club, are also for sale by the glass and bottle. There's a full-service deli and Italian Marketplace where free bites are offered, a barbecue stand selling grilled meats, and picnic tables overlooking the Carneros region, from vineyards to the bay's wetland marshes. The winery, which was founded and is run by Sam Sebastiani (of *the* wine-family Sebastianis), produces and pours up to 34 different wines, with several fine Italian-style options, like Dolcetto and Nebbiolo. Tours are offered by appointment for winery club members. *25200 Hwy 121, 3 miles N of Sears Point Raceway; 707/935-4700; open every day 9am–5:30pm summer, 10am–5pm winter.*

RESTAURANTS

CAFE LA HAYE ★★★

Located just off the main plaza, this light-filled cafe blends two sensual pleasures: art and food. Art exhibits rotate, but if you're lucky walls will be graced by the colorful and dreamlike works of owner/chef John McReynold's wife, who is also responsible for the larger-than-life fantasy nude floating across the women's room wall. The split-level dining room itself is simple, intimate, and romantic, with small-business charm. Not to be outdone, the food, which is miraculously created in a shoe box of an open kitchen, is also an unfussy but unique work of art. Brunch dishes offer surprising twists, like a poached egg with ham bobbing in a sea of white cheddar grits. Or try the ubiquitous eggs Benedict, updated here with roasted red peppers and shiitake mushrooms, served on an herb biscuit. Dinner offers a short menu of starters like savory spinach salad with bacon, oven-dried grapes, crumbled hard-boiled egg, and pine nuts. The half-dozen or so main courses lean toward rustic European cuisine. Simple, fresh tagliarini with sugar, pumpkin, prosciutto, and sage is bliss at its most basic. Grilled pork chop with herbed spaetzle and whole-grain mustard vinaigrette redefines comfort. More avant-garde choices include the seared black pepper–lavender fillet of beef with Gorgonzola potato gratin, and risotto and fish specials that change daily. The wine list is three times as long as the menu and, in keeping with the theme, offers some unusual Sonoma specialties. *140 Napa St E, Sonoma; 707/935-5994; $$; MC, V; local checks only; dinner Tues–Sat, brunch Sat–Sun; beer and wine; reservations not accepted for brunch, but recommended for dinner; just E of the plaza.*

DELLA SANTINA'S ★★↓

A fixture on the plaza for years, this popular local outpost of the Joe's restaurant dynasty in San Francisco was smart to move down the block into the digs vacated by the late Eastside Oyster Bar & Grill. In addition to the small, trattoria-style dining room, Della Santina's inherited the wonderful vine-laced brick patio tucked in back—the place to dine

Stroll Sonoma Plaza, grab coffee and a light breakfast, and head to Viansa Winery for wine tasting and an invigorating valley view. Head north to Ravenswood for some Zin, then move to downtown Glen Ellen. Stop by the Glen Ellen Village Market for picnic provisions, continue north to Chateau St. Jean, buy a bottle of wine to go with your feast, and dine at a picnic table or in the grass (bring sunscreen!). Return to Glen Ellen and visit either Jack London State Historic Park, Benziger Family Winery (take the tour), or both. Take a breather before finishing the evening with dinner at the girl & the fig.

when the weather is warm. The menu includes a good selection of light to heavy house-made pastas (the Gnocchi della Nonna with a tomato, basil, and garlic sauce would impress any Italian grandmother) and wonderful meats from the *rosticceria* (the chicken with fresh herbs is tender and perfectly spiced). Be sure to inquire about the *pasticceria* (homemade pastas)—and if panna cotta (a vanilla cream custard, here flavored with Italian rum) is among the offerings, nab it. Paired with an espresso, it's the perfect finale to a fine meal. *133 Napa St E, Sonoma; 707/935-0576; $$; AE, DIS, MC, V; local checks only; lunch, dinner every day; beer and wine; reservations recommended; off 2nd St.*

THE GIRL & THE FIG   ★★★

"Country food with French passion" doesn't get more inviting than at cozy the girl & the fig. Owner Sondra Bernstein's restaurant, celebrating among other things the decadent fig, became known while located in a small Glen Ellen dining room. But when a spot along Sonoma Square opened up she couldn't help but take advantage of the opportunity. Thus in 2000, her pots, pans, chef John Toulze, and figs moved into the new, warm, and charming location. (So as not to disappoint her Glen Ellen loyalists, she replaced the restaurant with new, Spanish-influenced the girl & the gaucho.) Tables surrounded by cheery yellow walls and wood paneling are a wee bit tight, but all the better to get a sneak preview from your neighbors of the lively fig salad with arugula, dried figs, pecans, chèvre, pancetta, and fig and port vinaigrette; aromatic steamed mussels with Pernod, garlic, leeks, fresh herbs, and croutons; or savory pan-seared striped bass with roasted shallot and chive vinaigrette and mashed potatoes. But patio seating is prime country dining when the weather's right. It'd be easy to fill up on a top sirloin burger with grilled onions and Brie, Cambazola, or cheddar and matchstick fries, or salmon niçoise. But it would be shameful not to splurge on the cheese menu, which showcases local productions such as Point Reyes Farmstead Cheese Original Blue and Redwood Hill Crottin goat cheese. If nothing else, forks should stand at attention for the sensuous lavender crème brûlée or delicate chilled Meyer lemon soufflé with whipped cream and fruit compote. Just as exciting as the food is the trend-setting wine list, which goes against the Sonoma grain with Rhône-style California wines, including plenty of by-the-glass choices, flights, and a fantastic selection of local Viognier and Syrah. *110 W Spain St, Sonoma; 707/938-3634; $$; AE, MC, V; checks OK; lunch, dinner every day; full bar; reservations recommended; www.thegirlandthefig.com; on Sonoma Plaza, on the ground floor of the Sonoma Hotel.* &

JUANITA JUANITA   ★ ✦

For the occasions when heaven is a roadside shack, cold beer, and a heaping plate of nachos, Juanita Juanita is your savior. Locals are loyal to this spray-painted-mural box of a restaurant, and no wonder. It's not every day that you can play Trivial Pursuit or admire toddlers' artwork while digging into a plastic bucket of thick, crisp tortilla chips and zesty salsa and waiting for your grilled chicken quesadilla, beef enchilada, or fish taco. The intentionally ramshackle mix of mismatched tables, Formica counter seating, and convivial dinnertime crowd are half the fun; the other half is the dependable fare, which is fresh, hearty, and served with a sarcastic wink. Hint: Come at off-hours to avoid the wait. *19114 Arnold Dr, Sonoma; 707/935-3981; $; no credit cards; local checks only; lunch, dinner every day; beer and wine; no reservations; from Sonoma Plaza head W on W Napa St,* *turn right on Arnold Dr, and continue until you see the shack on the left side of the street.*

MAYA ★★

The menu at this Yucatan grill-and-rotisserie restaurant justifiably warns, "Beware . . . some fun may occur." And that's not just because libations from the Temple of Tequila are flowing freely. Owners Craig and PJ Clark have taken great care in creating a festive Mayan-style restaurant dedicated to upscale Mexican food. The duo's experience at the region's Mustards Grill, Piatti, and General's Daughter plus degrees in architecture (Craig) and interior design (PJ) gave them plenty of insight into what the public wants, and the nightly crowds are indication they've translated it into the design and gestalt of this place. Amid the acid-washed concrete floors, bright walls, art, artifacts, and sky blue ceiling, guests dine on exotic appetizers of grilled vegetable empanadas with roasted tomatillo salsa; ravioli with butternut squash, sage brown butter, and Parmesan; guacamole made to order; and char-grilled tiger prawns. Dinner items are no less flavorful and include a well-spiced paella; juicy slow-roasted pork with cumin rice and pinto beans; and tender and zingy pan-roasted sea bass with blood orange vinaigrette, coconut rice, and a mixed vegetable salad. Meat eaters can't resist the grilled rib-eye steak adorned with jalapeño butter and paired with sweet potato gratin. Order a margarita with one of the few dozen blue agave tequilas, sample the half-shot tasting flight, or go the high-octane route with a potent Mexican coffee (tequila, Kahlua, coffee, and whipped cream). Expect noise levels associated with people having a good time, and don't miss out on classic Mexican flan or the creative Ibarra chocolate crème brûlée. *101 E Napa St, Sonoma; 707/935-3500; $$; MC, V; checks OK; reservations recommended; lunch, dinner Mon–Sat, dinner Sun; closed Mon Jan–Apr.*

MERITAGE ★★

Named after the style of cooking rather than a wine blend made with traditional Bordeaux varieties, Meritage has garnered a stellar reputation with chef/owner Carlo Cavallo's combo of southern French and northern Italian cuisines. The Italian-born former executive chef for Giorgio Armani Restaurant in Beverly Hills developed a fan club while chef at Piazza d'Angelo in Mill Valley. But it is in his Mediterranean-inspired downtown Sonoma dining room, with wrought-iron grapevine railing, distressed surfaces, and lots of wood and copper, that the chef has created a true dining destination. Whether seated at a cozy booth or on the new garden patio, diners are treated to a daily changing menu, which accentuates the freshest local ingredients. Those who continually return for the crispy polenta with wild mushrooms and Gorgonzola sauce, napoleon of escargots with Champagne and wild thyme, or classic Caesar might be enticed to change the agenda in favor of selections from the new oyster raw bar. Of course that shouldn't deter one from the pastas, such as a zesty thin spaghetti with sauteed chicken breast, baby spinach, and roasted tomatoes in a spicy garlic sauce, or the clean flavors of fresh salmon poached over spinach with roasted potatoes and aromatic herb aioli. The new take-out deli and marketplace is a delicious option for gourmands on the go, and breakfast and brunch feature classic eggs Benedict and omelets. *522 Broadway, Sonoma; 707/938-9430; $$; AE, MC, V; no checks; breakfast Wed–Sun, lunch, dinner Wed–Mon, brunch Sat–Sun; beer and wine; reservations recommended; S of Sonoma Plaza.* &

RIN'S THAI RESTAURANT ★ᛁ

Rarely does Thai food come accompanied by as appealing an environment as the modernized old-home-turned-restaurant known as Rin's. Not too cramped, not too sparse, the yellow-walled local favorite is just right for a casual, well-priced meal, as is the patio seating, which is open year-round except for winter. Well-seasoned starters include *tom yum*, the classic spicy and sour soup with lemongrass, galanga, and chili paste, and the savory satay of pork or chicken, served with addictive peanut sauce and refreshing cucumber salad. Pad thai, savory-sweet pan-fried rice noodles with shrimp, tofu, egg, and bean sprouts, is a must-have. But from there you'll be hard pressed to decide between the likes of *gai kraprao* (minced chicken breast,

Even if you're most interested in confining your visit to the boundaries of Sonoma Valley, consider popping up to Santa Rosa for a hot-air balloon flight. (See Santa Rosa section for details.)

basil, and fresh chiles in garlic sauce), *gang dang* (a red curry dish with choice of chicken, pork, beef, or vegetables that's almost as fun to say as it is to eat), or pork ribs seasoned in spices, charbroiled, and served with a chile-garlic dipping sauce. Do it right: start with the potent and sweet Thai iced tea or coffee and finish with fresh mango with coconut rice or fried banana with coconut ice cream. *139 E Napa St, Sonoma; 707/938-1462; $; MC, V; local checks only; lunch, dinner every day; beer and wine; reservations recommended; 1 block E of Sonoma Plaza.*

RISTORANTE PIATTI ★★

Another pleasant link in a chain of chic nouvelle Italian restaurants with outlets in touristy towns throughout Northern California. For a full review, see the Restaurants section of Yountville. *405 1st St W, Sonoma (and branches); 707/996-2351; $$; AE, MC, V; local checks only; lunch, dinner every day; full bar; reservations recommended; in El Dorado Hotel, at W Spain St, facing the plaza's W side.*

LODGINGS

BEST WESTERN SONOMA VALLEY INN ★

Okay, so Sonoma's Best Western isn't exactly romance central, but it's relatively inexpensive, it's in a good location near the town plaza, kids are welcome, and on summer weekends it may be the only place left with a vacancy (if you're lucky). Although the guests rooms are woefully plain, the free benefits are many: continental breakfast delivered to your room each morning, a gift bottle of local white table wine sitting in the refrigerator, cable TV with HBO, and either a balcony or a deck overlooking the inner courtyard. The hotel also has an enclosed outdoor pool and gazebo-covered spa, which come in really handy on typically scorching-hot summer afternoons. *5550 2nd St W, Sonoma; 707/938-9200 or 800/334-5784; $$; AE, CB, DC, MC, V; no checks; www.sonomavalleyinn.com; one and a half blocks W of Sonoma Plaza.*

EL DORADO HOTEL ★★

If you've had it with cutesy B&Bs, El Dorado Hotel is a welcome respite, offering 26 moderately priced rooms modestly decorated with terra-cotta tile floors, handcrafted furniture, and down comforters. Renovated by the team that created Napa Valley's ultra-exclusive Auberge du Soleil, each room has French doors leading to a small balcony overlooking the town square or the hotel's private courtyard—a pleasant, sunny spot where you can enjoy the complimentary continental breakfast. Not exactly fancy, but certainly worlds better than some of the area's cheap motels and funky-frilly older accommodations, El Dorado melds contemporary with country without being remotely offensive. There's also a heated outdoor lap pool, and concierge service to help you arrange your next Wine Country excursion. *405 1st St W, Sonoma; 707/996-3030 or 800/289-3031; $$$; AE, MC, V; checks OK; at W Spain St, on the plaza's W side.*

EL PUEBLO INN ★

If you're just looking for an inexpensive place to stay and you're not too concerned with prime location or goose-down pillows, consider the El Pueblo Inn, a modest little hotel located about eight blocks west of Sonoma Plaza. The guest rooms' exposed-brick walls, light-wood furnishings, and post-and-beam construction lend a sort of ersatz rusticity to them (but not much). The usual budget accommodation perks are included, such as air-conditioning, television, refrigerator, coffeemaker, and use of the inn's outdoor heated pool. Since this is one of the only budget lodgings in town, be sure to make reservations as far in advance as possible. *896 W Napa St, Sonoma; 707/996-3651 or 800/900-8844; $$; AE, DIS, MC, V; no checks; going N on Hwy 12/121, follow 12 into the plaza, turn left on W Napa St, and continue 1 mile.*

THE LODGE AT SONOMA ★★★

Big-city hotel meets Wine-Country living at this 182-room, privately owned resort managed by Marriott. Once past the spacious, light lobby, guests meander to one of the rooms in the main buildings or wander winding pathways dotted with maples, rosebushes, daisies, and dozens of blooms to two-story six-room cottages with sunny and rather conspicuous sitting areas. The sheer newness of the place makes it a boon for perfectionist visitors. Yet the decor doesn't disappoint. Quality reproductions of local artworks complement shades of brown and earth tones, many rooms have fireplaces, all have patios or balconies, and in the two-story main building, bathrooms with deep tubs have shutter doors opening to the bedroom. Even light fixtures are artistically designed. Though the rooms are appealing, there are many reasons to linger in the common areas. A charming courtyard with umbrella-shaded sitting areas makes for lovely alfresco dining; a large heated outdoor pool and hot tub beckon sun worshipers. A city-slick restaurant, Carneros, serves seasonal fresh cuisine and also hosts an impressive continental breakfast. At the end of the property the full-service spa offers facials, massage, body exfoliation, wraps, baths, and manicures and pedicures, and is landscaped for intimate tranquillity with fountains, more umbrella-shaded seating, and four outdoor pools tucked behind foliage. *1325 Broadway, Sonoma; 707/935-6600 or 888/710-8008; $$$$; AE, MC, V; checks OK; www.thelodgeatsonoma.com; heading N at junction of Hwy 116/121, bear right, then exit at Hwy 12 and continue to Sonoma; lodge is at corner of Leveroni and Broadway on Hwy 12.* &

MACARTHUR PLACE ★★★✦

The hottest new resort to hit fast-growing Sonoma is located four blocks off Sonoma Plaza. The property does such a good job of creating a sense of space and atmosphere that the 64 individually appointed rooms, most of which are in one- and two-story cottages scattered amid deliciously lush landscaped grounds, feel more like part of a charming village than a hotel. A quick wander through gardens adorned with sculpture and an astounding array of flora leads to the cozy library with a blazing fire, enviable works by local artists and artisans, plenty of hardback books, and nightly wine and cheese hour; a heated outdoor pool and whirlpool, exercise room, and adjoining spa complete with 30 treatments emphasizing elements from the garden (fruit, flowers, herbs, and earth); and the humorous Barn, where cowboy decor deftly straddles haute and kitsch. Within the Barn is Saddles Steakhouse, which specializes in, you guessed it, USDA prime beef—and the more modern accompaniment of martinis. Rooms are equally divine. The wisteria-draped historic Manor House, built in the 1860s and one of the oldest Victorian homes in Sonoma, holds 10 elegantly adorned guest rooms, which have artistic furnishings, four-poster beds with pillows and blankets properly fluffed, and original artworks. The cottages include suites with wood-burning fireplaces, wet bars, and hydrotherapy tubs with shutters that open into the bedroom. Furnishings are colorful, and coffeemakers and fridges add a few comforts of home. The too-sweet box of bath amenities in the bathroom (with a spacious shower) are second only to the Robe Works robes, which are delicious enough that management sagely includes a note stating that if the robe disappears with the guest an extra $135 will be added to the bill. All rooms are appointed with DVD and CD players (and access to a complimentary DVD and CD library), two-line data port phones, and voice mail. Rates include continental breakfast. *29 E MacArthur St, Sonoma; 707/938-2929 or 800/722-1866; $$$$; AE, MC, V; checks OK; www.macarthurplace.com; heading N on Hwy 121, take a right at the "Y" junction of Hwy 12/116, go left onto Hwy 12, and take a right at the second stoplight (MacArthur St).*

SONOMA CHALET   ★★

So close, and yet so far: every room in this secluded Swiss-style farmhouse overlooks the grassy hills of a 200-acre ranch, giving you the impression that you're way out in the country. Fact is, you're at the edge of a suburban neighborhood—three-quarters of a mile from Sonoma's town square. There are four rooms in the two-story 1940s chalet (two of them share a bath) and three adorable private cottages, each with its own little sitting area, feather bed, fireplace or wood-burning stove, and kitchen. All of the rooms have decks or balconies with views, and each boasts an assortment of Western antiques, quilts, and collectibles that complement the rustic surroundings. In the morning, proprietor Joe Leese serves complimentary pastries, juices, yogurt, and granola in the country kitchen or, if you prefer, in the privacy of your cottage. *18935 5th St W, Sonoma; 707/938-3129; $$; AE, MC, V; checks OK; www.sonomachalet.com; follow 5th St W to the end, then continue W on the gravel road.*

THE SONOMA HOTEL ★★

Historic 19th-century charm, modern amenities, a prime location on Sonoma Square, and a great downstairs restaurant make this a good pick for Sonoma visitors. You'll have to climb the stairs to all but one of the 16 nonsmoking rooms, which are located on the second floor. But the minimal effort gets great results, as rooms are generally sunny and well appointed with country French furnishings. Some have claw-footed tubs and attractive iron or carved-pine bed frames, and all have cheery yellow walls, clean bathrooms, hand-made soaps, data ports, and cable TV. Room 34, the cheapest, has its bathroom down the hall, and some rooms have small sitting areas with comfy overstuffed slipcovered furnishings. Continental breakfast and wine hour are included in the rates. Best of all: you need only step out the door and you're at the girl & the fig restaurant, one of Sonoma's gems. *110 W Spain St, Sonoma; 707/996-2996 or 800/468-6016; $$$; AE, MC, V; checks OK; www.sonomahotel.com; at the NW corner of Sonoma Plaza.*

SONOMA VALLEY INN ★

This 75-room hotel is part of the Best Western chain and is located off a busy street across from a supermarket, but you won't care about all that once you see how spacious, tidy, and well appointed the rooms are. Standard features include a private bath, cable TV, air-conditioning, minifridge, gift bottle of wine, continental breakfast delivered to your door, and a tiny enclosed patio. The floral bedspreads obviously didn't come from Sears, and even the art is more upscale than you'd expect in a chain hotel. In addition, most rooms have a wood-burning fireplace. The landscaped courtyard with a swimming pool, fountain, and gazebo-covered whirlpool will prompt you to scratch your head and wonder if you can actually afford to stay here. *550 2nd St W, Sonoma; 707/938-*

9200 or 800/334-5784; $$; AE, DC, DIS, MC, V; checks OK; www.sonomavalleyinn.com; off W Napa St.

VICTORIAN GARDEN INN   ★

This 1870s Greek Revival farmhouse with a wraparound veranda has one of the most inviting small gardens you'll ever see: lush bowers of roses, azaleas, and camellias encircle wonderful little tables and chairs, while flowering fruit trees bend low over Victorian benches. The inn's four guest rooms, decorated in white wicker and florals, are pretty, if a bit cloying. The most requested room is the Woodcutter's Cottage, favored for its comfy sofa and armchairs facing the fireplace and its private entrance and bath. In the evening, owner Donna Lewis pours glasses of wine and sherry to enjoy in front of the parlor fireplace. Complimentary breakfast, served at the dining table, in the garden, or in your room, consists of granola, croissants, gourmet coffee, and fruit picked right from the garden. A big bonus is the large swimming pool in the backyard—a blessing during Sonoma's typically hot summer days—plus a therapeutic spa located in the garden. *316 E Napa St, Sonoma; 707/996-5339; $$$; AE, DC, MC, V; checks OK; VGardeninn@aol.com; www.victoriangardeninn.com; between 3rd St E and 4th St E, 2 blocks from the plaza.*

BOYES HOT SPRINGS

This town would be nothing more than a thoroughfare with ramshackle businesses and blue-collar housing if it weren't for one thing: it also happens to be home to one of California's greatest and most expensive spa resorts.

ACTIVITIES

 Golf. The most upscale golf game in the valley is played at Sonoma Mission Inn's latest addition to its resort empire. The Sonoma Mission Inn Golf Club, a 2-minute drive from the pink palace itself, is backed by the Mayacamas Mountains and flanked by vineyards. Its 7,087-yard championship course ambles through 177 acres of mature oaks, eucalyptus, and redwoods, with three

Sonoma County is absolutely enormous. Try to see all of it in a few days and you'll never get out of the car. Consider staying a day or two in Sonoma Valley and then setting up camp in northern Sonoma County, in or near charming Healdsburg.

lakes, a creek, and 76 sand bunkers. Dress for success: wear a collared shirt and nonmetal spikes (required), and don't arrive wearing jeans. If you're up for playing this course and don't want to have to pay the steep room rates to stay at Sonoma Mission Inn, book a tee time as soon as you can; they're in the process of going private. (17700 Arnold Dr; from Sonoma Mission Inn turn left out of the parking lot, continue to Arnold Dr, take a right, and the entrance is on the left; 707/996-0300; www.sonomamissioninn.com; open every day; Mon–Thurs $85, $70 twilight; Fri–Sun and holidays $115, $80 twilight; cart $15 per player)

LODGINGS

SONOMA MISSION INN & SPA ★★★

With its ethereal, serene grounds and elegant pink stucco buildings, the Sonoma Mission Inn feels a bit like a convent—except that novitiates here wear white terry-cloth bathrobes or colorful running suits instead of nuns' habits. And except that indulgence, in body and spirit, is the order of the day. The recently renovated world-class European-style spa offers everything from aerobics classes and Swedish massage to aromatherapy facials, seaweed wraps, and tarot card readings in perfectly groomed surroundings (the likes of Barbra Streisand, Tom Cruise, and Harrison Ford come here to get pampered). You'll also find exercise rooms, saunas, whirlpool spas, a salon, yoga and meditation classes, and a swimming pool filled with artesian mineral water. While the luxurious spa is the main draw, the inn also recently reacquired its historic golf course, which had been sold during the Depression.

Thirty new suites were added in 2000; they offer every amenity, including Mission-style decor, and views of the gardens and fountain. Bathed in shades of light peach and pink, each of the more than 230 rooms features plantation-style shutters, ceiling fans, and down comforters. Some units have wood-burning fireplaces and luxe granite or marble bathrooms big enough for an impromptu tango. Also pleasing are the rooms overlooking the inn's swimming pool (a favorite, room 232, is in a turret), which are in the historic building. The inn's two restaurants, the recently remodeled Restaurant at Sonoma Mission Inn & Spa and the Big 3 Diner, are both basic Californian. The restaurant is one of the most expensive in Sonoma; the less-expensive Big 3 Diner offers such California-Mediterranean fare as light pastas, pizzas, and grilled items, as well as hearty breakfasts. *18140 Sonoma Hwy, Boyes Hot Springs; 707/938-9000 or 800/862-4945; $$$$; AE, DC, MC, V; checks OK; www.sonomamissioninn.com; on Hwy 12, at Boyes Blvd.*

GLEN ELLEN

It may have become best known for the affordable and widely distributed wine of the same name, but adorable Glen Ellen is anything but a big-business destination. Winding country roads lead to wineries and its few destination-worthy hotels and restaurants, all of which appropriately exude the tiny town's genuine country charm.

ACTIVITIES

 Historic Park. There are more places and things named after Jack London in Sonoma County than there are women named María in Mexico. This cult reaches its apex in Glen Ellen, where the writer built his aptly named Beauty Ranch, an 800-acre spread now known as Jack London State Historic Park (2400 London Ranch Rd, off Hwy 12; 707/938-5216). London's vineyards, piggery, and other ranch buildings are here, as well as a house-turned-museum containing his art collection and mementos (including a series of rejection letters London received from several publishers, who must have fallen over backwards in their cushy chairs the day they learned London had become the highest-paid author of his time). Ten miles of trails lead through oaks, madronas, and redwoods, including a grove of oaks shading London's grave. If you'd rather ride than walk through London's land, let the friendly folks at the Sonoma Cattle Company (located in Jack London State Historic Park; 707/996-8566) saddle up a horse for you. Call for the lowdown on their guided horseback trips, which can be arranged by reservation. (Open every day 9:30am–7pm summer, 9:30am–5:30pm winter; museum open 10am–5pm; admission $3 per car or $2 per seniors' car)

The Wine Country Film Festival, a three-week summer splurge of screenings and parties throughout Napa and Sonoma, is headquartered in the tiny town of Glen Ellen. Call 707/996-2536 for information.

Tiny Glen Ellen was the longtime home of the late celebrated food writer M.F.K. Fisher, whose books include **Map of Another Town** *and* **How to Cook a Wolf**.

WINERIES

Arrowood Vineyards and Winery. Perched on a vineyard-draped hillside, friendly Arrowood combines New England farmhouse charm with the flavors of highly respected Cabernet, Merlot, and Chardonnay as well as small productions of lovely Viognier and Syrah. The current tasting room debuted in 1998 and is warm and hospitable, with a fire blazing on cold days and a wraparound veranda beckoning during spring and summer. Helpful staff are as eager to answer questions about the valley as they are about the winery, which was acquired by Robert Mondavi. Richard Arrowood is still directly involved in the winemaking process and saw the opportunity as a way to allow more time to focus on what ends up in the bottle. *14347 Sonoma Hwy; 707/938-5947 or 800/938-5170; www.arrowoodvineyards.com; open every day 10am–4:30pm; tasting $3.*

Benziger Family Winery. Atmosphere, education, and good wines make this family winery a great stop for novices and connoisseurs. Guests interested in the full-blown experience can take the effortless tram ride tour, which runs numerous times daily and leads through the vineyards and the winery's history. Complimentary tastings of everything from Fumé Blanc to Zinfandel are held in the wine shop, as are $10 reserve tastings of special releases and library wines. Home to good Chardonnay and Cabernet Sauvignon, Benziger also operates the beautiful new Imagery Winery. *1883 London Ranch Rd; 707/935-3000 or 800/989-8890; open every day 10am–5pm, except major holidays; off Arnold Dr.*

B. R. Cohn Winery. A quintessential old-school Sonoma winery, B. R. Cohn shirks the fancy corporate image to stick with a classic laid-back wine-tasting experience. The small and funky tasting room is where you can sample highly regarded Chardonnays and Cabernets as well as fine Pinot Noir and Merlot. Tastings are free, but if you want to sip their high-end productions you'll have to kick over $3 to $5 per taste (fee waived with purchase), or $12 to sample the whole shebang. Winery-produced olive oils are available for sample and sale, but if you want to make full use of the umbrella-shaded picnic tables on the outdoor patio overlooking Chardonnay vineyards and olive trees, bring your own grub. And if, by chance, you're around the first weekend in October, find out which rocking band is headlining at the winery's annual concert to benefit local causes. Since B. R. Cohn is owned by the manager of the Doobie Brothers, the talent tends to be impressive. *15140 Sonoma Hwy; 707/938-4064 or 800/330-4064; tastings $3–$12; open every day 10am–5pm.*

Imagery Estate Winery. One of Sonoma's newest wine-tasting facilities, Imagery focuses on the symmetry between wine and art by displaying original works by artists commissioned to design their labels and pouring wines that inspire the masterpieces. Though the new winery is an extension of a fantastic long-standing program led by Benziger Family Winery, this modern property with a huge stone fireplace was recently dedicated to showcasing the art collection amassed with each Benziger release since 1985 and pouring nothing other than Imagery series wines. Now at the centerpiece bar guests can part with $5 to sample five tastes from over a dozen varietals, most of which are lesser known, such as Malbec, Cabernet Franc, Petite Sirah, Viognier, and Barbera. Along with the wine came a new visitor center, wine shop, and tasting room on the tranquil 20-acre grounds. *14335 Sonoma Hwy; 707/935-3000; www.imagerywinery.com; open every day 10am–4:30pm.*

RESTAURANTS

GLEN ELLEN INN   ★★

If you're staying in Glen Ellen, it's nice to know you don't have to go far to find a good meal. In fact, Christian and Karen Bertrand's tiny, romantic restaurant is worth a drive from farther afield. The menu changes frequently, but always features local cuisine at its freshest and in beautiful preparations. Dinner might include a jambalaya of prawns, bay shrimp, chicken, sausage, and honey-smoked ham, simmered in vegetables and fresh-from-the-garden herbs; expertly seared ahi tuna in a wasabi cream sauce with pickled ginger; or tender ricotta and pecorino cheese dumplings in a roasted bell pepper sauce with a garlic-infused tomato-basil salsa. The wine list features strictly Sonoma Valley labels. With just six white-clothed tables in the dining room and eight more outside in the herb garden, service is personal and attentive, almost as if you've been invited into the Bertrands' home. *13670 Arnold Dr, Glen Ellen; 707/996-6409; $$; AE, MC, V; local checks only; dinner Thurs–Tues; beer and wine; reservations recommended; at O'Donnell Ln.*

MUCCA ★★√

If rustic romance is your ideal atmosphere, there is no sweeter dining room than Mucca. Tucked amid redwoods and overlooking a creek, the barnlike room exudes ambience and genuine country charm without feeling overdone or contrived. It also does a good job of not taking itself too seriously: the cow-patterned bar in the funky, dark bar is a case in point. But at the white-linen-draped tables, many of which are in front of a blazing fire and all of which are situated on old hardwood floors, food, though fun, is a more serious matter. The handful of appetizers include homemade mozzarella with olive oil and thyme, a 1-pound bucket of steamed mussels, a delicious grilled garlic quail with warm potato salad, and a vibrant salad of grilled onions, mixed lettuces, blue cheese, apples, and Champagne vinaigrette. Main courses include three types of T-bones (grilled lamb, pork, and double-cut beef), which might come with hearty, comfort-food sides like risotto or white bean stew. Meanwhile, it's hard to pass up the whole rotisserie chicken for two with homemade fries and verjus jus and horseradish-aioli-crusted salmon with creamed leek mashed potatoes and spinach. Then again, when was the last time you had macaroni and cheese? During spring, the wisteria-draped deck is gorgeous. *14301 Arnold Dr, Glen Ellen; 707/938-3451; $$; MC, V; local checks only; dinner Thurs–Sun; full bar; reservations recommended; in Jack London Village, near Verano Ave.*

LODGINGS

BELTANE RANCH ★★√

Quintessential country lifestyle comes with the cost of a night's slumber at this beautiful two-story ranch house built in 1892. Amble up the winding road off Sonoma Highway to the cheery buttercup-yellow-and-white retreat on 1,600 acres overlooking vineyards, the Mayacamas Mountains, and the highway, and you're transported into yesteryear's pastoral paradise. Two resident cats wander along white-washed up- and downstairs verandas as if to lead the way to the most comfortable porch swing or idyllic vista points. Bountiful gardens overflow with bloom. Aromas of fresh-baked cookies waft from the wonderfully rustic country kitchen, where, seated at breakfast (more great bucolic views), guests can compare their bird sightings with the posted list of the species in the area. The natural surroundings, which include a well-hidden tennis court and plenty of hiking trails, are so enticing it would be hard to find reason to retreat to one of the five bedrooms were they not equally charming. Period furnishings, cozy seating areas, and thoughtful touches of home prove this is not just another funk-and-lace B&B (although the bathroom's whimsical, retro stained-glass-like linoleum floors give a fun if unintentional nod to kitsch). All have sitting areas, private baths, separate entrances, and a family antique or two. Ask for one of the upstairs rooms that opens onto the huge wraparound double-decker porch equipped with hammocks and a swing. *11775 Sonoma Hwy, Glen Ellen; 707/996-6501; $$$; no credit cards; checks OK; www.beltaneranch.com; on Hwy 12, 2.2 miles past the Glen Ellen turnoff.*

"We're nice. Everybody's nice," was B. R. Cohn Winery employee Sherri Hewitt's response to the question what's the best thing about Sonoma. The inferred comparison was to Napa, which she considers "the other four-letter word."

GAIGE HOUSE INN   ★★★✦

From the outside, the Gaige House looks like yet another spiffed-up Victorian mansion, inevitably filled with the ubiquitous dusty antiques and family heirlooms. Inside, however, the Victorian theme comes to a screeching halt. All 11 rooms are spectacular, and each is individually decorated in an Indonesian plantation style with an eclectic mix of modern art. Owners Ken Burnet Jr. and Greg Nemrow have added three new guest rooms, including one with a private Japanese garden and waterfall. An old favorite is the newly remodeled Gaige Suite, which features a king-size four-poster canopy bed; it's also known as the Oh Wow! Room (since that is what everyone instantaneously gasps as they enter the bathroom). The suite has an enormous blue-tiled bathroom centered by a deep tub, as well as a huge wraparound balcony. The three Garden Rooms, slightly smaller and less expensive, open onto a shaded deck and are within steps of a beautiful brick-lined 40-foot swimming pool surrounded by a large, perfectly manicured lawn. All come with the best robes on earth, fancy toiletries, and thoughtful touches around every corner. Included in the room rate—which is reasonable considering the caliber of the accommodations—is a two-course gourmet breakfast served at individual tables in the dining room or on the terrace, perhaps cantaloupe carpaccio followed by a poached egg atop a fabulously fluffy ricotta pancake. Another perk: evening wine and appetizers, which might include a mind-blowing oyster with ponzu served on individual Chinese soupspoons. With addictive fresh-baked cookies, coffee, tea, and sodas ever available in the breakfast room, don't be surprised if you're not the only one tiptoeing down the hall for a late-night snack. *13540 Arnold Dr, Glen Ellen; 707/935-0237 or 800/935-0237; $$$; AE, DIS, MC, V; checks OK; gaige@sprynet.com; www.gaige.com; from Hwy 12, take the Glen Ellen exit.*

GLENELLY INN ★★

A graceful grove of oak trees forms the backdrop for this exceedingly tranquil two-story French Colonial inn, originally built in 1916 as a lodging for railway travelers. The eight squeaky-clean guest rooms, each with a private entrance, down comforter, and private bathroom with claw-footed tubs, open onto the elaborate garden or the veranda, which offers a fine view of Sonoma Valley and the tree-covered mountains beyond. As if that weren't enough, thoughtful touches and extra perks abound. Guests are greeted each morning with a good old-fashioned country breakfast—the likes of winter garden quiche, lemon bread, and Champagne grape and melon compote, or stuffed French toast with apple cider sauce, chicken apple sausages, and cranberry poached pears—served in front of a wood-burning cobblestone fireplace or on the flagstone patio. After a long day of wine tasting there are few pleasures more indulgent than disappearing to your room, flicking on the overhead ceiling fan, cozying up amid antique and country furnishings, and living the simple life of yesteryear. Then again, the outdoor hot tub draped by grapevines and roses or the on-property spa services aren't exactly shabby, either. *5131 Warm Springs Rd, Glen Ellen; 707/996-6720; $$; MC, V; checks OK; www.glenelly.com; from Hwy 12 turn left on Arnold Dr and right onto Warm Springs Rd.*

JACK LONDON LODGE ★

For those who really want to get away from the city scene, this white, two-story, wisteria-draped lodge offers 22 quiet rooms next to rippling, tree-lined Sonoma Creek. The lodge is a short drive from the town of Sonoma, near several wineries and beautiful Jack London State Historic Park. The rates are reasonable, but as usual in Wine Country, they creep up in the summer. Ask for one of the upstairs rooms, with a view of the trees. The decor is simple if somewhat bland, and each unit has a brass bed (either one king-size or two queen-size), private bath, cable TV, a portable radiator, coffeemaker, refrigerator, blow dryer, and air-conditioning. A continental breakfast is included on weekends and holidays, and daily in the summer. The swimming pool sits alongside the creek, but its surrounding chain-link fence is an eyesore in spite of the vines of red roses planted all around. Next door is the Bistro, an attractive, moderately priced restaurant, and the wonderful Jack London Saloon, where you can admire London memorabilia and hoist a glass to the author's memory. *13740 Arnold Dr, Glen Ellen; 707/938-8510; $–$$; MC, V; checks OK; from Hwy 12 turn onto Arnold Dr, follow it to Glen Ellen.*

KENWOOD

The last little town in Sonoma Valley en route to northern neighbor Santa Rosa, sleepy Kenwood has little more to it than a few wineries and one highly regarded restaurant and hotel.

ACTIVITIES

 Nature Mecca. Annadel State Park is a large wilderness area of nearly 5,000 acres, encompassing 35 miles of horseback, hiking, and biking trails amid rolling hills, streams, meadows, and forests of Douglas fir. In springtime, wildflowers are in full bloom. During winter, the park is relatively quiet. However, even at its busiest moments, the park's massive size makes it a favorite among outdoor enthusiasts looking for solitude. Lake Llsanjo offers excellent fishing conditions for bluegill and black bass (601 Channel Dr; from Sonoma Hwy/Hwy 12 turn left at Mission Blvd, turn left on Montgomery Dr, go 2 miles, then turn right on Channel Dr to the park entrance; 707/539-3911; open every day 9:30am–sunset). Sugarloaf Ridge State Park, between Santa Rosa and Sonoma, covers much of the vast oak woodlands draining toward Sonoma Creek, but there are also some nice redwood groves here, along with 2,729-foot Bald Mountain, one of the valley's most prominent geologic features. You'll also find picnic facilities; biking, hiking, and equestrian trails; a campground; and even a pretty 30-foot waterfall on the creek, but be advised that much of the park is open and exposed to the elements. So don't head out on a long bike trek without being properly prepared. For more information call the park at 707/833-5712. (2.5 miles N of Hwy 12 on Adobe Canyon Rd, 8 miles E of Santa Rosa)

Golf. Golf in the Valley of the Moon by reserving a tee time at semiprivate Oakmont Golf Club. Its two 18-hole courses designed by Ted Robinson are located in a retirement community at the base of Hood Mountain and include the 72-par 6,000-yard West Course and par-63 4,300-yard East Course. (7025 Oakmont Dr, off Hwy 12; 707/539-0415; Mon–Thurs $30, Fri $35, Sat, Sun, holidays $45)

Nursery and Sculpture Gardens. Art and nature are yours with a flash of the credit card at Wildwood Farm. Flanked by vineyards and a hillside forest of oak and bay trees, the nursery known for its outstanding maples is a garden lover's muse thanks to curator Susan Alexander. Along with rare plants and Asian maples she incorporates wrought-iron gates and purchasable contemporary wood, clay, and ceramic sculpture into the gardens. (10300 Sonoma Hwy, just south of Kangaroo on Hwy 12; 707/833-1161; www.wildmaples.com; open Tues–Sun; call in advance)

WINERIES

Chateau St. Jean. You'll be hard-pressed to find a more civilized way to spend an afternoon than to sip a Chardonnay and savor some pâté, cheese, and crackers in a shady picnicking nook at grand and glorious (and unabashedly corporate) Chateau St. Jean. The culmination of idyllic Wine Country atmosphere is the 250-acre property's new visitor center, which opened in 2000 to accompany the original country mansion that was a private home before becoming a tasting room. While the original building is open for reserve tastings ($10), most of the action takes place in the new wing, which celebrates retail with abandon. At the long and bustling wine bar Chardonnay, Merlot, and Fumé Blanc are poured at $5 per person. At another end of the building a culinary leader, in chef whites, doles out samples of local smoked salmon and chèvre and advises guests which purchasable snacks and sandwiches will go best with each wine. And at every turn, there's more country-charm cookware, must-have wine books, table linens, and fancy wine-bottle stoppers. Some visitors can't shake the tradition of spreading out a blanket and setting up lunch on the vast lawn or at the few coveted tree-shaded picnic tables. But others migrate to the gorgeous and meticulously manicured gardens, where the gurgle of fountains is accentuated by clinking glasses and the hum of bees bumbling from one blossom to the next. *8555 Sonoma Hwy/Hwy 12; 707/833-4134; www.chateaustjean.com; open every day 10am–6pm.*

Kenwood Vineyards. Old-fashioned Sonoma is honored in the original refurbished, 22-acre 1906 winery now known as Kenwood. Within the quaint red wooden barn, red wines still rule. Classic varietals—Cabernet Sauvignon, Chardonnay, Zinfandel, Sauvignon Blanc, Pinot Noir, Gewürztraminer, and Merlot—are produced here, and the best of the Zinfandel and Cabernet grapes come from Jack London's old vineyard on Sonoma Mountain. *9592 Sonoma Hwy/Hwy 12; 707/833-5891; www.kenwood.com; open every day 10am–4:30pm, closed major holidays; tours every day at 10:30am and 2pm; tasting free.*

Kunde Estate Winery. An estate in the truest sense, Kunde is able to make all of its wines with estate-grown grapes from its 2,000-acre ranch. And if ever there were benefits to starting early, Kunde's living proof: Since the family, now in its fifth generation of winery owners and operators, started the winery in 1904, some of the Zinfandel vines here are more than a hundred years old. Not surprisingly, their old-vine reds get great rankings from the big-boy critics. But Cabernet, Chardonnay, and Syrah also get plenty of attention. A visit promises a picturesque wine-country setting, a cheery tasting room, and details on Kunde's seven vineyard designations, both in the glass and from the staff. Tours, which explore the caves and 32,000 square feet of tunnels in volcanic rock, are held every hour on the hour. Along with a long bar, the tasting room has a gift shop that sells everything from cookbooks and wine books to Kunde Estate Winery–branded mocha Merlot chocolate sauce and spicy seafood sauce. *10155 Sonoma Hwy/Hwy 12; 707/833-5501; www.kunde.com; open every day 10:30–4pm; tasting free.*

St. Francis Vineyards & Winery. Technically it's in Santa Rosa, but the new tasting room for St. Francis marks the northern end of Sonoma Valley Wine Country. The winery, founded in 1979, makes a fine Chardonnay, Zinfandel, and Cabernet Sauvignon and is best known for its Merlot. To a growing number of visitors the winery is sure to become reputed for its gift center since it is aiming to feature only the best-quality products. *500 Pythian Rd, Santa Rosa; 707/833-0248 or 800/543-7713; open every day 10am–4:30pm.*

RESTAURANTS

CAFE CITTI ★ɟ

Cafe Citti (pronounced CHEET-ee) is a roadside Italian trattoria that serves hearty, home-cooked Italian fare for low, low prices. It's a sort of do-it-yourself place: first you order from the huge menu board displayed above the open kitchen, then you find a vacant table inside or at the shaded patio, and wait for a server to bring your food. Some of our favorite dishes are the focaccia sandwiches, tangy Caesar salad, green bean salad, and the savory rotisserie chicken stuffed with rosemary and garlic. There's also an array of freshly made pastas that come with a variety of sauces such as zesty marinara. Everything on the menu is available to go and makes for excellent picnic fare, but if you can't wait you can evoke the picnic spirit at the outdoor tables. *9049 Sonoma Hwy, Kenwood; 707/833-2690; $; MC, V; no checks; lunch, dinner every day; beer and wine; no reservations; headed N from Glen Ellen, it's on the left side of Hwy 12.*

KENWOOD RESTAURANT AND BAR ★★⁴

What Mustards is to Napa, Kenwood is to Sonoma: a dependable mainstay where high-quality food is doled out without pretense. The large, sun-filled dining room with polished wood floors, a natural-pine ceiling, white linens, and bamboo chairs is the showcase for chef/owner Max Schacher's changing menu, which is likely to feature classics reflecting his Swiss heritage and time spent in Germany, France, and San Francisco. Thus, you might kick off a meal with sautéed sweetbreads with endive, mushrooms, and caper bordelaise, escargots with garlic parsley butter, or crab cakes with greens and herb mayonnaise. Main courses appeal to the straightforward palate (a good old-fashioned hamburger or a juicy grilled Angus New York steak with shallot herb butter and french fries), the European expat (calf liver with caramelized onions, bacon, and mashed potatoes; rabbit with grilled polenta), and, generally speaking, everyone who enjoys good cooking. Keeping with the time-honored classics, finish with a sweet and well-prepared tarte Tatin. *9900 Sonoma Hwy, Kenwood; 707/833-6326; $$; MC, V; no checks; lunch, dinner Wed–Sun; reservations recommended; on Hwy 12, 3 miles past Glen Ellen.* &

LODGINGS

KENWOOD INN & SPA ★★★

The romance of Tuscany comes with a room at country-luxurious Kenwood Inn. Beyond the patinaed salmon-colored walls dividing this pastoral paradise from the highway are 12 gorgeous guest rooms with private entrances that lead to the landscaped courtyard and pool. Each is lovingly adorned in idyllic Italian style with plastered walls, a fluffy feather bed, fireplace, and sitting area. Room 3, bathed in shades of burgundy and green paisley, has a pleasant private patio, and room 6 sports a sitting room with a stereo, whirlpool spa, and balcony overlooking the vineyards and the swimming pool. With nary a television in sight and a glistening centerpiece outdoor pool, relaxation is done the old-fashioned way: by lounging and enjoying the simpler things. A bountiful breakfast of perhaps fresh fruit, polenta with poached eggs, and buttery house-made croissants is served in the romantic and luminous dining room, which overlooks the gardens. Afterward, you needn't wander far to further your newfound sense of tranquillity: the six-room, full-service spa located just off the entryway pampers guests with such treatments as a Mediterranean scrub of lemon rind, rosemary, and salt followed by a massage. *10400 Sonoma Hwy, Kenwood; 707/833-1293; $$$; AE, MC, V; checks OK; www.kenwoodinn.com; on Hwy 12, 3 miles past Glen Ellen.*

NORTHERN
SONOMA
COUNTY

NORTHERN SONOMA COUNTY

If you were ever to custom-build a place for the sole purpose of basking in the sun and never wearing long pants all summer long, northern Sonoma County would be it. Part Wine Country, part swimmin' hole, and part lazy weekend paradise, this region seems to have a little bit of everything that is Northern California wrapped into one package. The Russian River itself is placid enough for canoeing and tubing, or just taking a dip. The beach scene can be *Baywatch*-esque during the height of summer. Go north of the resort town of Guerneville a short distance, however, and you'll swear you've reached Humboldt County, as the Armstrong Redwoods State Reserve is a nicely preserved redwood forest, perfect for slow, meandering walks or bike rides in the cool shadows of giants. Another California component to the Russian River experience is sociological rather than geographic: numerous resorts along the river cater primarily to the Bay Area gay community, who use the Sonoma Coast area as a weekend retreat. It is curious to see a relatively rural setting embrace a culture normally associated with big cities, but the blend works comfortably here, and therefore the river is also a popular family spot.

The sheer vastness of this area allows room for well over 100 wineries, which must be discovered along winding back roads, as well as a few truly charming towns and endless outdoor recreation. The downside is you'll have to do a decent amount of driving to cover this ground. On the plus side, because wineries and attractions are well dispersed and more remote than their southern neighbors, you won't spend your time in wine-tasting traffic— on the road *or* in the winery. Simultaneously, there's so much to do in the way of outdoor adventure, you can easily busy yourself for a week without ever stepping into a tasting room.

Get a better understanding of Sonoma County by visiting www.sonoma.com/regions/, a section of Sonoma.com, which tells you how the region's various areas differ and offers late-breaking tips on what's new.

SANTA ROSA

Santa Rosa is the closest thing Sonoma County has to a big city. Historically it's been more like a countrified suburb, but to make room for the 30.3 percent population growth from 1990 to 2000, it continues to undergo growing pains and urban expansion. The best parts about it for the Wine Country traveler are the abundance

In town from late July to early August? Check out the local crowd-pleaser Sonoma County Harvest Fair (1350 Bennett Valley Rd; 707/545-4200), an annual wine-tasting, food-gobbling orgy held at the fairgrounds.

of affordable hotels, B&Bs, and motels; a growing number of good restaurants; and things for the kids to do.

ACTIVITIES

Getting Acquainted. Sure it's fun to hit the country roads in search of adventure. But to ensure your path is best charted, it's worth contacting the Santa Rosa Convention and Visitors Bureau. Its comprehensive and friendly web site, which offers a cornucopia of information on the region, has an area where you can request the complimentary visitors' guide. You can also stop by the office anytime Monday through Friday from 8:30am to 5pm and weekends from 10am to 3pm (later during summer) to pick up the guide, along with endless brochures and walking-tour maps. (9 4th St, at Wilson; from Hwy 101 take 3rd St exit, turn right on Wilson; 800/404-ROSE; www.visitsantarosa.com)

Farmers Market. For music, magicians, and a plethora of fresh-from-the-farm food, head over to the wildly successful Thursday-night farmers market on downtown Santa Rosa's Fourth Street, which is closed to traffic every Thursday night for this festive event and draws folks from far and near from Memorial Day through Labor Day (call the visitors bureau, above, for more information). The year-round Veteran's Building version offers less in the way of entertainment and crafts, but farmers still bring their best produce to the Maple Avenue location (at Brookwood by the fairgrounds) on Wednesday and Saturday mornings from 8am to noon.

Golf. With the area's good deal of elbowroom and continuing onslaught of well-to-do professionals and vacationing weekenders looking for fun, Santa Rosa's got plenty of places to tee off. You'll find no frills at Fairgrounds Golf Center, a well-priced and well-kept municipal nine-hole course, which is compacted into the flat infield of the area's fairgrounds (1350 Bennett Valley Rd; off 5th St exit from Hwy 12; 707/577-0755; www.empiregolf.com; open every day 7am–6pm; $9 adults, $3 replay, $5 children). The Fountaingrove Club is another story. Its 18-hole semi-private par-72 championship course is carved into Santa Rosa's rolling hillsides and boasts gorgeous landscaping and challenging terrain (1525 Fountaingrove Pkwy; from Hwy 101 N take

Bicentennial exit E, follow for 2 miles; 707/579-4653; www.fountaingrovegolf.com; open every day 7am–6pm; Mon–Fri $75, Sat–Sun $95). Wikiup Golf Course, a nine-hole par-29 executive course, charges $10 for nine holes weekdays, $12 weekends, with $6 for replays. (5001 Carriage Ln; from Hwy 101 N take Guerneville Rd exit—first right after Luther Burbank Center, bear E to 4-way intersection, take left on Redwood Hwy, proceed 2.25 miles; 707/546-8787; open every day 7am–6pm, later during summer)

Camping and Fishing. Spring Lake Regional Park in Santa Rosa has 30 campsites at Spring Lake, a popular boating and rainbow fishing spot. The lake, also known as Santa Rosa Creek Reservoir, has a regular fish-stocking schedule during the outdoor season. Each site has a picnic table and fire pit, with piped water, showers, and flush toilets nearby. Boat rentals and shopping for basics are available on-site. Various RV lengths can be accommodated, but there are no hookups. Campsite reservations require Visa or MasterCard payment and 10 days to one year's notice; call 707/565-2267 weekdays 9am–3pm. (5585 Newanga Ave; from Hwy 101, take Hwy 12 E for 0.75 miles, continue 0.5 miles along Hoen Ave to Newanga Ave, head N 0.5 miles to park entrance; www.sonoma-county.org/camping; camground open every day May–Sept, weekends and holidays Oct–Apr; parking $3–$4)

Hot-Air Balloon Ride. It may be the stereotypical Wine Country thing to do, but there's a reason hot-air balloon rides are a popular way to tour this part of the state. From the comfort of a sturdy 2- to 16-person basket dangling below the brightly colored balloon, passengers get a bird's-eye view for thousands of acres, which include redwoods, the Russian River, the mountains, the Pacific Coast, and the San Francisco skyline. Provided weather conditions are good, the ride begins in Santa Rosa early in the morning, includes at least an hour in the air, and unwinds with a Champagne picnic brunch at Kendall-Jackson winery. (Starting points vary from Santa Rosa, instructions and directions are provided upon reservation; 707/538-7359 or 888/2FUN-FLY; www.balloontours.com; $195 per person)

 Plants. Botanists, gardeners, and other plant lovers will want to make a beeline for the popular gardens and greenhouse at the Luther Burbank Home & Gardens (corner of Santa Rosa and Sonoma Aves; 707/524-5445). Burbank was a world-renowned horticulturist who created 800 new strains of plants, fruits, and vegetables at the turn of the century.

Snoopy. Thanks to donations by the beagle's creator, Charles Schulz, who lived in Santa Rosa, pop-culture fans can visit Snoopy's Gallery & Gift Shop, a "Peanuts" cartoon museum opened in 1981 by the great cartoonist himself and featuring the world's largest collection of Snoopy memorabilia. Along with eyeing original artwork, a time line of "Peanuts" history, the first strip, and awards, you can stop into the gift shop to add the likes of a Waterford crystal bowl adorned with "Peanuts" characters, a Snoopy and Woodstock salt-and-pepper set, or a Joe Cool hairbrush to your collection. A larger memorial is being constructed across the street. (1665 W Steel Ln; from Hwy 101 N take W Steel Ln exit, go left at off-ramp, go straight until Range Ave, turn right, and take first left onto W Steel Ln; 707/546-3385; www.snoopygift.com; open every day 10am–6pm; closed major holidays; free admission)

WINERIES

De Loach Vineyards. Former San Francisco firefighter Cecil De Loach might just heat up your love for Zinfandel with his rendition, which is made from century-old vines. But then again, many consider his Chardonnay, Merlot, Pinot Noir, and Cabernet Sauvignon hot stuff too, especially the "O.F.S." label. (Publicly it stands for "Our Finest Selection," but insiders say it really means something else. Do ask about it when you drop by and see what they say.) Within the friendly tasting room hosts pour complimentary tastes, which you can savor as you admire the paintings by local artists, displayed alongside locally crafted ceramics, stemware, and logo-wear. Picnics are encouraged on the beautiful lawn area adjacent to the vineyards. Tours of the winery, production process (during harvest), and the daily goings-on are held every day at 11am and 2pm or by appointment. *1791 Olivet Rd; from Hwy 101 N take the River Rd exit, head W 5 miles to Olivet Rd, and turn left; 707/526-9111; www.deloachvineyards.com; open every day 10am–4:30pm.*

▣ **Ledson Winery & Vineyards.** The Ledsons, a fourth-generation Sonoma family, went all out when constructing an eye-catching place in which to showcase their wines. The 16,000-square-foot Gothic castle built in 1999 in French-Normandy style includes a custom-colored brick edifice, turrets, balconies, seven fireplaces, *Gone with the Wind*–style staircase, and numerous fountains. Designed by family member Steve Ledson and featuring ornate wood inlays and mosaics created by his son Mike, it really is a dramatic departure from your everyday casual, incognito Sonoma wine-tasting venue. The architecture and spectacular grounds, including an outstanding picnicking patio and rose garden, are enough reason to head to Ledson. But of course there's more: three tasting bars pour Chardonnay, Merlot, and Riesling, which are sold only at the winery. A gourmet marketplace arms you with plenty of picnic ammunition, and a gift shop beckons to the credit cards. *7335 Sonoma Hwy, just N of Kenwood; 707/833-2330; open every day 10am–5pm.*

▣ View **Matanzas Creek Winery.** A beautiful drive graced with fields of 4,500 lavender plants and surrounded by rolling vineyard-covered hills introduces Matanzas, one of Sonoma's prettiest wineries. Once inside the state-of-the-art facilities, you won't take long to discover they also make some pretty darned good wine. Three or more wines, which might include their highly regarded Chardonnay, Merlot, and Sauvignon Blanc, are yours for the tasting, along with the winery-exclusive blanc de blancs sparkling wine. If you want to know more about the property's spectacular flora you can pick up a garden booklet in the tasting room. Lovely mementos include the gift shop's estate-grown-lavender products for the kitchen, bed, and bath, but for even better memory-making, bring a lunch, purchase a bottle of wine, and picnic at one of the tables strategically placed in an oak grove. *6097 Bennett Valley Rd; heading N on Hwy 12 from Sonoma Valley, take Warm Springs Rd turnoff to Bennett Valley Rd; 707/528-6464; www.matanzascreek.com; open every day 10am–4:30pm; tasting $5, refunded with wine purchase.*

RESTAURANTS

HANA JAPANESE RESTAURANT ★★★

If Hana were the only attraction in this section of Northern California, it'd be reason enough to make the trip. Unbeknownst to most visitors this Japanese restaurant, located in a strip mall in Santa Rosa suburb Rohnert Park, is *the* place for sushi in Northern California. What it lacks in its almost motel-style decor it more than makes up for with mind-blowing raw and cooked fish dishes and astoundingly beautiful presentations. Chef Ken Tominaga presides over the exceedingly fresh and delicious standard nigiri sushi such as tuna, salmon, albacore, and yellowtail; rolls ranging from California or spicy salmon to tuna-belly-and-green-onion or softshell crab; as well as some of the most memorable specials you'll ever taste. Nothing is more indulgent than foie gras with unagi (eel), unless, of course, you are lucky enough to taste the sea urchin egg custard. Other addictions include outstanding Hawaiian ahi poke or buttery monkfish liver. For the sushi experience of your life, ask Ken to lead the way. But be sure to tell him how much you want to spend, because it's possible to blow around $100 per person here. Folks who aren't raw fish fans can choose from the huge lunch and dinner menu of light and crisp tempura, a juicy grilled steak (perhaps with shiitake mushrooms and soy-Cabernet sauce), grilled Atlantic salmon with creamy potatoes and saffron cream sauce, or chicken teriyaki. Wash it down with one of the great premium sakes or a Japanese beer and, trust us, you've gone to heaven. At lunch, the bento boxes, donburi, and udon meals, complete with miso soup, Japanese pickles, salad, and rice, are a great deal at $10.50 or less. While service is basic, it's friendly and speedy, which is important since you'll have a hard time waiting for the next edible treasure to make its way to the table. *101 Golf Course Dr, Rohnert Park; 707/586-0270; $$; AE, DIS, MC, V; no checks; lunch, dinner every day; beer and wine; reservations recommended; from Santa Rosa take Hwy 101 S, take Wilfred Ave exit toward Golf Course Dr, turn right on Redwood Dr, right on Commerce Blvd, left on Golf Course Dr,*

*left on Red Lion Dr, left toward DoubleTree hotel, left into Dou-
bleTree Plaza mini-mall, and drive to the back.* &

JOHN ASH & CO.   ★★★

This casually elegant restaurant, founded by Wine Country
cuisine guru John Ash (who has little to do with it anymore),
has topped the list of Santa Rosa's best restaurants for many
years. It's pricey, but the service is expert, the food is fabulous, and the serene dining room with cream-colored walls,
tall French windows, and a crackling fire will entice you to
settle in for a good long time. The menu, under the direction
of executive chef Jeffrey Madura, is a classic California
hybrid of French, Italian, Asian, and Southwestern cuisines.
A meal might begin with such luminous dishes as tuna
tartare and sashimi with spicy greens and potato gaufrettes
(wafers) or warm vegetable salad with grilled portobello
mushrooms and honey-lemon vinaigrette. About a dozen
entrees cover most of the cravings bases with the likes of al
dente orecchiette pasta with prawns, Brie cream sauce, sun-
dried tomato pesto, and dried jack cheese; coq au Zinfandel;
a decadent Sonoma-specific concoction of chicken, cremini
mushrooms, smoked bacon, and fried herb potatoes; and
roasted rack of lamb with truffled celery root purée, Swiss
chard, and hazelnut, honey, and thyme jus. For dessert, diners swoon over El Rey chocolate crème brûlée and flourless
chocolate cake with a layer of chocolate and house-made
peanut butter served with crème anglaise and peanut brit-
tle. The large, reasonably priced wine list, showcasing Napa
and Sonoma wines, also includes a good selection of ports,
sherries, and dessert wines. For a taste of delicious cuisine
at a fraction of the regular price, sit at the bar or on the patio
and order from the Vineyard Cafe menu. *4330 Barnes Rd,
Santa Rosa; 707/527-7687; $$$; AE, MC, V; local checks only;
lunch Mon–Fri, dinner every day, brunch Sun; full bar; reserva-
tions recommended; www.vintnersinn.com; next door to Vint-
ners Inn, off River Rd, at Hwy 101.*

LISA HEMENWAY'S   ★★

Don't let the rather drab shopping center setting fool you—
within that boxy brown shrine to the '70s is a refreshingly

light, airy restaurant with alfresco dining and an inviting menu. With cooking skills honed at the venerable John Ash & Co. restaurant (see review), combined with working vacations in Asia and Europe, owner/chef Lisa Hemenway has created an expansive and varied menu that runs the gamut from classic to exotic. While the culinary itinerary changes frequently, some tried-and-true classics might include baked herb Brie with fresh fruit, candied almonds, and cheese pastry twists; a rich and savory beef bourguignon; and the French standbys steak frites (a tender flatiron steak seared with mustard, herbs, and peppercorns, and served with red wine glace and pommes frites) and decadent coq au vin. Less traditional menu offerings include Hanoi spring rolls with mint, cilantro, rice noodles, and chili dipping sauce; rich crab fritters with green papaya salad and sambal aioli; and a vibrant salad of mixed greens, dried cranberries, candied pecans, red grapes, apples, blackberry balsamic vinaigrette, and baked goat cheese. Parents with kids in tow are in luck; the children's menu may be limited to a few items, but they are half the price of the entrees. If all this is too daunting for you, you can always loosen up at the wine bar, which proudly boasts numerous Awards of Excellence from *Wine Spectator* magazine. *714 Village Ct, Santa Rosa; 707/526-5111; $$; DC, DIS, MC, V; checks OK; lunch Mon–Sat, dinner every day; full bar; reservations recommended; www.sterba.com/sro/hemenway/; in the Village Court Mall/Montgomery Village at Farmers Ln and Sonoma Ave.*

SYRAH   ★★ɟ

Owners Josh and Regina Silvers preside over a local favorite serving French-inspired American cuisine. Within a casual-chic historic building with a beamed ceiling, an open kitchen, and a handful of patio seats, it's possible to watch chef Josh (previously of Mustards in Napa Valley) bake brioche and poached foie gras, which might be accompanied by marinated dried cherries, in a terra-cotta pot, or sauté crab cakes that will be lovingly placed on an arugula salad with roasted beets and horseradish vinaigrette. Other starters include a moist duck confit with beluga lentil salad and succulent pork tenderloin. *205 5th St, Santa Rosa; 707/568-4002; $$$; DIS,*

MC, V; no checks; lunch, dinner Tues–Sat; beer and wine; reservations recommended; www.syrahbistro.com; at Davis St.

WILLOWSIDE CAFE ★★★

Hiding out in a funky roadhouse a few miles from downtown Santa Rosa, Willowside may not receive ongoing recognition from national critics, but Bay Area residents have long been fans of one of Sonoma County's best-kept dining secrets. Inside, the mood is simple yet sophisticated, with pale yellow walls, copper-topped tables, and fresh flowers—the perfect match for chef Greg Markey's (previously of San Francisco's Masa's) French-inspired California cuisine. The menu, served by an attentive staff, changes with the seasons, but it always features five starters (such as seared king salmon with sorrel and pink peppercorns or cornmeal-crusted soft-shell crab with spicy port wine sauce) and five entrees (which might include day boat scallops with red lentils, citrus, and green garlic; baked halibut with potato pancakes, stewed leeks, and romesco sauce; or pan-roasted ostrich with foie gras and shiitake mushrooms). A favorite with local winemakers, Willowside offers 200 labels on its wine list, including hard-to-find California, French, and Australian bottles. *3535 Guerneville Rd, Santa Rosa; 707/523-4814; $$; MC, V; local checks only; dinner Wed–Sun; beer and wine; reservations recommended; at Willowside Rd.*

LODGINGS

VINTNERS INN ★★

The Vintners Inn combines the charm of a country inn with the conveniences of a modern hotel, which makes it a prime spot for corporate retreats as well as everyday travels. Its four Provençal-style buildings are clustered around a central courtyard set amid vineyards. The inn's 44 newly refurbished rooms have pine beds, plush carpets, antique armoires and desks, and separate sitting areas; many have wood-burning fireplaces, too. French doors open onto a balcony or patio with a view of the vineyards or the landscaped grounds (ask for a room with a vineyard view facing away from Highway 101). The young, courteous staff is very attentive, providing first-class service. A complimentary breakfast is served in the main building's sunny dining room until 10am on weekdays and 11am on weekends. Though there's also a fine deck for sunning and a whirlpool spa, the inn's best feature is its adjoining restaurant, John Ash & Co. (see review, above). Other pluses are its proximity to all the wine-country action and its newness, which goes a long way in an area rife with funky B&Bs and traditional inns. *4350 Barnes Rd, Santa Rosa; 707/575-7350 or 800/421-2584; $$$; AE, DC, MC, V; checks OK; www.vintnersinn.com; off River Rd, at Hwy 101.*

WINDSOR

It may be a one-block town, but there are a few good reasons to wind your way to sleepy Windsor.

WINERIES

Martinelli Winery. No, they're not the sparkling-apple-juice makers. Most guests who drop in on this charming old wooden hop-drying barn know it's the home of the family-owned winery's well-respected Chardonnay, which is poured freely by gregarious tasting room attendants and accompanied by a Gewürztraminer or two and a Pinot Noir. All of Martinelli's wines are handcrafted, unrefined and unfiltered, and all tastings are free, except for the "Jackass Hill Vineyard" Zinfandel, which costs $1 per coveted sample. You can set up camp at the picnic table out front, but if you want more than cheese and crackers you should bring your own grub. The food selection here is limited and surrounded by hand-painted oh-so-wine-country glassware. *3360 River Rd, between Chalkhill Rd and Healdsburg Ave; from Hwy 101 take River Rd exit W, go 3 miles; 707/525-0570; open every day 10am–5pm.*

RESTAURANTS

MARIPOSA   ★★★

Book a reservation well in advance, because more than a few food-savvy locals deem this tiny, charming restaurant the best in the region. The adorable cottage dining room offering the best of Wine Country cuisine is run and operated by chef Raymond Tang and his wife, Shawn. Each night diners, including many off-duty chefs, settle into the 26 inside seats, five bar stools, or a seat on the small seasonal patio to see what chef Tang is up to now. His menu changes weekly to celebrate whatever's in season, but delights invariably accentuate a skilled interpretation of French-American cuisine with a dab of Chinese influence (after all, Tang *is* Chinese). What that means to the lucky diner is perhaps an opportunity to sample his legendary sizzling black mussels, which have been poached, shelled, sautéed with pea sprouts in a dreamy coconut curry cream sauce, and then lovingly placed on a sizzling-hot cast-iron skillet. Or the evening's choices might include tender and aromatic tea-smoked duck breast paired with duck leg confit, Hudson Valley foie gras, wilted frisée, and duck gizzards, which could easily be the must-have were it not for a tantalizing house-cured pork tenderloin with baked black Thai rice, apples, and smoked bacon. Desserts are simply delicious and usually include a concise selection of gelato and house-made crème brûlée, apple crisp, and chèvre cheesecake with walnut crust. Service is friendly and polished. *275 Windsor River Rd, Windsor; 707/838-0162; $$$; DIS, MC, V; no checks; dinner Tues–Sat; closed 2 weeks in Feb; beer and wine; reservations recommended; mariposarestaurant.org; exit Hwy 101 N at Central Windsor, turn left from off-ramp, go 0.5 miles and the restaurant is on the right-hand side.*

GUERNEVILLE

Southwest of Healdsburg is the funky Russian River Valley town of Guerneville, which was explored by the Russians in the 1840s and grew into one of the busiest logging centers in the West by the 1880s. More recently, it was a haven for bikers (the sort who wear leather, not Lycra) before becoming a hangout for hippies. Now it's a summer mecca for gays and lesbians as well as naturalists drawn by the beauty of the land. The commercial center of town is about three blocks long and sprinkled with dive restaurants, gay bars, and basic provisions for residents. Surrounding it on all sides are cabins, campgrounds, cheap and tired hotels, rustic atmosphere, and the thing that pulls it all together: the Russian River. Come summertime, nothing's more fun than jumping into a canoe and paddling along the forest-flanked waters from beach to beach, occasionally dodging the renegade kid who's cannon-balling off a rope swing. The area also happens to be a good place to kick off a nature expedition or a tour of the local wineries.

ACTIVITIES

Getting Acquainted. Guerneville is easily accessed by taking the Highway 116/River Road exit off Highway 101 and following it west into town. Because the Russian River is paralleled by Guerneville's main road (River Road), it won't take long to familiarize yourself with the area. What is likely to be more challenging is finding accommodations during summer or learning about the interesting restaurants, attractions, and goings-on tucked into redwood groves and dotting the winding back roads. Give a call to the Guerneville Chamber of Commerce (707/869-9000) or the Russian River Chamber of Commerce (707/869-3533) for information on anything and everything the area has to offer.

Parks. Nestled in the rolling hills and valleys adjacent to the Russian River canyon are two contiguous parks, comprising some 6,000 acres of forested hills. The magnificent redwood grove at Armstrong Redwoods State Reserve contains a self-guided nature trail that meanders among the trees, some of which are well over 1,000 years old and stand over 300 feet tall. Exploring the cool, shaded, moist redwood grove at Armstrong is a true joy. If you are looking for a short stroll, check out Pioneer Trail, an easy 1.4-mile round-trip jaunt. The trail runs parallel to Fife Creek through the cool, dark, and damp redwood habitat. An alternate route back to the trailhead is via the Pool Ridge Trail and the Discovery Trail, which will add roughly 1 mile to your return trip. To venture through the forest on horseback, see "Horseback Riding and Pack Trips" below. (17000 Armstrong Woods Rd; from Santa Rosa, take Hwy 101 N, and turn W on Hwy 12—it becomes Hwy 116 at Forestville—to Guerneville; at Armstrong Woods Rd, turn right and drive 2.5 miles to entrance; 707/869-2015; open every day 8am–1 hour after sunset; day use $2 per car)

Austin Creek State Recreation Area, adjacent to Armstrong, contains grasslands, riparian habitats, chaparral, conifer, and oak woodland. The park's only campground sits on a high ridge overlooking the forest. From the 20 miles of hiking trails through the Austin Creek area, you're likely to see an array of wildlife, such as the rare California spotted owl. In contrast to the busy Armstrong Redwoods area, Austin Creek has several trails that are seldom traveled. One noteworthy choice, the Gilliam Creek Trail, is a moderate 8.2-mile round-trip walk; it starts at a 1,200-foot elevation and travels along the riparian habitat of Gilliam/Schoolhouse Creek down to a 200-foot elevation at the trail's end in Gilliam Creek Trail Campground (see camping information below). (Continue 3.5 miles through Armstrong Redwoods State Reserve to the entrance; 707/865-2391; open year-round except during high fire danger periods; camping $7 per site)

For more information about the Russian River area, contact the Guerneville Chamber of Commerce (707/869-9000) or the Russian River Chamber of Commerce (707/869-3533).

 Bicycle. Although it's tempting to jump in the car to get to the river and wineries, it's a heck of a lot more fun to absorb the flavor of the area by pedaling your way along the redwood-flanked roads. From Guerneville it's a flat and easy two-wheeling trip to Korbel. Ditto Armstrong Redwoods State Reserve, but those who want to break a sweat can go the uphill battle to the campgrounds. Russian River Bikes (14070 Mill St, next to the post office; from River Rd turn right on Mill St; 707/869-1455; www.russianriverbikes.com) rents 24-speed sport comfort bikes or 7-speed "classic cruisers" for $7 per hour and $25 per day and also offers information on great local routes.

More-passionate bicycle enthusiasts should take one of Adventure Bike Company's tours. After saddling up on a 21-speed hybrid bicycle and strapping on your helmet, you can embark on their Bike-n-Hike Champagne & Redwoods Tour, which departs Guerneville via bicycle in the morning, tours and tastes at Korbel Champagne Cellars, and pedals to Armstrong Redwoods State Reserve for a hike and delicious picnic. A little more strenuous on the glutes is the Dry Creek Valley tour, a wine-tasting adventure through some of the region's prettiest landscape to equally flavorful wineries, with a picnic lunch. No need to bring a backpack to fit that case or two of wine you're likely to buy; transportation of wine purchases to your hotel is included in the rates. (707/794-8594; www.adventurebikeco.com; call for schedules; reservations recommended; $89 per person)

A GOOD DAY IN . . . GUERNEVILLE

Enjoy a quick breakfast at **Korbel,** *grab lunch to go, and scurry to* **Burke's Canoes** *(in summer only) for a fun-filled day on the Russian River. By midafternoon you'll be more than ready for a refreshing shower and rest before dining at the* **Applewood Inn & Restaurant.** *If water sports aren't your thing, follow the Healdsburg itinerary; the town is a mere 20 minutes away and there are plenty of wineries along the way.*

Horseback Riding and Pack Trips. What better way to find respite from the exhausting pursuits of riverside sunning and back-road wine tasting than an invigorating horseback adventure? Laura and Jonathan Ayers's guided rides are more than just a few spins around the old corral. Their Pool Ridge ride begins with a short lesson on how to communicate with their well-trained horses before following a stream surrounded by huge redwoods and climbing the mountainside through five distinct biotic environments to a ridge with a 100-mile view. Half- and full-day excursions are also offered and cover beautiful, pristine Sonoma terrain. Saddle up before sunset, and after the sun slips beyond the Pacific you can wind down with a gourmet barbecue. And if you feel like you could ride for days, well, you can, because the Ayerses' overnight rides include cozy tepee camping and a gentler second-day ride. If you saddle up with Laura, who is also a naturalist, she can tell you interesting information about the redwoods and the nuances of the area's various flora and fauna. But as you meander through Armstrong Redwoods State Reserve, you won't need a specialist to point out the spectacular trees, many of which are wider than a VW bus, stand over 300 feet tall, and date back over 1,500 years. (Armstrong Woods Pack Station; 1 mile into Armstrong Redwoods State Reserve, follow "Horses for Hire" signs (left fork), and turn onto dirt road by Armstrong Tree; 707/887-2939; www.redwoodhorses.com; day ride $50–$150, overnight ride $225; parking $5 per day, or park free at the entrance and walk 1 mile to stables)

Beach. It's not exactly white sand and lapping sapphire blue water, but the gravelly stretch of shore called Johnson's Beach is as good as it gets in this area. Along with ample space to lay out your beach chair and towel amid families, gay suntanners, and summertime party kids, you'll also find a Russian River–style "resort," which includes a campground, rooms, and snack bar. The resort, open May to October, rents canoes, kayaks, and paddleboats (just under the main bridge; 707/869-2022; no dogs allowed). Its beach, open year-round, is also home to the wildly popular Russian River Jazz Festival, held every September (707/869-3940) as well as the Russian River Blues Festival, held in June (510/655-9471 for tickets; www.russianriverbluesfest.com).

Camping. Austin Creek State Recreation Area's 24 campsites accommodate tents or RVs and offer access to showers and toilets. RV campers take heed: there are no hookups and the maximum acceptable length of your ride is 20 feet. Hardcore naturalists can reserve a spot in the boondocks or one of the four primitive campsites (no water, pit toilets) 2.5 miles into the backcountry. However, be sure to get a backcountry camping permit from the ranger station. (From Santa Rosa, take Hwy 101 N and go W on Hwy 12, which becomes Hwy 116 at Forestville, to Guerneville; at Armstrong Woods Rd, turn right and drive 2.5 miles to Armstrong Redwoods State Reserve; continue 3.5 miles past entrance to Austin Creek area; campground is just past the main parking area; 707/865-2391; open year-round except during high fire danger periods; camping $7 per site)

The Faerie Ring Campground is a private campground in Guerneville. The 41 tent or RV sites have shower and toilet access, RV hookups, and water and sanitary disposal. Locationwise, this facility is in a central spot, just 1 mile from the Russian River and less than a mile from Armstrong Redwoods State Reserve. It's also reputed to be gay friendly. Note: RV length limit is 31 feet. (From Santa Rosa, take Hwy 101 N to River Rd exit, go left at the off-ramp stop sign, go 17 miles to Armstrong Woods Rd, turn right, and drive 1.8 miles to the campground; 707/869-2746)

Fishing. Fishing is a year-round sport on the Russian River, with access points at major resorts and bridge crossings. Recent endangered species listings continue to affect fishing regulations in the state, but the sport has yet to be completely outlawed. Current laws require barbless fishing, but you should get up-to-date information on regulations before setting out for the riverbanks. Bait-and-tackle dealers should have free copies of the latest amendments. In late September, chinook and coho salmon runs begin, but currently if you catch them in the river (as opposed to the ocean) you must throw them back. In November the steelhead runs begin on the Russian. Shad can be caught in May; in summer the popular catches are striped bass, large- and smallmouth bass, bluegill, and catfish. Kings Sport & Tackle in Guerneville arranges guided fishing tours on the river and also has information about current fishing conditions. (16258 Main St; 707/869-2156; every day 8am–6pm, opens 7am during abalone season)

Spa. Rose Mari's Russian River Spa & Massage Center is a far cry from five-star Sonoma Mission Inn, but what do you expect from ultra-laid-back Guerneville? By the same token, you won't pay five-star prices for your herbal wrap, facial, or massage. As a matter of fact, you can have a combo package that covers the gamut for about the price of one massage at one of the Wine Country's fancier retreats. (16370 1st St; at Mill St, just off River Rd; 707/869-3322; www.sonic.net/~pamg; open Thurs–Mon 10am–8pm)

WINERIES

Korbel Champagne Cellars. As you enter the town of Guerneville from Healdsburg it's impossible to miss Korbel's vineyards to the left and the ivy-covered gabled brick winery set in a redwood grove to the right. The informative tours walk you through their 115-plus-year-old winemaking business and the more recent brewery, which produces a selection of house-made suds under the Russian River Brewing Company label. The extensive and beautiful flower gardens are open for tours from May through September. An enormous gift shop sells the expected trinkets and wines, and the adjoining market and deli is the best in the area. *13250 River Rd; 707/824-7000; www.korbel.com; tasting room open every day 9am–5pm; deli open Mon–Fri 8am–6pm, Sat–Sun 9am–6pm; wine shop open every day 9am–5:30pm; tours every day 10am–3:45pm; garden tours Tues–Sun 11am, 1pm, and 3pm.*

RESTAURANTS

APPLEWOOD INN & RESTAURANT ★★★✦

Rarely does everything come together in a restaurant, but in Applewood Inn's rustic 60-seat second-floor dining room, ambience, service, California-Provençal cuisine, and wine come together in relaxed but perfect harmony. Executive chef Brian Gerritsen, who worked with famed chef Ken Frank at both Napa Valley's La Toque and FENIX at the Argyle Hotel in Hollywood, could give any big-city chef a run for the money with his unfussy fare and judicious use of excellent ingredients, many from his organic garden. Whether you order à la carte or from the six-course tasting menu, one thing is certain: few things in life are as heavenly as his tuna tartare provençale, the translucent red fish perfectly simple with preserved Meyer lemons, parsley-cumin flatbread, and crunch from a reserved sprinkle of sea salt. Gerritsen's lobster and mussel pithiviers (puff pastry) is a jewel of a dish with delicate seafood flavors that dance on the palate. Roasted pork tenderloin couldn't be more tender and flavorful, arriving on a savory pillowlike chick-pea–ricotta pancake with orange roasted beets and watercress; equally outstanding is the quail with prosciutto-wrapped figs, orec-chiette pasta, and dry sherry. An award-winning wine list makes it a delicious challenge to choose the night's wine. Dessert, also by chef Gerritsen, might feature outstanding panna cotta with Spanish sherry and figs roasted in orange caramel or a devilish chocolate pecan and browned butter tartlet with caramel-brandy ice cream. No need to wear a tie, but do your best not to arrive in shorts: the casual-chic French-barn-style room, where two river-rock fireplaces blaze beneath lofty beamed ceilings, is Guerneville-formal. *13555 Highway 16, Guerneville; 707/869-9093; $$$; AE, MC, V; no checks; dinner Tues–Sun; beer and wine; reservations rec-ommended; one mile S of downtown Guerneville, from River Rd headed toward downtown, turn left on Hwy 116 and follow it one mile; hotel driveway is on the left.*

KORBEL DELICATESSEN AND MARKET ★

Gourmet delis are few and far between in these parts. But Korbel is one dependable place where you can fill your picnic basket with everything from pasta salads and grilled chicken to a custom-ordered box lunch. Drop in unannounced to buy cheeses, pâtés, grilled meats and vegetables, and goodies like brownies. Call two days ahead to order from a variety of $14 gourmet feasts. Previous menus have included grilled Mediterranean vegetable chicken salad with penne pasta, bruschetta with rosemary, fresh fruit, and dessert, or beef tri-tip and caramelized onions on a sourdough baguette, red potato salad with capers and sour cream, fruit, and dessert. Each boxed lunch comes with plastic ware, a napkin, and a soft drink. However, you might be inclined to grab a six-pack or two of their house-made beers brewed under the Russian River Brewing Company label. Better yet, order a glass on tap, pull up a chair at the in- or outdoor seating overlooking the redwoods (and, unfortunately a bit of River Road), and enjoy. *13250 River Rd, Guerneville; 707/824-7313; $; AE, DIS, MC, V; no checks; breakfast, lunch every day; www.korbel.com; just E of downtown Guerneville.*

LODGINGS

APPLEWOOD INN & RESTAURANT ★★★

The quaint boutique hotel and destination restaurant set on 6 acres of forested hillside are worlds beyond Guerneville's other options. A 2-minute drive from downtown, the turn into the driveway of this beautiful salmon pink Mediterranean-style retreat is quick, but the change in ambience is dramatic. The three structures that comprise the 16-room compound surround a sweet and sunny courtyard. The original building, a 1922 California Mission Revival mansion with a formal dining room and lovely sitting areas, hosts a variety of rooms, all individually decorated with antiques, attractive fabrics, and tasteful colors. Its age shows in not-quite-even floors, small bathrooms, and a lack of central heating (there are space heaters). But that's a fair price to pay for rooms that revel in old-fashioned country charm, boast pastoral views, and have TVs, phones, Egyptian-cotton towels, down comforters, and, in one case, a lovely secluded redwood-shaded deck. Newer accommodations are equally charming, even a touch more modern, with fireplaces and small private decks or courtyards. The newest additions, two huge suites, are the most modern in decor, with bright colors, fireplaces, and huge bathrooms. An outdoor pool (heated spring through fall) and hot tub (heated year-round) tempt guests to linger on the property. And even those not staying here should come for dinner: the charming restaurant offers some of the best food in the region (see review in Restaurants). In keeping with casual Russian River style, it's completely appropriate to come and go in shorts and flip-flops (except at dinner, when casual-chic is more in order), but many visitors rightfully argue it's even more enjoyable to do it when you have such a nice place to return to. *13555 Hwy 116, Guerneville; 707/869-9093; $$$; AE, MC, V; checks OK; stay@applewoodinn.com; www.applewoodinn.com; 1 mile S of downtown Guerneville: from River Rd toward downtown, turn left on Hwy 116, follow it 1 mile, and hotel driveway is on the left.*

SANTA NELLA HOUSE ★★

This pretty 1870 Victorian farmhouse, hidden just off Highway 116, is one of the better B&Bs in the valley—and it's only a half-mile walk to a little beach on the Russian River. Santa Nella was built for Dr. Joseph Proseck, who (well before his modern-day counterparts) switched careers to become a producer of wine and olive oils from the 1890s to the 1920s. Today, his four turn-of-the-century guest rooms are run by hospitable on-property owner/hosts Kristine and Francis Tellefsen, who moved here from San Francisco when they purchased the 2-acre property in August 2000. They too switched gears—she from a corporate position at the Gap, he from school-teaching (he now teaches locally)—to take in the country air on a more permanent basis. In their restorations they took care to respect the building's original charm; now the painted lady wears a coat of off-white paint with green trim as she did in her heyday, and her newly repaired wraparound veranda is looking particularly dapper. The four rooms, two upstairs and two downstairs, are tastefully decorated, with period antiques, fireplaces, and private baths (two with the classic claw-footed tubs). The second-floor rooms are substantially larger and worth the minimal upgrade cost, since they afford a better view of the property's second-growth redwoods and neighboring Pinot Noir grapes. A tasty two-course breakfast of classic comfort foods like poached eggs with salmon béarnaise, chiles rellenos, or pancakes with fruit, coffee, and tea, as well as access to the outdoor hot tub, is included in the rates. *12130 Hwy 116, Guerneville; 707/869-9488 or 800/440-9031; $$; MC, V; checks OK; www.santanellahouse.com; 1.5 miles S of town.*

THE WILLOWS   ★

Gay-friendly Willows prides itself on its convivial, hang-loose atmosphere. What's most impressive about the 5-acre property is the absolutely immense lawn that sweeps down from the back of the lodge to the private dock on the Russian River—with in-season access to kayaks and canoes. The grounds are expansive enough to accommodate up to a whopping 130 campers, who are welcome to pitch tents for a small fee. (Usually there are far fewer folks sleeping under the stars, but on holiday weekends it can get cozy.) The house, built in the 1940s and showing its age, is up a flight of stairs, and a good thing, since this area has been known to flood on occasion. (Check out the photos at reception, which demonstrate how high the innocent-looking Russian River can climb.) The 12 guest rooms, which begin on the second floor (sorry, no elevator here), are simply decorated with wood furnishings and flowered quilts. Three rooms share baths, and everyone shares the outdoor hot tub and sauna. The least expensive units are on a par with your average no-frills motel room, but on the bright side, every room comes with a VCR and phone and a free continental breakfast each morning. The large back deck begs for suntanners, while the huge family room with a wall of books, large fireplace, and antiques is an ideal place to settle into a couch and learn about the adventures of fellow travelers. *15905 River Rd, Guerneville; 707/869-2824 or 800/953-2828; $; AE, DIS, MC, V; no checks; www.willowrussianriver.com; 0.5 miles*

E of the green bridge downtown.

FORESTVILLE

The tiny hamlet of Forestville, just around the bend from Guerneville, is surrounded by redwoods and makes a nice base for trips on the river.

ACTIVITIES

Canoeing and Kayaking. Canoeing doesn't get much easier than it does at Burke's Canoe Trips. Just pay your money, grab a paddle, point your canoe downstream, and 10 miles later the best canoeing outfit in the area picks you up in its complimentary shuttle and drives you back to your car. The voyage departs in Forestville, ends in Guerneville, and takes $3^1/2$ hours if you do a straight run. But of course you shouldn't. Make a day of it: pack a picnic (waterproof if possible, because tipping can happen), swim, and take shore breaks at the various small riverbank beaches along the way. Words of wisdom: Reserve a canoe in advance, don't bring anything that can't get wet, and remember sunscreen, a hat, and a waterproof camera. Kayaks are also available and follow the same fun course. (From Hwy 101 N, take Highway 116 W for 7 miles into Sebastopol, go another 7 miles to Forestville, turn right on Mirabel Rd at the Pit Stop gas station, and go 1 mile to entrance; 707/887-1222; www.burkescanoetrips.com; open May–Sept, weather and river conditions permitting; $40 per 3-person canoe)

Camping. Just a few miles outside of Forestville and Guerneville in Duncan Mills, Casini Ranch Family Campground is a private facility with 225 sites for tents, including some hookups for RVs (which must be 31 feet or less). Water, showers, toilets, a sanitary disposal station, a laundromat, a grocery store, propane, and boat and canoe rentals are available. Some facilities are wheelchair accessible. (From Santa Rosa, go W on Hwy 12 to Forestville, take Hwy 12/116 6 miles to Duncan Mills, turn left onto Moscow Rd, and drive 0.5 miles to the campground; 707/865-2255 or 800/451-8400; $20 tents, $24 RV partial hookup, $27 RV full hookup)

RESTAURANTS

TOPOLOS RUSSIAN RIVER VINEYARDS
RESTAURANT & WINERY ★★

A Greek restaurant on the Russian River? Well, why not—
especially when the chefs prepare the food the same way
you'd get it on the Mediterranean and it's served in a picturesque 120-year-old farmhouse setting? Despite the
divided dining room's old-fashioned charm, this romantic
spot is famous in the area for its patio dining—and wed-
dings, which happen almost every Saturday afternoon during summer. And no wonder. There are few sweeter places
in the area, especially when you factor in the native flowers
in the front yard, koi pond by the patio, century-old wisteria, cobblestoned rose garden, and big brick patio. Toss in a
bottle of vino from the family's adjoining winery, add a feast
of flaky filo triangles with feta cheese filling; chicken saltim-
boca (sautéed boneless breast with prosciutto, fresh sage,
Chardonnay, and kasseri cheese); classic moussaka; or not-
so-classic dishes like baby rack of lamb with lamb reduction, port, tarragon-roasted potatoes, and stuffed tomato,
and what's not to like? *5700 Gravenstein Hwy, Forestville;
707/887-1562; $$; AE, DIS, MC, V; local checks only; beer and
wine; reservations recommended; lunch, dinner Tues–Sat,
brunch Sun (winter: lunch, dinner Wed–Sat, brunch Sun); on
Hwy 116, 0.25 miles S of town.*

LODGINGS

THE FARMHOUSE INN AND RESTAURANT ★★

Before the Bartolomei family, fourth-generation Forestvil-
leans all, bought the Farmhouse Inn and its eight cottages,
the inn was already abundantly charming. But as of 2001,
these new owners have every intention of turning the 6-acre
property into a luxury destination. While renovations are in
the works, the status quo includes a sweet turn-of-the-19th-
century farmhouse complete with glistening outdoor pool
in a natural setting, fantastic European country–style
restaurant, lovely sundeck, and a row of cottages designed
to invoke English country architecture. Each accommoda-

tion may look modest from the outside, but step inside to find air-conditioning, whirlpool spa tubs, televisions, telephones, and in most rooms not only a fireplace but, if you can believe this, a sauna. Decor, which errs on the side of haphazardly modern, will soon be glorious if the Bartolomeis have their way. But even if it takes a while for a style evolution, the Farmhouse is a comfortable place to set up camp—and a decent deal, considering the options in the area. *7871 River Rd, Forestville; 707/887-3300 or 800/464-6642; $$$; AE, MC, V; checks OK; www.farmhouseinn.com; from Hwy 101 take River Rd exit E to the property.*

HEALDSBURG

Considering the notoriety of Napa and Sonoma Valley towns, it's surprising to stumble upon Healdsburg and discover that it's infinitely more charming and sophisticated than its better-known southern neighbors. Its allure, though certainly slanted toward tourists, seems completely unforced, and the upscale shops and restaurants in the area are in the best of taste. Perhaps this is the reason the growing country town has lured the big-business likes of New York chef Charlie Palmer, who is opening a restaurant here in late 2001. Or perchance it's the obvious: Healdsburg's sense of place and proximity to great wineries, hotels, shopping, outdoor adventure, and food make it an excellent place to spend some time.

ACTIVITIES

Getting Acquainted. The town of Healdsburg is just east of Highway 101, while the majority of its wineries are in the valley just west. Despite its laid-back nature, there's lots to do here, and the attractions are scattered, so it's advisable to stop by the Healdsburg Chamber of Commerce & Visitors Bureau to pick up lodging, dining, and winery guides as well as good maps. You can access the same information online (minus the personal service and one-on-one answers to questions) at www.healdsburg.org. (217 Healdsburg Ave, Healdsburg, CA 95448; 707/433-6935 or 800/648-9922 in CA; open Mon–Fri 9am–5pm, Sat–Sun 10am–2pm)

Shopping. More than any other Wine Country plaza, Healdsburg's offers serious danger to the shopaholic. The grassy central plaza's periphery is packed with quality (read: upscale) reasons to part with your money, whether it be food, drink, home furnishings, children's clothing, jewelry, or artwork. Great entertainers should pay a visit to Friends in the Country (114 Matheson St; 707/433-1615; open Mon–Sat 10:30am–5:30pm, Sun noon–4pm) for its attractive selection of European dinnerware (including Quimper), linens and lace, pine, and wicker. Even if you don't have kids of your own, the clothing, toys, antiques, and accessories at Scout (125 Matheson St; 707/431-0903; open Mon–Sat 10am–6pm, Sun 11am–4pm) are so insanely cute you'll figure out a reason to buy something. For one-of-a-kind artistic mementos head to Art and All That Jazz (119A Plaza St; 707/433-7900; www.artandallthatjazz.com; open Mon–Sat 10am–6pm, Sun 11am–5pm), which has a nice selection of jewelry, art glass, paintings, and ceramics. Levin & Company (306 Center St; 707/433-1118; open Sun–Thurs 9am–9pm, Fri 9am–9:30pm, Sat 9am–10pm) combines culture with a great selection of great reads and resource books, plus select music and a second-floor art gallery. Just off the plaza, the furnishings and home accessories at Kajul (387 Healdsburg Ave; 707/431-8855; open Mon–Sat 10am–6pm, Sun 11am–4pm) are original works of art of teak, leather, and wicker that celebrate organic forms and hand-carved craftsmanship.

Antiquing. With a growing number of savvy-shopper residents and visitors you won't find the same deals here you would have years ago, but that doesn't mean you can't load up the backseat with a few new heirlooms from local antique shops. Circa (314 Matheson St; 707/433-3788) supplies 18th- and 19th-century French and English furnishings and accessories to a showroom in San Francisco and sells retail out of its warehouse by appointment only. Healdsburg Classics (226 Healdsburg Ave, half a block S of the square; 707/433-4315; open every day 10am–5pm) sells furniture dating from 1790 to 1950, glassware, china, and jewelry. With 16 vendors stocking stalls that showcase everything from 50-cent vintage Valentine's Day cards to $3,200 cowhide chairs, you'll have to be selective at Vintage Antiques (328 Healdsburg Ave; 707/433-7461; open every day 10am–5pm).

The eclectic collection at Irish Cottage (112 Matheson St, at Healdsburg Ave; 707/433-4850; open every day 10:30am–5pm summer, closed Tues in winter) includes a good selection of sterling silver, fine glassware, and European pine furnishings designed in the late 1800s.

 Canoeing. You don't have to worry about people with a death wish shooting down Class V rapids when you visit the Russian River. Virtually its entire length is more suitable for canoes, sea kayaks, and even inflatable tubes. That makes the river a popular summer water-play area for families with children. Pack a picnic, bring plenty of sunscreen, and leave everything valuable onshore; tipping over, intentionally or by accident, is half the fun of this classic Russian River adventure. Canoes are available to rent from W. C. "Bob" Trowbridge Canoe Trips, which shuttles canoers to various starting points in the area and either picks them up at the end or arranges for passengers to leave a car at their final destination. (20 Healdsburg Ave; 707/433-7247 or 800/640-1386; open every day 9am–5pm mid-Apr–2nd week of Oct; reservations required; $55 per 3-person canoe)

Hot-Air Ballooning. There are few good reasons to rise with the sun while on a leisurely vacation, but hot-air ballooning is one of them. A gentler ride than even the elevator, coasting in a balloon with Aerostat Adventures is an ideal way for explorers to get that wide view of the Russian River canyon. The

Even in the thick of Wine Country summer heat, nothing beats a cold brew and a shaded patio table. Get both at Healdsburg's Bear Republic Brewing Company (345 Healdsburg Ave; 707/433-2337), where house-made ales and standard pub grub taste just as good in the dead of winter. And on weekend nights, if you still have energy after that satiating Wine Country meal, head here for live music.

catch is you must embark early to ensure the best weather conditions. But no matter. If the relaxing ride across Russian River, Dry Creek, and Alexander Valley doesn't wake you up, the aromas of the sparkling-wine breakfast with made-to-order omelets, fresh fruits, breads, orange juice, coffee, tea, and plenty of bubbly served in the picturesque picnic grounds of J Winery will perk up the senses. Balloons accommodate up to eight, and passengers receive both a photo of their balloon over the vineyards and a digital photo of their departure, which is forwarded via email upon their return. Balloons depart from J Wine Company/Rodney Strong Vineyards in Healdsburg. (707/433-3777 or 800/579-0183; www.aerostat-adventures.com; open every day year-round, departure times vary by season; $195 per person)

Bicycling. Maximize your time in the country air by touring the region on a bike. Healdsburg Spoke Folk Cyclery rents tandems, touring bikes, and hybrids and provides maps to great riding trails as well as the best winery routes that require the least effort. (249 Center St, at Mill St; 707/433-7171; open Mon–Fri 10am–6pm, Sat–Sun 10am–5pm; hybrids $7 per hour, $35 per day; touring bikes $30 per day; tandems $60 per day)

Spa. As if being in Healdsburg weren't relaxing enough, Spa Off the Plaza is one more way to ensure you are properly pampered during your Wine Country visit. The clean and tranquil day spa features facials, massages, foot reflexology, salt scrubs, and truly indulgent spa packages. Be sure to make a reservation, as this place books up in advance. (706 Healdsburg Ave, 4 blocks N of the plaza at Lincoln St; 707/431-7938; www.spaofftheplaza.com; open Wed–Sun 10am–6pm)

Farmers Market. No matter how many restaurant reservations you have, it's a good idea to stop at the farmers market, where locals, local farmers, and tourists merge to pick over the region's bounty of fresh fruits, flowers, and vegetables as well as artisan creations like birdhouses and gourds. (Parking lot on Vine St and North St, just W of the plaza: May–Nov, Sat 9am–noon; Healdsburg Plaza: Jun–Oct, Tues 4pm–6pm; 707/431-1956)

 Movie. If you're in need of a respite from your activity-packed day trips, catch a flick at the Raven Theater (115

North St, 707/433-5448), Sonoma Wine Country's best movie house for new releases and art films.

Golf. Swing through your leisure vacation with a tee time at Tayman Park Golf Course. The hilly par-35 nine-hole course boasts small greens and affordable rates. (7 S Fitch Mountain Rd; from Hwy 101 N take Central Healdsburg exit to third stoplight, Matheson, take a right, and go 1 mile to entrance; 707/433-4275; open every day 6am–dark; 9 holes $11 weekdays, $13 weekends; 18 holes $17 weekdays, $19 weekends; $5 per person per cart)

Country Store. It's hard to believe a store can have enough charm to make it an attraction in itself, but one visit to the Jimtown Store and you'll understand its allure. Not only is the adorable country shack of a shop a must-stop for hungry and thirsty bicyclists, it's also a draw for anyone in need of a to-go gourmet breakfast, lunch, dinner, or treat (you can also sit in the funky enclosed patio); house-made condiments; retro toys and candy; antiques; and fantastic gift items. The adorable adjoining barn hosts very affordable antiques. (6706 Hwy 128, at Alexander Valley Rd; from Healdsburg Plaza go north on Healdsburg Ave past Simi Winery, turn right on Alexander Valley Rd, continue 3.7 miles; 707/433-1212; www.jimtown.com)

Gourmet Goodies. Foodies will flip over the cornucopia of gourmet products, foods, and wines overflowing throughout practically every inch of Oakville Grocery. This outpost of Napa Valley's original shop has far more elbow room, which allows for greater access to fantastic meats, cheeses, olives, crackers, breads, sandwiches, pizza, salads, pasta salads, rotisserie chicken, cookies, coffees, and every possible condiment you can think of. Take it to go or plunk yourself down at one of the patio tables; the latter is preferable since it's not likely you'll be able to bear the anticipation anyway. (124 Matheson St, on Healdsburg Plaza; 707/433-3200; Sun–Thurs 10am–6:30pm, Fri–Sat 10am–7pm).

Jump-start your day with coffee, pastries, or lunch snacks at local java hut Healdsburg Coffee Co., on the plaza at 312 Center Street (707/431-7941). Sweeten up any afternoon at neighboring Downtown Bakery & Creamery (308-A Center St; 707/431-2719), where big fluffy cakes, hefty cookies, fresh-baked bread, and ice cream are calling your name.

WINERIES

Alexander Valley Winery. The vineyard property that originally belonged to 19th-century pioneer Cyrus Alexander, the northern Sonoma County explorer after whom the valley is named, is now the winery of Harry and Maggie Wetzel, who restored the grounds and planted 150 acres of grapevines. Flavorful results of their efforts are evident in complimentary tastes of around nine wines, which may include Chardonnay, Cabernet Sauvignon, and Merlot plus limited bottlings of Chenin Blanc, Gewürztraminer, Cabernet Franc, Pinot Noir, Syrah, and Zinfandel. Reserve tastings range in price from $3 to $5 each. Tours of the property, including wine caves and some background history, are available by appointment, but the picnic table is yours so long as someone hasn't beaten you to it. *8644 Hwy 128; 707/433-7209; open every day 10am–5pm.*

Chalk Hill Estate Vineyards and Winery. The winery of the same name as the Chalk Hill appellation occupies 1,200 acres of backcountry between the cooler Russian River Valley to the west and the warmer Alexander Valley to the northeast. The winery is known for its Sauvignon Blanc, Chardonnay, and Merlot. Tastings and tours are available weekdays only and only by appointment. *10300 Chalk Hill Rd; from Hwy 101 N take the Shiloh exit, proceed E on Shiloh Rd, turn left on Old Redwood Hwy, continue 1.3 miles, turn right on Pleasant Ave, left on Chalk Hill Rd, and proceed. 2.2 miles; 707/838-4306; open Mon–Fri 8am–5pm, closed weekends and holidays.*

Ferrari-Carano Vineyards & Winery. Astoundingly beautiful grounds, which if you're lucky enough to come in spring include thousands of bulbs and an explosion of purple wisteria, are reason enough to pull into the parking lot of Ferrari-Carano. The formal garden to the right of the path leading to the stately winery beckons with an enviable collection of rhododendron, statice, cypress, Chinese tallow trees, Japanese-style bridges, boxwood, maples, saucer magnolia, an impressive rose garden, and a wooden pagoda. And there's much, much more. All greenery and lawns, backed by picture-perfect vistas of vineyard-draped hillsides, lead to the tastefully decorated yet obviously big-business tasting room, where up to four wines, perhaps including Sauvignon Blanc, Fumé Blanc, Chardonnay, Zinfandel, "Siena" (a Sangiovese and Cabernet blend), or Merlot, are poured. Tastes will set you back $2.50, which, as with most wineries, is refundable with any wine purchase. But don't put your wallet away yet. The spacious and airy tasting room also offers a slew of gourmet oils, sauces, olives, and logo items. *8761 Dry Creek Rd; from Hwy 101 N take Dry Creek Rd exit, turn left at the end of off-ramp, and go 9 miles to entrance on left; 707/433-6700; www.ferrari-carano.com; open every day 10am–5pm; tasting $2.50.*

Lambert Bridge. This family-owned winery's friendly down-home redwood barn is the perfect setting for savoring complimentary tastes of Sauvignon Blanc, Chardonnay, Merlot, and well-rated Zinfandel. In between sips you can peruse the selection of logo shirts, peek through a big picture window into the barrel room, and sample flavored olive oils or other gourmet food products amassed here. *4085 W Dry Creek Rd, between Lambert Bridge Rd and Mill St; 800/975-0555; wines@lambert.com; www.lambertbridge.com; open every day 10:30am–4:30pm.*

Preston of Dry Creek. Every single aspect of a visit to Preston is charming. The drive is a meandering cruise along narrow roads where a sign demands, "Slower!" so as to not disturb the neighboring grapes. Dry Creek, which may or may not be dry, serves as a reminder that you're in the heart of Dry Creek Valley. The grounds welcome you with a wheelbarrow full of blooms and a rustic grassy courtyard garden with picnic tables and shading trees. Just when you think it can't get any more quaint, you pass into the old-fashioned, country-kitchen-style, Victorian farmhouse tasting room that's hands down the most charming in the valley. The beauty of this place is that nothing feels contrived amid the combination of the old kitchen furnishings, the neon sign reading "Drink Zin," the hardwood floors, and the artfully displayed books on baking, wine, and food. "Choose four," the chalkboard recommends, and you should. There's some great wine being made here, and we're not talking your everyday Chardonnay. Here varietals range from Sémillon, Zinfandel, Barbera, and Syrah to a house Rhône blend called Faux. Winemaker Lou Preston is likely to be on the premises; if you can't see him, it's likely you'll smell the aromas of his latest passion, which happens to be bread baking. The most recent

You can stumble on many of Dry Creek Valley's wineries by following one main road. In this case, it's a narrow, winding path called West Dry Creek Road, which is accessible from Geyserville and Healdsburg and runs parallel and west of Highway 101. Once you're on your way, signs point you toward various tasting rooms.

winery addition is the huge baking room, complete with a new top-of-the-line wood-burning brick oven. Take our advice and buy a load of his "freeform hearth loaf," a country white sourdough. Meanwhile, he hasn't turned his attention away from wines, so take a few bottles to go. *9282 W Dry Creek Rd; from Hwy 101 N take the Dry Creek Rd exit, turn left at Yoakim Bridge Rd and right at W Dry Creek Rd; 707/433-3372; www.prestonvineyards.com; open every day 11am–4:30pm; tasting free.*

Quivira Vineyards. Classic quirky Dry Creek hospitality combined with delicious Zinfandel and Sauvignon Blanc make this postmodern barn in a quiet vineyard setting a perfect stop. Behind the small wood bar there's likely to be one person pouring the day's complimentary tastes. Equally dependable at "Kee-veer-a" is background lounge music—the staff prides itself on its selection. Good attitude and a sense of humor are dispensed as freely as the wine, of which 15,000 cases are produced annually. Another refreshing element is the lack of retail diversions here: apart from the glowing purple neon "Club Q" announcing the establishment's wine club and a few mugs and shirts, there's little in the way of Wine Country knickknacks. And good thing: you're likely to want to spend your extra dollars on a case or two, which are discounted substantially when you're a club member. Tours venture through the vineyard and winery, are likely to include barrel tasting, and are available by appointment. Exceedingly welcoming rows of umbrella-shaded picnic tables between the tasting room and vineyards beg for you to break out the picnic basket. *4900 W Dry Creek Rd, between Lambert Bridge and Yoakim Bridge Rds; 707/431-8333; www. quivirawine.com; open every day 11am–5pm; closed major holidays.*

Rochioli Vineyard & Winery. This no-nonsense family winery has good reason to limit the amount of wine you can purchase. First off, they produce only around 10,000 cases of Sauvignon Blanc, Chardonnay, and Pinot Noir per year. Second, the stuff is damn good and a number of people know it. The Rochiolis' dedication to good wine and nothing other than good wine is evident in the refreshingly sparse but polished and warm tasting room, where, aside from a few select pieces of rotating local artwork, there's only a tiny display shelf showcasing handdyed silk scarves. You can peer beyond the bar at the vineyards, picnic at the strategically placed tables, linger in the small land-scaped courtyard, and taste for free. But try as you might, the staff won't let you depart with more than two bottles each of the whites and a single 750-milliliter of red. Yet this policy of moderation is not so bad; it makes you appreciate the wine that much more, and improves the chances of availability next time you arrive with credit card in hand. *6192 Westside Rd, near Sweetwater Springs Rd; 707/433-2305; open every day 11am–4pm.*

Windsor Vineyards. If ever there comes a time when you don't have it in you to hit the wine trails, there's always Windsor Vineyards, whose modern, spiffy, and rather corporate tasting room on the plaza makes it absolutely effortless to raise a glass. In fact, there's nowhere else in the area you can taste these particular wines, nine of which are poured free of charge and all of which are sold exclusively out of three tasting rooms in California. Here the focus is on custom labels rather than small-business charm. You can have a personalized label made and applied to any of the wines, provided you purchase at least three. *308B Center St; Healdsburg; 707/433-2822 or 800/204-9463; www.windsorvineyards.com; open Mon–Fri 10am–5pm, Sat–Sun 10am–6pm.*

RESTAURANTS

BISTRO RALPH ★★★

In a town where restaurants have been afflicted with the revolving-door syndrome, simple yet sleek-modern Bistro Ralph continues to thrive. Housed in a slender storefront on the square, Ralph Tingle's intimate bistro serves consistently excellent food, with a focus on local ingredients. Choice starters include grilled portobello mushrooms with white truffle oil and crispy Sichuan pepper calamari seasoned with lemon and ginger and accompanied by soy dipping sauce. Lamb dishes are always good, particularly the hearty spring lamb stew à la Provençal and the lamb shanks with crème fraîche–horseradish mashed potatoes. Yet fish entrees, such as grilled salmon with lentils, spinach, and carrot-ginger broth or roasted halibut with saffron rouille, warm potatoes, asparagus, and pea-shoot salad, make deciding a definite challenge. Throw in an extra side of addictive shoe-string fries and sautéed spinach with lemon and garlic and you've got yourself one darned satisfying meal. The lunch menu focuses on upscale salads and sandwiches, such as the grilled ahi or salmon sandwich and the popular lamb burger on a fresh roll, all three served with the famed fries. But there's also a tangy and rich chicken paillard, which is a lemon-caper-brown-butter delight, again with fries. The decor has a cozy, slightly industrial feel, with a dozen or so linen-topped tables, white brick walls, and a long concrete counter where you can watch chef Tingle perform culinary magic in the small open kitchen. The staff is Healdsburg-casual, yet appropriately cordial and efficient. *109 Plaza St E, Healdsburg; 707/433-1380; $$; MC, V; local checks only; lunch Mon–Fri, dinner every day; beer and wine; reservations recommended; on the plaza.*

FELIX & LOUIE'S ★⌐

No other spot on the plaza takes such great pains to be a casual, fun place to be. You need only peer through the glass windows at the scuffed wood floors, unfussy wooden tables, brown-barn-like color palette, spacious seating, high ceil-ings, and diners huddled at tables or saddled up at the bar and it's obvious: Felix & Louie's combo of laid-back atmos-phere and low-price, quality food does the trick. On the seri-ous foodie scale the mostly Italian menu is not that remarkable. It goes out on a limb with the likes of sautéed frog legs with garlic, parsley, white wine, and lemon or grilled boneless trout with almonds, currants, brown but-ter, and lemon. But it sticks to the standards with fresh, fla-vorful bruschetta topped with tomato, basil, and garlic; zesty pizzas with the likes of pepperoni, onions, and bell pepper; house-made rigatoni bolognese; and a good old "Healdsburger" with grilled potatoes. Though the restau-rant is run by Ralph Tingle of Bistro Ralph, the similarities stop there. This place is much larger and cheaper and also offers live jazz on Wednesday nights and during Sunday brunch. Even when the band's jamming, there's no cover, and the kids are welcome, too. *106 Matheson St, Healdsburg;*

707/433-6966; $$; MC, V; local checks only; lunch, dinner every day; full bar; reservations recommended; on the plaza.

MADRONA MANOR ★★★

A completely unique and exceedingly romantic dining experience happens nightly within this Victorian mansion's stunning, intimate dining spaces. Complementing its historic surroundings, the candlelit dining rooms are ornately decorated in period style and lavishly appointed with deep red wallpaper, linens, china, and beautiful garden views. Covered terrace seating, with heat lamps when necessary, is a prime place to lean over a glass of Sonoma wine and honey-roasted beet salad with fennel, arugula, blood oranges, goat cheese, and pomegranate vinaigrette and whisper vacation nothings to a loved one. On weekend nights the menu features a prix-fixe feast to remember. Monday through Thursday an à la carte menu is also offered and might include such other temptations as delicate Dungeness crab ravioli with roasted red bell pepper, chives, and Riesling–Meyer lemon sauce, or tender and savory grilled pork tenderloin with root vegetables, foie-gras-stuffed dried plums, fava bean leaves, and green peppercorn sauce. Perhaps the only thing sweeter than your dinner companion are the desserts; you may just fall in love all over again with one forkful of the warm chocolate soufflé cake with crème anglaise and raspberries or the Napoleon of poached pear, maple-chestnut cream, and pecan praline. An award-winning wine list rounds out a near-perfect Wine Country meal. *1001 Westside Rd, Healdsburg; 707/433-4231; $$$; MC, V; dinner every day; beer and wine; reservations recommended; info@madronamanor.com; www.madronamanor.com; from Hwy 101 N take the Central Healdsburg exit, go left on Mill St, which becomes Westside Rd, and continue 0.7 miles.*

ZIN ★★

Located just off Healdsburg's main plaza, Zin opened in 1999 and has been a welcome addition to the local food scene. The menu specializes in updated versions of American classics and each day features a blue plate special, such as meat loaf or St. Louis–style barbecued ribs. The dishes

The Russian River area's wine appellations include Dry Creek Valley, which is famous for its Zinfandels; Alexander Valley; Chalk Hill (where Chardonnay reigns); and Russian River Valley and Green Valley, both of which are renowned for Chardonnay and Pinot Noir.

are particularly well suited to pairing with Zinfandels, and the wine list features a whole page of them—a fitting tribute, considering Sonoma is prime Zin country. Grilled cheese bruschetta with dry jack, goat cheese, and marinated tomatoes make for a great evening kickoff. Entrees include a succulent fettuccine with prosciutto, spring peas, and braised leeks seasoned with a zesty lemon cream sauce and sprinkled with fresh Parmesan; luxurious osso buco with saffron and rosemary risotto cake, wilted spinach, and lemon-garlic vinaigrette; or wasabi-crusted salmon with Asian noodle salad in pickled ginger vinaigrette. This is a great place for hearty appetites, because portions are huge. Feel free to indulge, because, frankly, desserts can be a disappointing conclusion to the meal. Zin's architecture is Postmodern California Bomb Shelter—a concrete bunker trimmed in redwood—which, thankfully, has little to do with the aesthetic of the food. *344 Center St, Healdsburg; 707/473-0946; $$$; AE, MC, V; local checks only; lunch Mon, Wed–Fri, dinner Wed–Mon; beer and wine; reservations recommended; 1 block from the plaza.*

LODGINGS

BELLE DE JOUR INN ★★★

In a region where rampant Victoriana is all the rage, Belle de Jour's four romantic Italianate hillside cottages and large carriage house have a refreshingly spare, uncluttered feel. From the bedroom of the cottage called the Terrace Room, you can savor a fine view of the valley from the comfort of a giant whirlpool. Also recommended is the Caretaker's Suite with its lace-canopied four-poster bed, private deck with vine-covered trellis, and blue-tiled whirlpool tub. All of the accommodations have a fireplace or a wood-burning stove, ceiling fans, and refrigerators and are air-conditioned—a big plus around here in the summer. Innkeepers Tom and Brenda Hearn whip up a bountiful country breakfast in their beautiful state-of-the-art kitchen and serve it on the deck of the main house. Also available to guests for an hourly fee is a chauffeured backroads winery tour in the Hearns' 1925 Star touring car—something to consider if wine tasting makes you tipsy. (Note: Both the inside and outside of the inn are nonsmoking.) *16276 Healdsburg Ave, Healdsburg; 707/431-9777; $$$; MC, V; checks OK; 1 mile N of Dry Creek Rd, across from Simi Winery; www.belledejourinn.com.*

HAYDON STREET INN ★★

This pretty blue 1912 Queen Anne Victorian inn with a large veranda set behind a white picket fence offers eight cheery guest rooms, all of which have private baths, and the hospitality of owners Dick and Pat Bertapelle. All rooms are charming, but your best bet is to rent one of the two larger ones in the Victorian cottage tucked behind the main house; these spacious quarters have vaulted ceilings, queen-size beds, high dormer windows, big whirlpool tubs, and loads of charm. In the morning you'll find a full country breakfast featuring such treats as a scramble casserole with mushroom wine sauce, vegetables, cheese, and herbs; fresh fruit or baked apples; and plenty of house-made muffins and croissants. Only the cottage suite has a television and phone, but guests have access to both in the main house. *321 Haydon St, Healdsburg; 707/433-5228; $$; MC, V; checks OK; www.haydon.com; at Fitch St.*

HEALDSBURG INN ON THE PLAZA ★★↗

Originally built as a Wells Fargo Express office in 1900, this quiet Victorian inn comes as a bit of a surprise, as it is tucked into a row of storefronts on the plaza and accessed by passing through a first-floor art and jewelry gallery. You'll have to hoof it up the 24 stairs to the second floor to get to the 10 attractive guest rooms, all of which have high ceilings. The four rooms facing the plaza have beautiful bay windows; particularly engaging is the spacious pale yellow and white Song of the Rose Room, which has a queen-size white iron and brass bed, as well as a comfy oak rocker set in front of the fireplace. The largest room is the Garden Suite, with a whirlpool tub, king-size bed, and private patio bedecked with flowers. All rooms have private baths with showers, TVs with VCRs (and access to a video library), and air-conditioning, and all but three have gas-log fireplaces and clawfooted bathtubs. Early risers can grab a quick continental breakfast, but it's advisable to wait around until 8:30am when a full-blown champagne breakfast is served at tables for two in the glass-enclosed solarium. Meander in before dinner and you're just in time for wine tasting and appetizers. Ensuring that guests never go hungry, a bottomless cookie jar is accompanied by ever-available coffee, tea, sodas, and juices. *110 Matheson St, Healdsburg; 707/433-6991 or 800/431-8663; $$$; MC, V; checks OK; www.healdsburginn.com; on the plaza's S side.*

MADRONA MANOR   ★★✈

Victorian grandeur is optimized within this three-story 1881 estate and its gardens, cottages, and restaurant located in Healdsburg's pastoral Dry Creek area. This towering painted lady received a fresh coat of yellow paint with red and green trim in 2001, so she's looking particularly impressive, standing tall amid a small orange orchard, fabulous manicured gardens, and redwoods. Many of the 21 rooms are located in the main house, which is Victorian through and through, starting with the ground-floor parlor, which has 16-foot ceilings, a sitting area, a fireplace, chessboard, and a variety of stuffed animals and statues suggesting that someone here really likes rabbits. Down the hall is the restaurant, one of the most romantic and gorgeous in the region, which also happens to serve impressive food and boast outstanding veranda seating (with heat lamps). Take the stairs to the second or third floor, where the bygone elegance extends to the guest rooms, most of which have crown molding and bathrooms with Aveda products and claw-footed tubs. Second-floor rooms, all grand and adorned with lovely antiques within their 14-foot-high walls, come with private baths, king beds, and gas fireplaces. Third-floor rooms have 12-foot ceilings and wood-burning fireplaces. Rooms in the nearby Carriage House, a two-story 1881 building, now feature more Asian and European antiques and reproductions; most have fireplaces and two have balconies. The suite here has a whirlpool tub for two. The newest structure, the School House, features two suites with private entrances; newly remodeled, each cozy and spacious room has a private garden patio, a view of the forest, a large bedroom with a fireplace, and a marble bath with a two-person whirlpool tub and a bidet. With its pastoral charm, easy access to Healdsburg and Guerneville, and swimming pool heated May through October, it's no wonder this place is a preferred wedding site. TV addicts take note: there are no boob tubes here. *1001 Westside Rd, Healdsburg; 707/433-4231 or 800/258-4003; $$$; MC, V; checks OK; info@madronamanor.com; www.madronamanor.com; from Hwy 101 N take the Central Healdsburg exit, go left on Mill St, which changes to Westside Rd, and continue 0.7 miles.*

GEYSERVILLE

When you take the Highway 101 turnoff to downtown Geyserville and arrive in the bland two-block town you might wonder why you even made the detour. But not so fast. The draw here isn't the commercial center, but the winery-dense strip of Highway 128 east of town. Known as Alexander Valley, it attracts wine lovers from the world over.

WINERIES

 Château Souverain. Signs and a clear view of the building from Highway 101 make it impossible to miss this landmark winery, which also happens to be one of the only major attractions in tiny Geyserville itself. The impressive structure housing the winery, tasting room, and restaurant (see "Restaurants" for review) evokes the European countryside, but inside, the tastefully done room is clearly big business. Step up to the tasting-room bar with the postcard-perfect view out its back window to sample four wines for $3, which is credited toward any wine purchase you might make. Varietals include a bright, no-oak Sauvignon Blanc, toasty Chardonnay, Syrah, Zinfandel, Merlot, and Cabernet Sauvignon. Reserve tastings are $2 each. Anyone who enjoys entertaining should stop in if only to browse the great collection of table-setting books, place mats, and other dinner-table accoutrements, and wine books. *400 Souverain Rd; from Hwy 101 follow the signs to the winery just off the freeway; 888/80-WINES; www.chateausouverain.com; open every day 10am–5pm.*

Clos du Bois. The winery did a good job of branding itself with its fun, unintimidating ad campaign, but the

If you want to hit a bunch of wineries without doing too much backtracking or head-scratching over directions and maps, get on Highway 28 at Geyserville and follow it east. This stretch is prime Alexander Valley Wine Country, with close to two dozen wineries within a 20-minute drive.

real reason "Clo-dew-bwah" is on the tips of people's tongues is its extremely popular Chardonnay. Visit the large visitor facility, which adjoins the Alexander Valley winery, and you can taste for yourself the nuances between the numerous barrel-fermented Chardonnays as well as fine productions of Sauvignon Blanc, Cabernet Sauvignon, Merlot, Zinfandel, and Pinot Noir. The winery makes great efforts to simplify food and wine pairing, so it makes sense to buy a bottle of wine, take the staff's advice on what meats, cheeses, and crackers from the deli will go well with it, and enjoy your feast alfresco on the lawn or at the picnic tables in the gazebo. *19410 Geyserville Ave; from Hwy 101 N take Geyserville's Independence Lane exit E to Geyserville Ave, turn left on Geyserville Ave, and it's the second winery on the right; 707/857-3100 or 800/222-3189; www.closdubois.com; open every day 10am–4:30pm, closed major holidays.*

Geyser Peak Winery. The wood-paneled tasting room is a little on the corporate side, but Geyser Peak's ivy-covered stone facility is centrally located and doles out free samples of everything from pleasant Gewürztraminer and Riesling to Sauvignon Blanc, Chardonnay, Merlot, and Cabernet Franc. You can kick over $5 for a reserve tasting and also depart with etched stemware, logo attire, and wines available only at the winery, such as its Petite Sirah, Cabernet Franc, Petit Verdot, Malbec, and sparkling Shiraz. The beautiful picnic area across the highway is available by reservation. *22281 Chianti Rd; from Hwy 101 N take the Canyon Rd exit, turn left from the off-ramp and right on Chianti Rd; 707/857-9463; www.geyserpeakwinery.com; open every day 9am–5pm.*

Murphy-Goode Estate Winery. Grape growers Tim Murphy and Dale Goode and wine marketer Dave Ready are the brains and brawn behind this modern family-owned winery along the beautiful and pastoral Alexander Valley wine trail. They're best known for their Fumé Blanc but also make fine Chardonnay, Merlot, Cabernet Sauvignon, Pinot Noir, and Zinfandel. Taste them all on the house if you stop by any day between 10:30am and 4:30pm. *4001 Hwy 128, N of Alexander Valley Rd; 707/431-7644.*

RESTAURANTS

CHATEAU SOUVERAIN CAFE
AT THE WINERY   ★★✦

 Aside from Napa Valley's Domaine Chandon, this captivating dining room holds the only major winery restaurant in Northern California. Pass the tasting room to the grand, airy space anytime during lunch or the weekend dinner hour, and the magic begins: everything about the place says elegant yet comfortably luxurious Wine Country. Beneath vaulted ceilings, rich hues of brown and beige, thick fabrics, and a huge fireplace with ornamental hearth warm the large room. Even when the sunny and spectacular terrace is closed, huge picture windows ensure that every indoor seat has a view to remember. Cast your view toward the menu and you'll find fresh seasonal fare, which ranges from fine to fantastic and can be paired with wines from the company's portfolio (they don't serve beer; it's wine and wine alone). Start with the generous serving of Souverain Pâté accompanied by garlic toast and cornichons, or a crisp salad of greens, roasted walnuts, and shaved Carmody cheese with Chardonnay dressing. Seafood lovers will appreciate the delicate poached northern halibut with saffron rice pilaf, fresh-cut chive crème fraîche, and julienne of vegetables—if, that is, they can pass up the wonderful Dungeness crab cakes, which share the plate with spicy greens, curried vinaigrette, and a mango purée. On one recent visit the flavor of the Sonoma duck confit salad with frisée and roasted garlic dressing was great, but the meat was a little overcooked and the sidekick five-spice candied almonds were missing their crunch. Grilled lamb T-bone over adzuki bean ragout finished with an aromatic garnish of gremolata is a safer bet. Desserts such as chocolate gâteau with cheesecake layer and almond crème fraîche are tempting. *400 Souverain Rd, Geyserville; 707/433-3141; $$$; AE, DC, MC, V; no checks; lunch every day, dinner Fri–Sun; wine only; reservations recommended; www.chateausouverain.com; from Hwy 101 take the Independence Ln exit, turn left, and the entrance is straight ahead.* ♿

Make sure to drive Dry Creek Road and West Dry Creek Road, both of which parallel Highway 101 between Geyserville and Healdsburg. The drive, though winding and slow, gives you a gorgeous tour of quintessential Wine Country scenery and passes a number of fantastic wineries.

LODGINGS

HOPE-BOSWORTH HOUSE ★★

Across the street from its showier cousin, the Hope-Merrill House (see below), the 1904 Hope-Bosworth House provides a cheery, informal, and less expensive place to stay. This Queen Anne–style Victorian inn has four bedrooms, three of which have full baths, including one with a whirlpool tub. The downstairs Sun Porch Room has the dry, woody fragrance of a summer cottage, and it reverberates each morning with birdsong from the backyard. Everyone's favorite, however, is the sunny and spacious Wicker Room with its old-fashioned white-and-pink-flowered wallpaper. Guests are treated to the same elaborate breakfast as their neighbors across the way, and they also have access to the pool and other facilities at the Hope-Merrill House. *21238 Geyserville Ave, Geyserville; 707/857-3356 or 800/825-4233; $$; AE, MC, V; checks OK; from Hwy 101, take the Geyserville exit.*

HOPE-MERRILL HOUSE ★★★

Since nearly every mediocre shack built in the late 19th century gets dubbed "Victorian," it's easy to forget the dizzying architectural and design heights reached during that period. This beautifully restored 1870 Eastlake Gothic will remind you: the three-story brown and cream Hope-Merrill House has expansive bay windows and a back veranda furnished with comfortable cane chairs. The landscaping is formal and strictly symmetrical, with box hedges and weeping mulberries. The inn offers eight individually decorated guest rooms with private baths and queen-size beds. The fairest of all is the Peacock Room: images of gold, rose, and gray-blue peacocks strut around a ceiling border, a wood-burning fireplace dominates one wall, and French doors open into a bathroom with an immense marble-topped whirlpool tub. For the best views, ask for the Vineyard View Room or the Bradbury Room, which have fireplaces, two-person showers, and views of the swimming pool and the pretty gardens. A hearty breakfast is included in the rates. *21253 Geyserville Ave, Geyserville; 707/857-3356 or 800/825-4233; $$; AE, MC, V; checks OK; from Hwy 101, take the Geyserville exit.*

CLOVERDALE

Quaint, rural, and heavily agricultural, Cloverdale is little more than a gateway to east Mendocino County's Anderson Valley.

WINERIES

Fritz Winery. Fritz is what a back-road California winery should be: a funky, quirky, picturesque hillside stop with good wine and an equally good attitude. When you see the groovy 1979 California-style redwood structure built into the mountainside and camouflaged by overgrown yet managed landscaping, you'll know you've arrived. Step into the aromatic tasting room for free samples of everything from single-vineyard Chardonnay, Melon de Bourgogne, and Sauvignon Blanc to Zinfandel and Cabernet Sauvignon. If you want to learn about the local *terroir*, ask these folks: they are committed to producing fruitful results by carefully selecting grapes that grow best in various vineyards throughout the Russian River and Dry Creek Valleys. Tours of the tanks, crush pads, and barrels are available by appointment, and the lone picnic table overlooking the wilderness would be ideal were it not right next to the dirt parking lot. *24691 Dutcher Creek Rd, just W of Hwy 101; 800/418-9463; www.fritzwinery.com; call for open hours.*

RESTAURANTS

WORLD FAMOUS HAMBURGER RANCH AND PASTA FARM ★

If you've hit Cloverdale you've been on quite a road trip, and there may be no better way to celebrate your drive than classic dive roadside dining at the funky-fun Ranch. The only thing this place has in common with a farm is the level of (in)formality. And that's exactly the beauty of it. Rave reviews from satisfied customers all over the world paper the walls of this converted service station, which was voted the purveyor of Sonoma County's Best Burger by readers of the *Santa Rosa Press Democrat*. When the sun's shining, grab a patio seat overlooking the barbecue pit and neighboring mountains or a deck seat overlooking the road and indulge in juicy burgers done anyway you like 'em. Options, which number more than you can count on both hands, include British (bacon cheese), Italian Fungi (mushrooms and jack), Latin Lover (jack and jalapeños), and Cackle (chicken) burgers, as well as American classics like steak sandwiches and fries, and pastas such as fettuccine Alfredo and pasta marinara thrown in for good measure. *31195 Redwood Hwy, Cloverdale; 707/894-5616; $; no checks; MC, V; lunch, dinner every day; beer and wine; no reservations; at the N end of town at the top of the hill.*

LODGINGS

VINTAGE TOWERS BED AND BREAKFAST INN ★★

Listed on the National Register of Historic Places, this beautiful mansion located on a quiet residential street holds seven air-conditioned guest rooms with private baths. The three corner suites have tower sitting rooms (one round, one square, and one octagonal), separate sleeping quarters, and private baths. Particularly unusual is the Vintage Tower Suite, which has its own private porch complete with a telescope for stargazing and a spiral staircase that descends to the yard. Downstairs you'll find a large dining room with a fireplace, a parlor, and a library. In the morning, friendly innkeeper Polly Grant serves a full gourmet breakfast in the dining room, including juice, fruit, fresh homemade bread, and an entree like eggs Benedict. The second-floor hospitality room is stocked with drinks and coffee and tea provisions, and the ground-floor veranda is the spot for lounging with a good book in the afternoon; with no TVs or phones in the rooms there's that much less to come between you and that long-neglected paperback. *302 N Main St, Cloverdale; 707/894-4535; $$; AE, DIS, MC, V; checks OK; www.vintagetowers.com; at 3rd St, off Cloverdale Blvd.*

MENDOCINO COUNTY

MENDOCINO COUNTY

If you think Sonoma is mellow, wait until you get to Mendocino Wine Country. Not only is it a slow and winding drive to Anderson Valley's two tiny towns and country wineries nestled in a landscape of vineyards and pristine country views, but there's also very little in the way of distractions. If your idea of a perfect vacation is simple living—maybe a good book and a streamside seat—plus leisurely visits to a dozen or so casual backcountry wineries, Anderson Valley's for you. Closer to Highway 101, there are around a dozen more wineries sprinkled around the agricultural towns of Hopland and Ukiah, though that area doesn't have the same bucolic charm as the more remote country towns. If you're itching for action, ultrafancy lodgings, or gourmet dinners, turn around and head back to Healdsburg, because truly, folks, it doesn't get any quieter and tamer than this part of Northern California.

Once noted only for sheep, apples, and timber, Anderson Valley has become the premier producer of cool-climate California wines such as Chardonnay, Gewürztraminer, Riesling, and Pinot Noir. The enological future of this valley, whose climate is almost identical to that of the Champagne region of France, may also reside in the production of sparkling wine, now that some of France's best Champagne makers have successfully set up shop here.

GETTING THERE

While Mendocino proper is on the rugged northern California coastline, the majority of Mendocino wine country lies inland, about a half hour west of Highway 101 and Cloverdale. Unless you've got all the time in the world or are making a stop in Mendocino, you won't want to drive from the coast inland; albeit beautiful, the roads are slow, winding, and sleepy. From Highway 101, the rolling, overgrown hillsides and valleys that lead to the wine trail and small towns of Boonville and Philo are not a quick jaunt, either. But in truth, driving past the ramshackle barns and abandoned and rusted tractors en route from Sonoma County is a welcome attraction in itself.

BOONVILLE

Provided you're not following a lagging motor home or big rig, it's about a half-hour drive from Cloverdale (see Northern Sonoma County chapter) to Boonville through tight turns carved into unadulterated hillsides rich with wildflowers, oaks, and the occasional dilapidated barn or herd of grazing sheep. Suddenly the valley opens up and before you know it you're in Boonville, a speck of a town in the heart of the magnificently pristine Anderson Valley. It's best known for a regional dialect called Boontling,

While you're in town, grab a copy of the Anderson Valley Advertiser, a rollicking, crusading (some say muckraking) small-town paper with avid readers from as far away as San Francisco and the Oregon border.

developed by townfolk at the beginning of the 1900s. No one really speaks Boontling anymore, though a few old-timers remember the lingo. As in most private languages, a large percentage of the words refer to sex, a fact glossed over in most touristy brochures on the topic.

ACTIVITIES

Farmers Market. From May through October the Boonville Hotel and Restaurant's parking lot becomes the site of the festive Boonville Farmers Market, held every Saturday from 9am to noon. Here you can purchase wonderful produce, handmade soaps, wool, and even the occasional billy goat. (Hwy 128 at Lambert Ln, center of town; 707/895-2210)

Hiking and Camping. You may share Hendy Woods State Park's stunning wilderness of old-growth redwoods and hiking trails with other fortunate souls who had the wisdom to pitch their tent in this little patch of paradise. But with plenty of elbowroom and hiking trails, a stay at more than half of the 92 campsites affords complete privacy and a total sense of getting away from it all. Picnic adjacent to the Navarro River, pick up that long-abandoned book under the shade of a giant redwood, walk Big Hendy Grove, or make s'mores at the campfire (rangers have wood for purchase but you'll have to bring your own graham crackers, chocolate, and marshmallows) and watch all your cares dissipate with the morning fog. Contact ParkNet (800/444-PARK; www.nps.gov) for reservations and information. (3 miles W of Philo off Hwy 128)

Brewery and Saloon. Most people don't know what the Boontling word for beer is, but the folks at the Anderson Valley Brewing Company, a microbrewery producing fine hand-crafted beers, probably do. The brewery set up shop in downtown Boonville (if you can call a few commercial blocks "downtown"), but as demand for its house-brewed beers increased, the management realized a larger facility was in order. The new 30-barrel Bavarian-style brew house, which opened in 2000, is a testament to the quality of the sensational suds. Take the tour offered daily at 1:30pm and 4pm and you'll get a glimpse of the copper brew kettles that owner Ken Allen imported from defunct German

THE SPORTING LIFE OF LAKE MENDOCINO

While one could easily occupy a week or more with wine tasting in Mendocino, an even more relaxing pursuit is exploring the banks of Lake Mendocino. An ideal fishing lake, it was created on the Russian River's east fork more than 40 years ago, covers some 1,800 acres, and supports a healthy fishery of striped, largemouth, and smallmouth bass, bluegill, catfish, and crappie. There are two public boat-launch areas on the lake, both with six lanes. One is at the Che-Ka-Ka section of the south shore on Lake Mendocino Drive; the other is at Lake Mendocino Marina, just east of Calpella on the north end of the lake, on Marina Drive. The marina also has boat and equipment rentals and slips and is the main gathering spot for those interested in sports such as waterskiing. For information, contact the U.S. Army Corps of Engineers office in Ukiah (707/462-7581) or the marina (707/485-8644). (Head E on Hwy 20 from Calpella on the Hwy 101 corridor; the lake is S of the highway at Lake Ridge Dr)

Naturally, there are a number of obvious options when it comes to tackle and outfitters in an area where bass fishing is so central. Our favorite way to scrounge up bait, however, is to scoop up crayfish living in the still, coved areas of the lake and just whittle them down into chunks. This is particularly effective in summer catfish season, but if you want to go the easy route, stop by Ron's Grocery & Tackle in Ukiah (800 Lake Mendocino Dr; 707/462-2622).

breweries. Ask 'em about their secret language and they're likely to tell you, but if you want to sample the secrets to their brewery success you'll have to taste them on tap at the Buckhorn Saloon (14081 Hwy 128; 707/895-3369; lunch, dinner every day, closed Tues–Wed in winter) in downtown Boonville. There's also a gift shop on the same block selling a sampler six-pack including an amber, porter, and IPA. (17700 Hwy 128; corner of Hwys 128 and 253, 1 mile outside Boonville; 707/895-BEER or 800/207-BEER; www.avbc.com; open every day at 1:30pm and 4pm)

Boont Berry Farm
(13981 Hwy 128;
707/895-3576), an
organic-produce
market and deli in
a small, weathered-
wood building,
turns out terrific
treats.

LODGINGS

ANDERSON CREEK INN ★★

This neck of the backwoods doesn't have much in the way of hotels, so B&Bs such as Jim and Grace Minton's five-room ranch-style getaway are in high demand. Set on 16 acres and surrounded by rolling hills and majestic oaks and redwoods, Anderson Creek is what country living is all about: tranquillity and small-town hospitality. Rooms are clean and country-modern in style, and each has a king-size bed, private bath, and picturesque valley views; three have wood-burning fireplaces. Romantics may want to opt for the Courtyard Room, which boasts a pretty netting-draped four-poster bed, a love seat in front of the fireplace, and a claw-footed tub. The bright Meadow Room is larger, with a fireplace and expansive views. A full breakfast is served in the courtyard or dining room. When weather permits, the place to be later in the day is the outdoor pool, which over-looks the valley. Kids will appreciate the horses, sheep, lla-mas, and goats, but due to the rusticity of the area, this place is not the best bet for families with young children. Also, note that the place is nonsmoking and there's a two-night minimum during high season (June through October). *12050 Anderson Valley Wy, Boonville; 707/895-3091 or 800/552-6202; $$; MC, V; checks OK; innkeeper@anderson-creekinn.com; www.andersoncreekinn.com; from Boonville, take Hwy 128 W for 1.5 miles, go left onto Anderson Valley Wy, and continue 1.7 miles.*

THE BOONVILLE HOTEL AND RESTAURANT ★★★

After a roller-coaster history of highs and lows, the 10-room Boonville Hotel languished for a few years until current owner John Schmitt brought it back to life as a small restau-rant and inn. The decor of the Old West–style hotel is pleas-antly austere, but feels more Shaker than Northern California. Half of the rooms have private balconies, although two overlook the busy highway. Two newer suites offer spacious separate sitting areas, making them well suited to those with kids in tow. (The staff hasn't seemed to figure out, however, that the bare hardwood floors of the old hotel are *not* suited to the clomping of small children, a fact that can make sleep near impossible for the other guests.) The smaller rooms at the back of the hotel are quieter than the ones in front and less expensive, but here the inn's minimalist decor heads toward bleak. Medium-size room 3, with its unique iron bed, strikes a good, compromise balance of price, spaciousness, and peacefulness. Guests are treated to a continental breakfast in the sunny dining room. A deck overlooks the beautiful 2-acre vegetable and herb garden behind the hotel.

The restaurant, a gathering spot for local winemakers, is still one of the best north of the Napa Valley. Chef Schmitt (who for years cooked with his mother when she owned the French Laundry restaurant in Yountville) offers a fresh mix of California, Southwestern, and backwoods regional cuisine, such as sliced pork tenderloin with cumin, cilantro, and oranges, and chicken breast with roasted-tomato–mint salsa. The restaurant is open for dinner only five nights a week; call for more information. Note: The inn rooms have no phones or TVs, so plan for a weekend of romance or R&R. *14050 Hwy 128, Boonville; 707/895-2210; $$$; MC, V; checks OK; usually closed Jan; www.boonvillehotel.com; at Lambert Ln, in the center of town.*

PHILO

Pronounced "File-oh," rather than "Feel-oh," this quaint country town on the two-lane highway (and only major road) is a great home base for exploring the dozen or so wineries in the vicinity. It's also a prime place for embarking on the area's other top activity: relaxing and getting a taste of what life was like before the likes of Macintosh and McDonald's.

WINERIES

Claudia Springs. After the county planning commission vetoed Claudia Springs' long-standing informal tastings and sales at the winery (because the place is on a private road), the winery set up shop in a gussied-up warehouse on Highway 128. At the 100-year-old bar, which was once part of a soda fountain, you can now enjoy more adult types of treats, as in award-winning

About 2 miles west of Philo is Gowan's Oak Tree (6350 Hwy 128; 707/895-3353), a great family-run roadside fruit-and-vegetable stand with a few picnic tables in back and a swing for road-weary tots.

Pinot Noir and Zinfandel as well as lovely Chardonnay. If during your visit to the area you've been dreaming of escaping your life and opening a winery here, ask the staff the story of Claudia Springs. Friends Claudia and Bob Klindt and Claudia and Warren Hein did exactly that in 1989; more than a decade later they're squeezing 3,000 barrels and plenty of awards out of their Anderson Valley grapes. An even newer tasting room called Mendocino Specialty Vineyards is in the works, which will share space with Lonetree and Rayes Hill wineries; call the winery to find out if they've moved yet. *1810 Hwy 128, next to the Floodgate Store, 1 mile W of Handley Cellars; 707/895-3993; open every day 11am–5pm, winter hours vary so call ahead; tasting free.*

Greenwood Ridge Vineyards. Named after the coastal ridge where its grapes are grown, pretty, pastoral Greenwood Ridge is known for white Riesling, but it also produces barrel-fermented Chardonnay, Sauvignon Blanc, estate-grown and -bottled Cabernet Sauvignon, and Merlot, Zinfandel, and a lovely Pinot Noir. The 16 acres of vineyards overlook Anderson Valley, and the expansive grounds, which include a friendly tasting room, are also the site of the annual California Wine Tasting Championships (for novices and pros) held on the last weekend of July. If you're in town during the event, don't miss the opportunity to join in on the international chocolate tasting and cheese tasting contests, or kick back and listen to live music, taste olive oils, and watch contestants try to identify wines by varietal name. Any other time of year it's still a nice place to linger, especially if you bring lunch and park yourself at the picnic area by their pond. *5501 Hwy 128; 707/895-2002; www. greenwoodridge.com; everybody@greenwoodridge.com; open 10am–5pm winter, 10am–6pm summer; tasting free, reserve wines $5.*

Handley Cellars. By using grapes from Anderson Valley and Dry Creek, Handley Cellars is able to produce a variety of wines that accentuate the unique *terroir* of the Mendocino and Sonoma regions. Most noteworthy are the award-winning Pinot Noir and Chardonnay, but don't let that stop you from sampling the slew of other complimentary options, which might include award-winning sparkling wines as well as Gewürztraminer and Sauvignon Blanc. Even if you're not in the mood to sample wines, it's worth stopping by to take in the sweet country surroundings, check out the tasting room full of exotic artifacts from around the world, or make use of the prime picnic area in a garden courtyard. *3151 Hwy 128; 707/895-3876; www.handleycellars.com; open every day 11am–5pm, closed Thanksgiving and Christmas.*

Husch Vineyards. Follow the road west of Philo and 5 miles later you'll see Husch's adorable rustic brown-shingled tasting room, which was once used to house farm animals and grains. As the oldest winery in Anderson Valley (founded in 1971), Husch appropriately maintains an ambience of old-fashioned charm and hospitality. Within the tasting room you can sample Chardonnay, Pinot Noir, and Gewürztraminer, along with wines from its Ukiah vineyards, all of which are made from grapes grown on family-owned vineyards. You can also purchase wines that are not available anywhere else. A self-guided tour meanders through the vineyards, and perfect picnic spots abound on the tasting room's deck, under a number of grape arbors, and in the gazebo overlooking a pond. *4400 Hwy 128; 707/895-3216; www.huschvineyards.com; open every day 10am–6pm summer and 10am–5pm winter; tours available by appointment.*

Navarro Vineyards. This small, family-owned winery founded in 1973 pioneered the region's trademark wine (dry, fruity, spicy Alsatian-style Gewürztraminer) and produces excellent Chardonnay, Pinot Noir, Petite Sirah, and white Riesling. Navarro wines are sold only by mail order and at the winery, which offers a surprisingly large tasting menu as well as nonalcoholic grape juice. *5601 Hwy 128; 707/895-3686 or 800/537-9463; www.navarrowine.com; open every day 10am–6pm summer and 10am–5pm winter; tastings free.*

Pacific Echo Cellars. In 1991 Scharffenberger Cellars (yes, it's the same folks with the fab chocolate) was sold to Moët Hennessey, which has since begun bottling its traditional French sparkling wine under the generic-sounding label Pacific Echo Cellars. The company still produces excellent brut, blanc de blancs, brut rosé, and crémant. Taste what they're up to in their remodeled farmhouse, where you can also embark on a tour highlighting winery production. *8501 Hwy 128; 707/895-2957; open every day 11am–5pm; tours by reservation only; tasting $3.*

Roederer Estate. If ever there was proof that rustic Anderson Valley is globally recognized as prized grape-growing territory, it's that in 1981, Roederer, one of France's most prestigious Champagne producers, chose to put down roots on 580 acres here (around 350 acres are vineyards). The big-business winery—barely visible from the road since it's surrounded by vineyards nestled in between rolling hills—is intentionally modest, blending in well with the pristine landscape and laid-back rural community. Visitors are welcome to drop by the polished tasting salon's antique French zinc-topped bar and sip complimentary (with wine purchase) tastes of Anderson Valley brut, brut rosé, and Roederer Estate's *tête de cuvée*, L'Ermitage, all of which are made from estate-grown grapes. Guests can also make a reservation to tour the state-of-the-art production facilities and learn about the sparkling-winemaking process. *4501 Hwy 128; 707/895-2288; www.roederer-estate.com; open every day 11am–5pm; tasting $3, refunded with wine purchase.*

LODGINGS

HIGHLAND RANCH   ★★✦

The price may be a big bump up from other options in the area, but you needn't pull out your wallet ever again during your stay at George Gaines's all-inclusive private luxury ranch. The property, on 250 acres, accommodates up to 22 guests, who have access to the community reading room, living room with large stone fireplace, country-style dining room, redwood deck, pool, two tennis courts, fishing poles, and 2-acre bass lake. Those who find the gumption to get active can jump on one of the ranch's 19 horses and explore the 100 miles of trails through redwood forests, pristine meadows, and ridges above Anderson Valley. Then again, it's just as alluring to loll around in any of the 10 private cabins, each of which includes a private bath, fireplace, telephone, and covered porch with rocking chairs. To ensure you don't have to lift even one weary finger, daily housekeeping service keeps things in order, while a chef whips up country breakfasts and lunches and European-influenced American dinners (accompanied, of course, by wines from the region and across the globe or, for those who want something a little stronger, cocktails from a full bar). Because the ranch positions itself as the perfect place for family reunions and business retreats as well as individual rentals, they go the distance with the extras, which means cribs are available for the little ones, and for a little extra money you can grab cartridges and clay pigeons for shooting on-property, use the on-site tennis courts, take private riding lessons, get a massage, or make long-distance phone calls. They even accommodate pets. *18941 Philo-Greenwood Rd, Philo; 707/895-3600; $$$; AE, DC, MC, V; checks OK; 2-night minimum; www.highlandranch.com; from Philo go W on Hwy 128, turn left on Philo-Greenwood Rd, continue 1 mile to sign, and follow dirt road 4 miles.* &

PHILO POTTERY INN ★★

This 1888 redwood farmhouse is pure and authentic country—no frilly ruffles, no overdressed dolls, just a lavender-filled English garden in the front yard and bright handmade quilts and sturdy frontier furnishings in each of the five guest rooms. You may linger in the library downstairs or snooze in the bent-willow loungers on the rustic front porch. Evaline's and Donna's Rooms are the lightest and most spacious, but the favored unit is the cozy one-room cottage with a detached private bath, a wood-burning stove, and a back porch. Staff will direct you to all the best hiking and biking trails and will happily arrange private tastings at the valley's many small private wineries. A complimentary continental breakfast, featuring many homemade coffee cakes and granola, is served in the dining room. *8550 Hwy 128, Philo; 707/895-3069; $$; MC, V; checks OK; in town.*

HOPLAND

Back on Highway 101 just southeast of Boonville is a small town whose name originated from hops, an herb used to flavor beer. Hop vines once covered the region, from the 1860s until mildew wiped out the crop in the 1940s. The only legacy left of that era today is the hops growing in the beer garden of Mendocino Brewing Company, a location that's also home to several award-winning microbrews. Today, Hopland's rich alluvial soil is dedicated to the production of wine grapes and Bartlett pears, which you can see flanking the highway. Though this town surrounding the highway lacks the rural charm of Boonville and Philo, there are a number of wineries worth exploration should you happen to be in the area.

WINERIES

Brutocao Cellars Hopland Tasting Room. The Brutocao family, originally from Venice, Italy, married into an American farming family and the next thing you knew they were doing one of the things Italians do best: making wine. Over a decade later they're still getting good juice from their 475 acres of vineyards in southern Mendocino County. Drop by the friendly facilities and taste the full spectrum of wines, from Sauvignon Blanc and Chardonnay to unrefined and unfiltered reds like Cabernet Sauvignon, Pinot Noir, Zinfandel, and Merlot. All are made from estate-grown grapes that haven't been subjected to synthetic chemicals, and all are also estate bottled. The gift shop is packed with locally made ceramics, glassware, and the like. An adjoining American restaurant serves lunch and dinner, and six bocce ball courts are waiting for you to get a game going. *13500 S Hwy 101, just N of Mountain House Rd; 707/744-1664; www.brutocellars.com; open every day 10am–5pm.*

Fetzer Vineyards. A big company with a huge production output and lots of money translates to a very picturesque and polished wine-tasting experience at Fetzer Vineyards. In the rather corporate tasting room you'll find everything you could possibly want: complimentary pours of Sauvignon Blanc, Chardonnay, Cabernet Sauvignon, Merlot, and Zinfandel; a friendly staff; plenty of logo gifts; and, in keeping with their dedication to wine and food pairing, gourmet foods and an extensive gourmet deli. Especially great for gourmands is the enormous organic garden, from which award-winning chef/author and Fetzer culinary director John Ash harvests ingredients during cooking demonstrations (call for schedules; he travels frequently). Take the tour and you'll enjoy a vineyard and garden tasting, or be leisurely and relax at one of the beautiful picnic spots. *13601*

Eastside Rd; from Hwy 101 take Hwy 175 E for less than 1 mile; 800/846-8637; www.fetzer.com; open every day 10am–5pm.

Milone Family Winery. Founded in 1977 by Jim Milone ("MI-low-nee"), great-grandson of Achilles Rosetti, who operated the first winery in Hopland, this rustic and down-home family-owned winery produces around 3,000 of cases Zinfandel, Chardonnay, a reserve Bordeaux blend of Cabernet Sauvignon, Merlot, a Petit Verdot called Echo, and small amounts of port. *14594 S Hwy 101, S of Mountain House Rd; 707/744-1396; www. milonefamilywinery.com; open every day 10am–5pm, winter hours vary.*

Most of Anderson Valley's wineries line the narrow stretch of Highway 128 that winds through this gorgeous, verdant, 25-mile-long valley before it reaches the Pacific Coast.

RESTAURANTS

HOPLAND BREWERY PUB & RESTAURANT AT THE MENDOCINO BREWING COMPANY ★

California's first brew pub since Prohibition (and the second in the nation), the Hopland Brewery is a refreshing break from the crushed-grape circuit. This quintessential brew pub has tasty grub, foot-stomping live music on most Saturdays (everything from the blues to Cajun), and five fine beers brewed on the premises. The classic beer garden has long tables shaded by trellised hops, as well as a sandbox to keep the kids amused while you chow down on the large burgers served on house-made buns or the Red Tail chili—a heavenly mash of fresh vegetables, sirloin steak, and a generous splash of Red Tail Ale. *13351 S Hwy 101, Hopland; 707/744-1361; $; MC, V; no checks; lunch, dinner every day; beer and wine; reservations recommended; www.mendobrew.com; downtown.*

LODGINGS

THATCHER INN ★★

Built as a stage stop in 1890, this haughty cream-colored combination of Gothic spires and gabled windows still looks like a luxurious frontier saloon-hotel, thanks to an $800,000 restoration in 1990. The lobby is dominated by a long, mirrored, polished wood bar; the gorgeous dark-wood-paneled library is filled with interesting old books, velvet settees, and shiny brass reading lamps. A wide, curving wood stairway leads from the lobby to 20 charmingly decorated guest rooms on the second and third floors—all with private baths. The quietest rooms with the best views are on the south side of the hotel overlooking the backyard patio with a fountain, wrought-iron lampposts, and a giant oak tree. A full breakfast, usually served alfresco and perhaps including eggs, bacon or sausage, house-made muffins and breads, and cheese pancakes (a traditional Romanian recipe from the owners), is included in the rate. The hotel's Thatcher Inn Restaurant serves acceptable but uninspired California cuisine. *13401 Hwy 101, Hopland; 707/744-1890 or 800/266-1891; $$$; AE, MC, V; checks OK; downtown across from Mendocino Brewing Co.*

UKIAH

Located in the upper reaches of the California Wine Country, Ukiah is still what Napa, Sonoma, and Healdsburg used to be—a sleepy little agricultural town surrounded by vineyards and apple and pear orchards. Peopled by an odd mix of farmers, loggers, and back-to-the-landers, Ukiah is a down-to-earth little burg with few traces of Wine-Country gentrification. That doesn't mean there isn't any wine, however.

ACTIVITIES

Hot Springs. Soak away the aches and pains of your long drive (Ukiah is a bit of a schlep from almost anywhere) at clothing-optional and very affordable Orr Hot Springs, 13 miles outside of Ukiah. Don't think too touchy-feely here. This wonderfully wooded place is laid-back with a fun, friendly, and very casual vibe. Along with several indoor tubs there's a redwood hot tub, outdoor pools, sauna, and steam room, all of which are heated (or chilled) by none other than Mother Nature. You can also splurge for a massage. If you're so relaxed you can't leave, you may just be in luck: they have 14 rooms (hostel-like accommodations) as well as campsites, two private cottages, and a shared kitchen. (13201 Orr Springs Rd; from Hwy 101 N in Ukiah, exit right on N State St, and turn left on Orr Springs Rd; 707/462-6277)

Hiking. Hikers will want to stretch their legs at Montgomery Woods State Park, which features 1,142 acres of coastal redwoods (both the taller coastal *Sequoia sempervirens* and the Sierra *Sequoia gigantea*) and fern forest with a self-guided nature trail along Montgomery Creek Reserve. (On Orr Springs Rd, off Hwy 101, 15 miles NW of Ukiah)

Museum. In town, the main attraction is the Grace Hudson Museum, which offers a historical look into the area's history. Grace Hudson (1865–1936), daughter of a local pioneer and painter, created many beautiful artworks depicting the Pomo Indians. You can also view her family's collection of Pomo baskets, historical items, and her Craftsman bungalow's study, front room, and dining room. (431 S Main St; from Hwy 101 N take Gobbi St exit W, and turn right at S Main St; 707/467-2836; www.gracehudsonmuseum.org; open Wed–Sat 10am–4:30pm, Sun noon–4:30pm)

WINERIES

Frey Vineyards. Continue up the road a bit to Redwood Valley and you'll find Frey, which holds the undisputed claim as the oldest and largest organic winery in the United States and the first in the country to produce biodynamic wines (i.e., the grapes are grown in accordance with the Demeter Association, an internationally recognized biodynamic certification agency, and are made with no added sulfites). Sample the Frey family's Petite Sirah, Cabernet, and Sauvignon Blanc. *14000 Tomki Rd; from Hwy 101 take West Rd to Tomki Rd, turn left and left again at the sign; 707/485-5177 or 800/760-3739; call for hours; tastings free.*

Jepson Vineyards. Set just off Highway 101 and backed by Mendocino County's rolling hills, 1,240-acre Jepson is highly regarded for its Chardonnay, Sauvignon Blanc, sparkling wines, Viognier, Merlot, and recently increased production of Zinfandel and Syrah. They also produce a lovely brandy, distilled in a copper alembic. *10400 Hwy 101; 707/468-8936; www.jepsonwine. com; open every day 10am–5pm, tours by appointment; tastings free.*

Parducci Wine Estates. Mendocino County's oldest winery, founded in 1932, is best known for affordability, but it does garner attention from the critics for its old-vine Chardonnay and Charbono as well as Pinot Noir and Petite Sirah. Drop by and you can decide which you like best—or perhaps you're partial to the Sauvignon Blanc, Chardonnay, or Syrah. Either way, the best part is these wines are so well priced you won't feel guilty if you set a case or two in the trunk. *501 Parducci Rd, off N State St; 707/462-WINE; www.parducci.com; call for hours.*

RESTAURANTS

SCHAT'S COURTHOUSE BAKERY AND CAFE ★

Schat's Courthouse Bakery has been open in Ukiah since 1990, but its history dates back to Holland in the early 1800s—which is as far back as the fifth-generation baker brothers Zach and Brian Schat can trace the roots of a very long line of Schat bakers. In 1948, the Schat clan emigrated to California, bringing with them the hallowed family recipe for their signature Sheepherder's Bread, a semi-sour, dairy- and sugar-free round loaf that's so popular it's been featured in *Sunset* magazine's "Best of the West" column. What really separates Schat's Courthouse Bakery from the rest are the huge, more-than-you-can-possibly-eat lunch items: made-to-order sandwiches, build-your-own baked potatoes, house-made soups, tangy Caesar salad, and huge slices of vegetarian quiche (served with bread and a salad), all for around five bucks. Located just off Highway 101, this is a great spot to load up on munchies while exploring the local Wine Country. Schat's stays open for lunch until 6pm during the week and 4:30pm on Saturday. *113 W Perkins St, Ukiah; 707/462-1670; $; no credit cards; local checks only; light breakfast, lunch Mon–Sat; from Hwy 101 take the Perkins St exit W; ¹/₂ block W of State St, across from the courthouse.*

LODGINGS

SANFORD HOUSE BED AND BREAKFAST ★★

There's something indisputably small-town about this tall, yellow Victorian inn on a tree-lined street just west of Ukiah's Mayberry-like downtown. Peaceful, unhurried, and bucolic,

Sanford House boasts only one Gothic turret, but it does have a big front porch dotted with white wicker chairs and an old-fashioned baby buggy, plus an English garden complete with a koi pond. Inside, antiques grace every room and everything is freshly painted, but it's far too comfortable and unpretentious to be called a showplace. The five guest rooms are named after turn-of-the-century presidents; the Taft Room, with its dark four-poster bed, floral fabrics, and a sort of spooky Princess Di doll in a wedding dress, is the most elegant, but equally pleasant is the spacious cream-and-green Wilson Room with its floral wallpaper, beautiful armoire, and sunny turret sitting area. Innkeeper Dorsey Manogue serves a breakfast feast every morning in the dining room using fresh, mostly organic ingredients, and in the evening she offers homemade biscotti (dipped in white and dark chocolate) and wine in the parlor. *306 Pine St S, Ukiah; 707/462-1653; $$; MC, V; checks OK; from Hwy 101, take the Perkins St exit, head W, and turn left on Pine St.*

If you have Internet access, check out www.mendocinoguide.com for a calendar of events and a plethora of information on the region's attractions.

VICHY SPRINGS RESORT ★

Although the rejuvenating effect of the naturally carbonated mineral pools at Vichy Springs had been known by the Pomo Indians for hundreds of years, it wasn't until the mid-1800s that others caught on to the idea. Since then, this California Historic Landmark has attracted the likes of Ulysses S. Grant, Teddy Roosevelt, Mark Twain, and Jack London, who all soaked their famous bones in North America's only naturally carbonated mineral baths—which have a mineral content identical to the famed pools in Vichy, France. With such a remarkable distinction and luminous history, one would expect the resort to be ringed by four-star accommodations and fancy bathhouses. Ironically, the estate was practically a disaster area for years, littered with rusting cars and machinery, until proprietors Gilbert and Marjorie Ashoff completely refurbished the 700-acre property and reopened it in 1989.

Even with its face-lift, the resort is far from posh, though five new creekside rooms, all with private baths, and the two-bedroom Jack London Cottage bring the accommodations up a notch. Twelve more small, simply decorated guest rooms—all with private baths and most with queen-size beds—line a long ranch-house-style building. If you're visiting with children, consider staying at one of the three private cottages, each fully equipped with a kitchen, a wood-burning stove, and a shaded porch. Built more than 130 years ago, the eight indoor and outdoor baths remain basically unchanged (bathing suits required). Also on the grounds are a nonchlorinated Olympic-size pool filled with the therapeutic bubbly, a modern whirlpool bath, a playground, a barbecue, a small cabin where Swedish massages are administered, and 6 miles of ranch roads available to hikers and mountain bikers. Room rates include an expanded continental breakfast and unlimited use of the pools, which are rarely crowded. The baths are available for day use, too, and the resort has basic services for business travelers. *2605 Vichy Springs Rd, Ukiah; 707/462-9515; $$$; AE, DC, DIS, MC, V; checks OK; www.vichysprings.com; from Hwy 101, take the Vichy Springs Rd exit and head W.*

REDWOOD VALLEY

It may be just another rural highway-side town, but Redwood Valley also is a good stop for beef lovers in need of a red-meat fix.

RESTAURANTS

BROILER STEAK HOUSE ★★

The Broiler is more than a steak house—it's a temple to meat. If you arrive without a reservation, expect to wait a while in the giant cocktail lounge—a good place to catch up on the latest Western fashions. Eventually you'll be ushered into the inner sanctum, where, if you're a true believer, you'll order a juicy steak grilled (to your exact specifications, of course) over an oak-wood pit. All entrees include a mammoth baked potato with butter, sour cream, and chives, plus a garden-fresh dinner salad the size of your head. *8400 Uva Dr, Redwood Valley; 707/485-7301; $$; AE, DIS, MC, V; checks OK; dinner every day; full bar; reservations recommended; from Ukiah, go 7 miles N on Hwy 101, take the West Rd exit, and turn left.* &

LAKE COUNTY

LAKE COUNTY

Although only a 2-hour drive northeast from San Francisco, Lake County is miles apart from the city's urban landscape. Twisting, undulating highways cut through the densely forested Mayaca-mas Mountains, leading from one quaint town to another. The main attraction for visitors to Lake County is, by no coincidence, California's largest natural freshwater lake—64-square-mile Clear Lake.

In 1919, Prohibition nearly eliminated Lake County's 5,000 acres of vineyards, which dated back to the early 1870s. Even when Prohibition was repealed in 1924, Lake County vineyards did not rebound quickly; farmers had replanted their acres mainly with pears. Slowly but surely, vineyards regained their size due to the pear pressure of competing prices from the San Joaquin Valley, as farmers came to value the steady, predictable prices for wine grapes. Meanwhile, growers from the heavily planted Napa and Sonoma growing areas also sought new sources for inexpensive vineyards. As a result, lately wineries have mounted a comeback, and Lake County is poised to become another Northern California winery destination—but it's not there yet. Thus visitors today can get a glimpse of how Napa and Sonoma once were before the mass popularity and subsequent skyrocketing prices kicked in. In addition to wine, Lake County is a destination for boating, fishing, water sports, camping, hiking, bicycling, and cultural activities, and with its vast, forested, mountainous terrain is also a hot spot for agriculture and geothermal power. All of which means that for the Lake County visitor, winery-hopping is just one of the many activities to plan.

ACTIVITIES

Getting Acquainted. Lake County is accessible from the San Francisco Bay Area by taking Highway 101 north to Novato, heading east on Highway 37 to Vallejo, then following Highway 29 north to Middletown. From Santa Rosa, take Highway 101 to Mark West Springs Road W, which turns into Porter Creek Road and ultimately Petrified Forest Road, which leads to Highway 29. Take Highway 29 north through Calistoga to Middletown. From Ukiah, take Highway 101 north to Highway 20 east to Highway 29.

A GOOD DAY IN . . .
LAKE COUNTY

Begin the day with a hearty breakfast at Middletown's Beulah's Café. From there, head to the sprawling estate of Guenoc Winery to take in the serene winery vistas over sips of Lake County's premier wine. Head north to Kelseyville, a one-road town that is home to some antique shops and a world-class dive bar, the Brick Tavern. Spend the rest of the day at the 120-acre Konocti Harbor Resort & Spa, where you can picnic at a table by the lake, rent a boat or jet ski, and enjoy the full-service spa. Stay for dinner (who wants to drive now?), and watch a great show under the stars at the Konocti Field Amphitheater or indoors at the renowned Joe Mazzola Classic Concert Hall.

Follow Highway 29 south to Lakeport. Though Lake County is sizable, most activities there are not far away from any of the major towns. Especially if your plans involve Clear Lake itself, staying in one of the towns in the area—Middletown, Lakeport, Kelseyville, Nice, Lower Lake, or the town of Clear Lake—is a good option; all are within a short drive of each other. Other activities such as wine tasting, hiking, visiting parks, bicycling, and golfing fall within reach wherever you are.

For more information on Clear Lake and its surrounding towns and wineries, call or drop by the Lake County Visitor Information Center (875 Lakeport Blvd, Vista Point, Lakeport; 707/263-9544 or 800/LAKESIDE).

Parks. Clear Lake State Park sits on the south banks of Clear Lake, and, as you might imagine, much of the park's activity revolves around boating and fishing. Camping and hiking are other outdoor activities that predominate in this 500-acre park. Mount Konocti, an active volcano that has been quiet for the past 10,000 years or so, stands 4,200 feet above water level, but doesn't cast a shadow on the simmering summer sun that draws tanning revelers from all directions to the water's edge. While the shore can get quite crowded in prime season, the park's steep elevations of 1,320 to 1,600 feet keep most visitors away from the interior reaches, where campgrounds and nature trails beckon to adventurous souls. (From Napa, take Hwy 29 N to Hwy

175 N to Kelseyville, turn right on Main St, turn right on Gaddy Ln, turn right on Soda Bay Rd, and proceed to the park entrance; 707/279-4293)

The 1,000 acres encompassing Anderson Marsh State Historic Park on Clear Lake (also see Wildlife, below) contain freshwater marshes, grasslands, oak woodlands, and riparian woodlands. The diverse habitats within the park make it a nature lover's paradise. The park's most outstanding feature by far is its marsh: while 84 percent of Clear Lake's marshland has been destroyed, Anderson Marsh provides breeding areas for many species of bird, mammal, reptile, and amphibian. Popular indigenous creatures include great blue herons, egrets, various hawks, foxes, and the occasional bald eagle. (From Hwy 53 N, a parking lot is at park headquarters on the left side of the road; 707/994-0688; open Wed–Sun 10am–5pm)

Wildlife. Come to the Clear Lake area at certain times in the summer and you'll swear the only wildlife here is the plain ol' mosquito. Bring repellent along, however, and there are plenty of other creatures to watch, observe, and enjoy. The best bet for bird-watchers is to hit the trails at Anderson Marsh State Historic Park on Clear Lake, where mallards and western grebes make their foraging grounds. The riparian woodlands adjacent to the marsh house a wide variety of birds, including great horned owls, bald eagles in the winter, and great blue herons. Also along the marsh and riparian woods at Anderson, watch for pond turtles, muskrats, river otters, and gray foxes. Within the park's oak woodlands, find deer and squirrels, black-tailed hares, and rattlesnakes. (From Hwy 53 N, a parking lot is at park headquarters on the left side of the road; 707/994-0688; open Wed–Sun 10am–5pm)

Hiking. For hikers looking to experience the sights and scenery of a freshwater marsh, there is no better place than Anderson Marsh State Historic Park (see Parks and Wildlife, above). Cache Creek Nature Trail, an easy 2.2-mile round trip, is a level hiking trail that meanders through the park's riparian ecological community, along the banks of a creek flowing into the marshland. The Ridge and Marsh Trails, together an easy 2.5-mile round trip, travel along the marsh and up through a higher elevation of oak woodland, providing an up-close glimpse into the unique and rapidly diminishing freshwater marsh habitat. (To reach the trailheads for all of these trails, take Hwy 53 north to the park's headquarters and parking facility on the west side of the road; 707/944-0688)

Another great place to work the old calves is Clear Lake State Park. It's relatively small at 500 acres, but it does have a few trails that meander about its hilly terrain, as well as ranger-guided morning nature walks. Dorn Trail, an easy 2-mile round trip that begins at the visitor center, winds through oak woodlands and affords hikers beautiful views over the lake. Indian Nature Trail, another piece-of-cake meander and a painless 0.25-mile round trip, is a self-guiding nature trail that starts at the park office, with explanations of how the local Indians used the native plants for their daily needs. (Take Hwy 29 N to Kelseyville, turn right on Main St, right on Gaddy Ln, right on Soda Bay Rd, and proceed to park entrance; 707/279-4293)

Camping. Clear Lake State Park has 150 sites distributed among four general locations around the lake's western shores, among oak woods, and near a boat launch and good fishing spots. Each site has a picnic table and fire grill, with rest rooms, showers, and running water nearby. Contact Reserve America (800/444-7275 or www.reserveamerica.com) to secure a spot, particularly during summer. For general directions, call the park at 707/279-4293. (To reach the campground, take Highway 29 W from the town of Lower Lake for 8.5 miles to Soda Bay Road. Continue north on Soda Bay another 9.5 miles to the park entrance, on the east side of the road. Note there are no hookups for RVs, but varying RV lengths can be accommodated)

Blue Oak Camp has 6 sites, again with no RV hookups, but room to park and stay a while. The setting here is in oak woods on the western banks of a nice fishing lake at Indian Valley Reservoir, just east of Clear Lake. Not surprisingly, it's popular with bass anglers who don't want to contend with crowds. Each site has a picnic table and fire pit, with running water and pit toilets nearby. There is a smaller camp on the east side of the lake, with just 1 site for tents only. The camp is a dirt road, so call ahead for conditions before taking the drive up. (No reservations; take Hwy 20 18 miles E of Clearlake Oaks, go 4 miles N on Walker Ridge Rd, go W at 4-way intersection, and continue 3 miles to campground on N side of the road; 707/468-4000)

GONE FISHIN'

Spend a lazy, warm Clear Lake afternoon in an aluminum fishing boat, bobbing around in the waters of a shady cove, and the best way to keep track of time is to count the number of catfish you've snagged. More than a few fishermen will tell you it's no sweat to catch over a dozen in just a few hours. In fact, the biting can be so regular and predictable it could border on annoying, since half the fun is the chase (or the wait). Clear Lake, the largest natural lake in the state, prides itself on its famed bass fishery anyway, so a bucket full of catfish is really nothing to brag about. At one time this was primarily a resort area that cleared out during the off-season. But with an increasing number of year-round residents—many of them retirees who have waited their whole lives for the day they could fish and do little else—the region is undergoing a metamorphosis of sorts. It now grapples with many of the same problems the big city must contend with—crime, unemployment, and environmental issues like loss of natural wetlands. With a large number of private resorts and some well-appointed public recreation areas to choose from, however, this is among the best non-alpine lake settings anglers can hope to stumble on.

Cycling. Cycling enthusiasts should check the Lake County Visitor Information Center in Lakeport (875 Lakeport Blvd, Vista Point, Lakeport; 707/263-9544 or 800/LAKESIDE) for the "Lake County Pathway Maps"—a series of great rides covering the county. There is a catch, however. Lake County is BYOB, as in bring your own bike: the businesses that previously provided bikes for rent no longer do so. Mountain bike enthusiasts clamor to tackle the challenging Boggs Mountain Demonstration State Forest (Hwy 175, Cobb Mountain; 707/928-4378).

Boating and Water Sports. So long as the sun is shining down on Lake County, we're betting the glistening waters of enormous Clear Lake are calling your name. And since surely you didn't come all this way to remain landlocked, it's a good idea to head straight to Disney's Watersports, where you can pick your playtime poison: ski boats, touring boats, patio boats, jet boats, wave runners, water skis, tubes, kneeboards, wakeboards, and pedal boats are all available by the hour, day, or, for the die-hard water sports fan, multi-days. (401 S Main St, Lakeport; 707/263-0969; www.disneyswatersports.com; open every day 10am–5pm, longer in summer)

Fishing and Boating. Clear Lake, at nearly 70 square miles, is the largest natural lake in California, and because it tends to fill up faster than it drains during heavy rains, sometimes it literally overflows like a plugged kitchen sink. With more than 100 miles of shoreline, it contains one of the finest bass fisheries in the state. Nighttime fishing under the full moon of summer is particularly rewarding here. While bass is the main fare, the bluegill, catfish, and crappie also bite a good percentage of the time. Clear Lake State Park (707/279-4293) and Horseshoe Bend, which lies to the east of the state park, are considered the best fishing spots for bass in early March through mid-June. These areas are also the main access points for recreation on the lake. Public boat ramps are located all around the lake: at Redbud *access to a cafeteria-style restaurant for breakfast and dinner, featuring vegetarian dishes as well as chicken and fish entrees (no alcohol allowed). Harbin also offers free movies every evening, along with activities like meditations, moon ceremonies, and massages. Although the resort has a definite touchy-feely, aging-hippie flavor, it attracts plenty of more conventional types who just want to relax (albeit in the nude). The Harbin staff take great pride in the tranquil environment they have created (telephones, TVs, and alarm clocks are purposely kept out of the rooms) and, indeed, it's so peaceful you're apt to see deer and their fawns lounging alongside guests on the lush lawns. If you're not comfortable around a lot of nudity, though, Harbin is not for you. (PO Box 782, Middletown, CA 95461; 707/987-2477; $–$$$; www.harbin.org; take Hwy 175 to Middletown, turn right on Barnes St and go about 1 mile, turn left on Harbin Springs Rd, which leads directly to property)*

Park in the town of Clearlake on Lakeshore Drive (707/994-8201); at Lakeside County Park in Kelseyville, on Park Drive; at five locations along the waterfront in Lakeport; at Lucerne Harbor County Park off Highway 20 in Lucerne; and at H.V. Keeling County Park on Lakeshore Boulevard in Nice.

There are numerous marinas and resorts around the lake with full bait-and-tackle shops, slips, and boat rentals. Among the most reputable are Ferndale Resort & Marina (6190 Soda Bay Rd, Kelseyville; 707/279-4866) and Talley's Family Resort (3827 Hwy 20, Nice; 707/274-1177).

Another great fishing spot is Indian Valley Reservoir, about 15 miles east of Clear Lake. The reservoir was formed in 1974 when Cache Creek was dammed. The lake is a bit smaller and less visited than Clear Lake because of its location off the main highway and its relative lack of amenities. As at Clear Lake, however, the bass and bluegill fishing, particularly top fishing at night, are quite good in the spring. There is a boat ramp and tackle facility near the dam; it's up to you to bring the rest. The lake's northern edge is a popular fishing spot in spring; in summer the west shore is more crowded. The U.S. Bureau of Land Management (BLM) runs a campground on the lake (see Camping, above). Most

If you like music, be sure to give a call to Konocti Harbor Resort at 800/660-5253 to find who's performing at the indoor Joe Mazzola Classic Concert Hall or the outdoor Konocti Field Amphitheater. They're known for bringing in surprisingly good talent. You can also get the scoop at www.konoctiharbor.com.

camping facilities are near the dam. (From the town of Clearlake, take Hwy 53 E, and exit N to Indian Valley; 707/468-4000)

Rafting. The main river action in this part of the state is on the upper section of Cache Creek, which flows southeast through the canyons of the northern Sacramento Valley from just below Clear Lake. Good runs are possible all summer if timed correctly with controlled flows out of Indian Valley Reservoir. The run is best taken on a 2-day trip, mostly paralleling Highway 16 between the towns of Rumsey and Madison. The creek is ideal for beginners who are not quite ready for the white-water death-drops found on other Northern California rivers. One good outfitter running regularly scheduled trips on the Cache is Whitewater Adventures of Napa (707/944-2222; www.whitewater-adv.com). Trips are usually scheduled through September in normal water-level years. To run the creek freestyle, take Highway 16 west from Woodland or east from Clear Lake, and look for put-ins at Rumsey, Guinda, and Brooks.

Bird's-Eye Views. Crazy Creek Soaring offers piloted glider flights that climb the omnipresent thermals above Lake County. Choose between the standard flight for one (there's a 240-pound maximum for passengers, so if you're getting close, skip dessert the night before) or two people (a 340-pound maximum) or the Acrobatic flight (one person only, who must be under 200 pounds), which is truly hairy. In town for a while? Crazy Creek Soaring will also teach you how to glide. Imagine the commuting possibilities. (18896 Grange Rd, 3 miles N of Middletown; 707/987-9112)

MIDDLETOWN

Formerly dubbed Middle Station, Middletown was a mere stagecoach stop halfway between Calistoga and Clear Lake for pioneers, miners, and ranchers in the mid-1800s. Today, Middletown stands as the southern gateway to Clear Lake but is more than just a great place to fill the gas tank and stock up on food. One can easily access all of Lake County's attractions in a day's trip from here.

ACTIVITIES

Spas. If mountain-biking Cobb Mountain left you sore and dirty, clean up your act with your choice of various spa packages at LaDonn's Day Spa and Salon or order from a menu that includes hairstyling, waxing, manicures, pedicures, body wraps, facials, and massage. Although it's best to call for an appointment, walk-ins are accepted during business hours, Tuesday through Saturday between 9am and 5pm (21108 Calistoga St; 707/987-3949). If they can't squeeze you in or you're in a more spiritual state of mind, give a call to Middletown Massage and Herb Collective, where you can get a complete tune-up for body and mind. They feature massage and bodywork techniques ranging from acupuncture to deep-tissue shiatsu, Chinese herbal consultations, yoga classes, hypnotherapy, astrology, and chiropractic alignment. Calling ahead is recommended, but walk-ins are welcome. (21158 Calistoga St; 707/987-7310; open Mon–Fri 10am–6pm, flexible weekend hours)

WINERIES

Guenoc and Langtry Estate Vineyards and Winery. The gem of Lake County, Guenoc has a rich viticultural history dating back to 1888, when famed stage actress Lillie Langtry first planted vineyards on the 23,000-acre estate. Completely dedicated to French Bordeaux varietals, the winery releases over a dozen labels every year. The tasting room is a warm, laid-back, stand-up bar where one can sip the estate wines for free or pony up $4 to taste several of the coveted reserve whites and reds (worth the cost, as the Guenoc Beckstoffer IV Cabernet Sauvignon and the Langtry Meritage Red are stunning). Tours are available daily and large groups must call ahead for a reservation. The tour consists of a walk-through of the winemaking facility with friendly, knowledgeable staff who toss in Lillie Langtry tidbits along the way. If you brought your own victuals, spread out the tablecloth on one of the many picnic tables perched under the wisteria canopy, complete with beautiful vistas of vineyards and the Mayacamas Mountains. If you're looking for a party when in town, check the winery's web site, as they frequently host special events. Finally, for a complete vacation experience, the Langtry House, which

Do you believe in ghosts? Some say the Langtry house has a permanent yet low-maintenance guest who is very light on her feet. Bring a Ouija board and have a chat.

accommodates 6 guests, and Freddie's Lodge, which sleeps up to 20, are available for rent. *21000 Butts Canyon Rd; 707/987-2385; www.guenoc.com; from Middletown, take Hwy 29 N, then go E 6 miles on Butts Canyon Rd; open every day 11:30am–5pm.*

RESTAURANTS

BEULAH'S CAFE

If you're looking for diner cuisine at its best, head to Beulah's Café, a postage stamp of an eatery in downtown Middletown. Due to popularity with locals, motorcyclers, boaters, and just about everyone in need of a heap of food with a greasy-good edge, chances are you will wait for your turn for a table. The ridiculously generous portions are compounded by affordable prices—even for the fill-'er-up breakfast-for-gluttons called the Garbage Omelet, a fluffy egg pouch containing just about everything within the chef's reach. Lunch-goers go for the hefty Beulah Burger that shamelessly weighs in at three-quarters of a pound, and that's not including the fixin's. Under new ownership, the cafe is now serving evening-only Mexican dishes that neither ease in size nor wane in affordability. *21147 Calistoga St, Middletown; 707/987-0473; $; MC, V; local checks only; breakfast, lunch every day, dinner Thurs–Sun; beer and wine; no reservations; downtown Middletown at the corner of Hwy 175.*

BOAR'S BREATH RESTAURANT & OVEN ★★

Smack in the middle of Middletown, this charming eatery is more in line with trendy metropolitan Bay Area dining rooms than the nearby roadside squat-and-gobbles. Serving dinner only, the Boar's Breath chef/proprietors, husband-and-wife team Frank and Suzette Stephenson, churn out classic oven-baked pizzas, hearty pastas, assorted salads, and serious cuts of meat and fish entrees. Menu mainstays include the zesty pizza Margherite (extra-virgin olive oil, garlic, Roma tomatoes, red sauce, and basil oil), Boar's Breath onion soup (savory braised onion in beef broth with roasted garlic and Gruyère crostini), good ol' spaghetti and meatballs, and a juicy center-cut pork chop, which is grilled and oven-roasted with apple, pancetta, and prune pan reduction sauce. If that's not enough, the friendly staff will explain the daily specials. But know in advance: Friday and Saturday have been permanently declared Prime Rib nights by popular demand. The old building, graced by craggy stone walls, high ceilings, and hardwood floors, is a combination of historic Middletown and contemporary modern design. A long, inviting bar, pouring top-shelf cocktails, wine, and beer, gives way to an open kitchen opposite a long, sleek wooden banquette, with simple wooden tables occupying the spaces in between. Adding emphasis to the restaurant's name are the two snarling (or smiling?) wild boar busts (one was a gift—and most likely a former barbecue "guest"—from Guenoc winery, and the other came from a local patron) mounted high on the back wall, their mouths stuffed with petrified pizzas. The full menu is available from the bar. *21148 Calistoga St, Middletown; 707/987-9491; $$; AE, DIS, MC, V; checks OK; dinner every day; full bar; reservations recommended; from Hwy 29 N enter Middletown (Hwy 29 becomes Calistoga St) and go to intersection of Hwy 175.*

BOHEMIA

Recently opened by a wife and husband with a Czech-ered (Czechoslovakian) past, Bohemia offers a deli experience by day and a single rotating dinner entree by night. For lunch, you can order from the assorted meats, cheeses, fresh-baked breads and desserts, and deli snacks. Enjoy them in the small, quaint Bavarian-style room or venture outside to the wisteria-covered pergola for an impromptu picnic accompanied by the gurgle of the patio fountain. Dinner is altogether different; at Bohemia the nightly nosh is a collaboration of Czech-influenced cooking by Amy and Mirek Volmuth. Each week they serve one dish, and one dish only, which might be schnitzel, chicken paprikash, stuffed cabbage, or Czechoslovakian dumplings. *20763 St. Helena Ln, Middletown; 707/987-4673; $; AE, DIS, MC, V; local checks OK; lunch, dinner every day; no reservations; beer and wine; 1 mile N of Middletown, slightly E of intersection of Hwy 29 and Butts Canyon Rd.*

MOUNT ST. HELENA BREWING COMPANY ★

If it's suds you seek, stroll into the Mount St. Helena Brewing Company for a cold one. The on-premise brewery is a local lunch and dinner hangout, a roomy, barnlike structure where they serve up everything from house-specialty pizzas, pastas, and burgers to house-smoked baby back ribs and fish and chips. Complementing the fare are four draughts: Palisades Pale Ale, Honey Wheat Ale, Brown Ale, and Imperial Stout. Seasonally, a few more specialty, small-batch brews make the list. The cozy, knotty-pine-walled bar, with additional table seating and good views of the TV, is a pleasant place to belly up and catch sporting events; diners seated in the main room can view brew masters at work through the large windows overlooking the brewery. *21167 Calistoga St, Middletown; 707/987-2106; $; DIS, MC, V; checks OK; lunch, dinner every day; beer and wine; reservations recommended; www.mtsthelenabrew.com; between Bush and Armstrong Sts, on the W side of street.*

LODGINGS

BACKYARD GARDEN OASIS ★★

Just minutes before Middletown as you drive from Calistoga is a bright yellow house announcing a backyard garden oasis of the same name. The three cottages and main house are tidily tucked away in the woodsy Collayomi Valley at the base of majestic Mount St. Helena. Rustic and cozy, each cabin is equipped with a king-size bed strategically placed under a skylight, gas fireplace, air-conditioning, spacious shower, refrigerator, coffeemaker, television (with direct satellite link), VCR (with access to an ample video library), and phones with data ports. While away the time with a good book in the gardens, play a smashing game of croquet (donning whites is not necessary), bird-watch, or soak away stress in the outdoor hot tub. Each morning you'll wake to fresh coffee delivered to your cottage before you make your way to the dining room for a full country breakfast of pancakes, eggs, frittata, bacon, and fresh, organic fruits grown on the property. Also available by arrangement through innkeeper Greta Zeit are ever-relaxing in-room massages. Think twice before bringing the kids: the Backyard Garden Oasis is clearly designed for adults in need of a time-out. *24019 Hilderbrand Dr, Middletown; 707/987-0505; $$; DIS, MC, V; no checks; www.jnb.com/~bygoasis; 4 miles S of Middletown (2 miles inside Lake County border), go E on Hilderbrand Dr, third driveway on the left.* &

WILLOW OAK PLANTATION INN ★★★

If it weren't for the ample oaks and rugged mountains, Willow Oaks would make you swear you'd stepped back in time to the Old South's glory days. Despite their ironic-under-the-circumstances surname, Bob and Elise Richmond pour on the Southern hospitality in this relaxed, roomy bed-and-breakfast. Outside, the beautifully manicured grounds greet you with a 100-year-old oak and a 40-year-old willow standing sentry for the 5,600-square-foot Greek Revival estate, designed from a blueprint of an original Southern plantation home. The plush lawns meander around the back, leading to the confines of the swimming pool or the nap-inspiring hammock that dangles under another willow, allowing its occupant to survey the adjacent vineyard. Inside, grab a book and relax in the library, which is complete with a large-screen television and furnished with Elise's family heirlooms from the South. If you dare leave the comfort of your room and its bathroom's radiant-heated marble floors, a Southern breakfast is served in the very Southern formal dining room or, weather permitting, outdoors. Breakfast features choices of eggs any style, buttermilk biscuits and sausage gravy made with genuine Lily flour imported from Tennessee (a touch of Elvis), pecan sour cream coffee cake, and the family secret—Aunt Patsy Love's Charleston grits. Soothe the rigors of exploring Lake County in the Jacuzzi room or at the wine happy hour every Friday and Saturday (during the busy summer season, almost every day) from 5 to 6:30pm. Bob and Elise go the extra mile, literally, by offering a ride to dinner at any of Middletown's restaurants. Mix in some lemonade on the patio with Uncle Remus and you'll sing zip-a-dee-doo-dah all day long. The Willow Oak Plantation is not an ideal place

For tours of wineries and tasting rooms all over Lake County, contact Jim at Eleven Roses Ranch, who will arrange for a private coach so you can safely travel the country roads. They also offer a variety of other theme tours (707/ 998-4471; www. elevenrosesranch.com).

for children, being designed for quiet, serene, adult relaxation—and bringing your pet is not a good idea either. *20650 Hwy 29, Middletown; 707/987-9000 or 800/856-4454; $$$$; AE, MC, V; no checks; www.willowoakplantation.com; about 1 mile N of downtown, on Hwy 29 near Butts Canyon Rd.*

KELSEYVILLE

Early settlers had to do little more than erect a U.S. post office here in order to put this place on the map. In 1882, however, some townspeople came to their senses and changed the name from Uncle Sam to Kelseyville, honoring the area's early pioneering family. A tiny, one-street town, Kelseyville is tucked into the base of the imposing dormant volcano Mount Konocti on the east side of Clear Lake. But it's definitely not in the shadows; today it appears to be right at the heart of Lake County's vineyard and winery revival. In fact, it's even arguable that over time Kelseyville will be much more than a stop to make while visiting the popular Konocti Harbor Resort.

ACTIVITIES

Watering Hole. Although every town in Lake County has its requisite dive bar, the Brick Tavern in Kelseyville stands out as a local historic monument. Built in 1872 while the town was still known as Uncle Sam, the tavern was once a full-service brothel with rooms upstairs available, we assume, by the hour. A step through the front door is a step back in time, in a room with wagon-wheel chandeliers, imposing wall-mounted stuffed animal busts, a pool table, a long, straight bar, and not much else. It may be missing the dual swinging tavern doors, but the 360-degree mural depicting local wilderness is classic. (4015 Main St, next to the Brick Grill; 707/279-4964; open Mon–Fri 9am–2am, Sat–Sun 10am–2am)

WINERIES

Steele Winery. Well regarded for making outstanding wines as well as experimenting with lesser-known grapes, Steele is a must-stop for the wine aficionado. Founder Jed Steele is legendary for bailing out of then-up-and-coming winery Kendall-

Jackson: as the story goes, Jess Jackson was so furious with Steele for leaving, he threatened to sue over the "secret Chardonnay formula." Apparently none existed or ever will, and Jed was on his way to his own success. That said, if you are looking for glorious tasting rooms, fountains, exotic gardens, or a parking lot full of Jaguars and Mercedeses, go back to Napa Valley. Steele Winery's tasting room, pouring the Steele label and the winery's second brand, Shooting Star, is all about the wine itself. The strip-mall-gone-bad atmosphere (with funky merchandise on either side of the small stand-up bar) might serve as a hint to buy a bottle and picnic with friends at one of the tables outside. In fact, try to do so on a Saturday, when a community farmers market is hosted outside from 8am to 5pm. Tasting the numerous wines will set you back $2, but they'll throw in the logo glass (rather than wash it). Among the highly regarded bottlings are the Pinot Noir, Zinfandel, and Syrah. Tours, available by appointment, include a view of the winery's production facility and the inefficient mouser, Ozgar the cat. *Hwy 29 and Thomas Dr; 707/279-9475; open Mon–Fri 11am–5pm, call for extended summer hours.*

Load your picnic basket or stock the fridge with the freshest of produce from the local farmers market each Saturday from 8am to 5pm at Steele Winery (Hwy 29 and Thomas Dr; 707/279-9475).

🍷 **Wildhurst Vineyards.** The Wildhurst tasting room brings a little country culture to downtown Kelseyville. With the charm of an old general store, the tasting bar offers complimentary samples of several wines, including limited Plunkett Creek reserves. Wander the room and peruse some of the locally crafted oils and sauces as well as wine accessories. *3855 Main St, between 1st and 2nd St; 707/279-4302; open every day 10am–5pm, closed major holidays.*

RESTAURANTS

THE BRICK GRILL

This breakfast and lunch stop is a simple little cafe serving generous portions for small prices. Breakfast consists of the usual suspects like fresh eggs, sausage, bacon, biscuits and gravy, and hotcakes. The real morning eye-opener is the Build a Brick omelet, wherein the diner selects from a laundry list of components designed to make breakfast last well into dinner. Lunch at the grill does not break new culinary ground with its selection of burgers, hot sandwiches, soups, and salads. However, locals hunker down with the juicy Philly cheese steak sandwich for their midday food paralysis. Although it may be early in the day, beer and nondescript wines are available and often enjoyed. *4015-B Main St, Kelseyville; 707/279-2213; $; AE, DIS, MC, V; no checks; breakfast, lunch every day; beer and wine; no reservations; Hwy 175 becomes Main St in town; between 2nd and 3rd St.*

THE SAWSHOP GALLERY BISTRO

Art gallery owner Maria Steele apparently decided that Kelseyville needed a dose of food culture as well when she redesigned her viewing space into a hip, artsy bistro, which was about to open when this book went to press. Maintaining a venue for local artists, Steele integrated their pieces into her charming, bright, and airy room with hardwood floors and high ceilings. The sleek banquette, welcoming bar, and simple wood tables add just the right amount of contemporary flair. Plans are for the edible art from the kitchen to consist of everything from sushi, pizzas, soup, and salads to roasted chicken and the requisite steak. *3825 Main St, Kelseyville; 707/278-0149; $$; MC, V; local checks OK; lunch, dinner Tues–Sat; full bar; reservations recommended; Hwy 175 becomes Main St in town; between 1st and 2nd St.* &

LODGINGS

KONOCTI HARBOR RESORT & SPA ★★

The top all-around attraction in Lake County, the Konocti Harbor Resort and Spa is a multifaceted property featuring accommodations that range from no-frills to swanky, indoor and outdoor concert venues, a full-service marina, and a world-class spa. Resting on 120 acres just a few miles northeast of Kelseyville, the property has recently undergone a million-dollar renovation. Long known for some of the best concerts on the West Coast, the resort features the intimate 1,000-seat indoor Joe Mazzola Classic Concert Hall as well as the 5,000-seat outdoor Konocti Field Amphitheater. The performing artists are generally world class; for information and dates, check the web site at www.konoctiharbor.com or call 800/660-5253. To stay at the resort, families, groups,

Day use of the Dancing Springs Spa and Fitness Center at Konocti Harbor Resort & Spa is available to nonguests for $10, or free when you buy any spa treatment. Also, day boaters who are not guests at the resort can launch their boat at Konocti Harbor for $5.

and couples can choose from options including affordable hotel rooms, secluded apartments, beachfront cottages, and VIP suites. All rooms have televisions, in-room movies, phones, air-conditioning and heat, and a coffeemaker. The apartments, beachfront cottages, and VIP suites all have full kitchens, while the deluxe hotel rooms and the apartments feature fireplaces. If you want to splurge, go nuts on the VIP suite complete with wet bar, private deck, and barbecue. While at the resort, take advantage of the multitude of services such as the complete fitness center, water-sports rentals at the marina, fishing accessories and equipment rentals, tennis courts, horseshoe pit, volleyball courts, swimming pool, peewee golf, and, of course, the beach. *8727 Soda Bay Rd, Kelseyville; 707/279-4281 or 800/660-5253; $$–$$$$; AE, DIS, MC, V; checks OK; www.konoctiharbor.com; off Hwy 29.* &

LAKEPORT

Originally named Forbestown after big-shot pioneer William Forbes, the town of Lakeport serves as the county seat and hub for most of the visitors seeking recreation on Clear Lake. With its cute, historic downtown, Lakeport is best seen as a drive-through, as top-notch accommodations and restaurants are few.

RESTAURANTS

PARK PLACE ★

A stone's throw from the northern shore of Clear Lake, Park Place stands alone atop Lakeport's food chain. In this laid-back lakeside setting with homey country decor, diners can kick back inside or take advantage of good weather on the patio or upstairs on the roof deck. As the sunshine warms the outside, the house-specialty homemade pasta dishes warm the soul with fettucine smothered in marinara, Alfredo, or clam sauce, or ravioli and tortellini with a variety of savory sauces. Also noteworthy are the seafood dishes and big, juicy burgers. Desserts are locally made delights, so save some room for the finale. *50 3rd St, Lakeport; 707/263-0444; $$; MC, V; checks OK; lunch, dinner every day; beer and wine; reservations recommended; off Main St, near the lake.*

LODGINGS

THE FORBESTOWN INN ★

Located only a few blocks from the lake, this wisteria-draped Victorian farmhouse dates back to 1863, when Lakeport was still known as Forbestown. Each of the inn's four guest rooms is pleasantly decorated with fine American antiques, Laura Ashley fabrics, and piles of hand-stitched pillows atop queen- and king-size beds. *825 Forbes St, Lakeport; 707/987-9000; $$; AE, MC, V; no checks; www.forbestowninn.com; 1 block W of Main St.*

NICE

In truth, the little shabby town of Nice ("neece") is not so nice. But it is on the lake and has one interesting place to stay.

LODGINGS

FEATHERBED RAILROAD COMPANY ★

Nine cabooses that look as though they would be right at home in Disneyland are spread out underneath a grove of oak trees at this gimmicky but fun bed-and-breakfast. The freight-train cars are burdened with cutesy names, but they're equipped with quilt-covered feather beds, private baths (some with whirlpool tubs), and other amenities that make up for the silliness. Favorite train cars include two new cabooses, the Orient Express (with a private deck) and the Casablanca (complete with a piano and bar), but it's the black-and-maroon La Loose Caboose, tackiest of them all, with bordello decor and a mirror over the bed, that's always booked. The Rosebud Caboose has two small bunk beds for the kids, and there's only a $10 charge per child. Breakfast is served at the Main Station, a century-old ranch house, in front of a cozy fire or on the porch overlooking the lake. A small pool and spa adjoin the house. *2870 Lakeshore Blvd, Nice; 707/274-8378 or 800/966-6322; $$; AE, MC, V; checks OK; www.featherbedrailroad.com; off Hwy 20, at the SW end of town.*

BEST PLACES
DESTINATIONS
CALIFORNIA WINE COUNTRY
REPORT FORM

Based on my personal experience, I wish to nominate the following restaurant or place of lodging; or confirm/correct/disagree with the current review.

_____

_____

_____

_____

(Please include address and telephone number of establishment, if convenient.)

REPORT

Please describe food, service, style, comfort, value, date of visit, and other aspects of your experience; continue on another piece of paper if necessary.

_____

_____

_____

_____

_____

_____

_____

I am not concerned, directly or indirectly, with the management or ownership of this establishment.

_____
SIGNED

_____
ADDRESS

_____

_____
PHONE   DATE

Please address to Best Places Destinations and send to:

SASQUATCH BOOKS
615 Second Avenue, Suite 260
Seattle, WA 98104
Feel free to email feedback as well: books@sasquatchbooks.com

BEST PLACES
DESTINATIONS
CALIFORNIA WINE COUNTRY
REPORT FORM

Based on my personal experience, I wish to nominate the following restaurant or place of lodging; or confirm/correct/disagree with the current review.

_____
_____
_____
_____

(Please include address and telephone number of establishment, if convenient.)

REPORT

Please describe food, service, style, comfort, value, date of visit, and other aspects of your experience; continue on another piece of paper if necessary.

_____
_____
_____
_____
_____
_____
_____

I am not concerned, directly or indirectly, with the management or ownership of this establishment.

_____
SIGNED

_____
ADDRESS

_____
_____

_____
PHONE   DATE

Please address to Best Places Destinations and send to:

SASQUATCH BOOKS
615 Second Avenue, Suite 260
Seattle, WA 98104
Feel free to email feedback as well: books@sasquatchbooks.com

TRUST THE LOCALS
BEST PLACES®

REGIONAL GUIDES

**Best Places
Southern California**
$19.95

**Best Places
Northwest**
$19.95

**Best Places
Northern California**
$19.95

**Best Places
Alaska**
$21.95

CITY GUIDES

**Best Places
San Diego**
$18.95

**Best Places
Las Vegas**
$18.95

**Best Places
San Francisco**
$18.95

**Best Places
Seattle**
$18.95

**Best Places
Los Angeles**
$18.95

**Best Places
Phoenix**
$18.95

**Best Places
Portland**
$18.95

**Best Places
Vancouver**
$18.95

ADVENTURE TRAVEL

**Inside Out
Southern
California**
$21.95

**Inside Out
Oregon**
$21.95

**Inside Out
British Columbia**
$21.95

**Inside Out
Northern
California**
$21.95

**Inside Out
Washington**
$21.95

**Inside Out
Northern Rockies**
$21.95

BEST PLACES DESTINATIONS

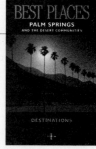

**Northern
California Coast**
$12.95

**San Juan
& Gulf Islands**
$12.95

Oregon Coast
$11.95

**California
Wine Country**
$14.95

**Olympic
Peninsula**
$12.95

Palm Springs
$14.95

All Best Places® guidebooks are available at bookstores, travel stores, and other retailers.
Call toll-free 1-800-775-0817 or visit www.BestPlaces.com.

Best Places® is a registered imprint of Sasquatch Books.